Culinary verbs in Middle English

STUDIES IN ENGLISH MEDIEVAL LANGUAGE AND LITERATURE

Edited by Jacek Fisiak

Advisory Board:
John Anderson (Methoni, Greece), Ulrich Busse (Halle),
Olga Fischer (Amsterdam), Marcin Krygier (Poznań),
Roger Lass (Cape Town), Peter Lucas (Cambridge),
Donka Minkova (Los Angeles), Akio Oizumi (Kyoto),
Katherine O'Brien O'Keeffe (UC Berkeley, USA),
Matti Rissanen (Helsinki), Hans Sauer (Munich),
Liliana Sikorska (Poznań), Jeremy Smith (Glasgow),
Jerzy Wełna (Warsaw)

Vol. 46

Magdalena Bator

Culinary verbs in Middle English

Bibliographic Information published by the Deutsche Nationalbibliothek
The Deutsche Nationalbibliothek lists this publication in the Deutsche Nationalbibliografie; detailed bibliographic data is available in the internet at http://dnb.d-nb.de.

Library of Congress Cataloging-in-Publication Data
Bator, Magdalena.
  Culinary verbs in Middle English / Magdalena Bator. – Peter Lang Edition.
    pages cm. – (Studies in English Medieval Language and Literature; Vol. 46)
  Includes bibliographical references and index.
  ISBN 978-3-631-65428-6 (Print) – ISBN 978-3-653-04576-5 (E-Book)
  1. English language–Middle English, 1100-1500--Verb. 2. English language–Middle English, 1100-1500–Vowel gradation. 3. Food–Terminology. 4. England–Languages. I. Title.
  PE587.B28 2014
  427'.02–dc23
                                                                    2014019168

This publication was financially supported
by the University of Social Sciences.

ISSN 1436-7521
ISBN 978-3-631-65428-6 (Print)
E-ISBN 978-3-653-04576-5 (E-Book)
DOI 10.3726/978-3-653-04576-5

© Peter Lang GmbH
Internationaler Verlag der Wissenschaften
Frankfurt am Main 2014
All rights reserved.

Peter Lang Edition is an Imprint of Peter Lang GmbH.

Peter Lang – Frankfurt am Main · Bern · Bruxelles · New York ·
Oxford · Warszawa · Wien

All parts of this publication are protected by copyright. Any utilisation outside the strict limits of the copyright law, without the permission of the publisher, is forbidden and liable to prosecution. This applies in particular to reproductions, translations, microfilming, and storage and processing in electronic retrieval systems.

This publication has been peer reviewed.

www.peterlang.com

Table of contents

List of Tables 9

List of Figures 13

List of abbreviations 15

Acknowledgements 17

Chapter One: Introduction 19
  1.1 Medieval recipes – an overview of the available sources 19
        1.1.1   The 14th-century collections 22
        1.1.2   The 15th-century collections 23
  1.2 Medieval recipes – a brief look at their characteristics 27
  1.3 The recipe as a text type 31
  1.4 An outline of the study 33

Chapter Two: Medieval food and drink 37
  2.1 Medieval foodstuffs 37
        2.1.1   Meat and fish 38
        2.1.2   Fruit and vegetables 43
        2.1.3   Dairy products 45
        2.1.4   Grains 47
        2.1.5   Herbs and spices 50
        2.1.6   Grease 54
        2.1.7   Beverages and liquids 54
  2.2 Food preparation 57
        2.2.1   Cutting 57
        2.2.2   Cooking 58
        2.2.3   Serving 62
        2.2.4   Preserving 63
                2.2.4.1   Salting and pickling 63
                2.2.4.2   Drying 65
                2.2.4.3   Smoking 65

Chapter Three: Verbs of cutting 67
  3.1 Introduction 67

3.2 Dividing verbs 70
　3.2.1 The corpus 70
　　　3.2.1.1　*break₁* 71
　　　3.2.1.2　*carve* 73
　　　3.2.1.3　*chop₁* 74
　　　3.2.1.4　*cut₁* 75
　　　3.2.1.5　*(de)part* 77
　　　3.2.1.6　*dice* 78
　　　3.2.1.7　*hack* 79
　　　3.2.1.8　*hew* 79
　　　3.2.1.9　*leach* 80
　　　3.2.1.10 *quarter* 81
　　　3.2.1.11 *shred* 82
　　　3.2.1.12 *slit₁* 82
　　　3.2.1.13 *smite* 82
　　　3.2.1.14 *tease* 83
　　　3.2.1.15 Peripheral verbs 83
　　　　　　(a)　*bard / baud* 83
　　　　　　(b)　*chine* 84
　　　　　　(c)　*cleave* 84
　　　　　　(d)　*culpon* 85
　　　　　　(e)　*dismember* 85
　　　　　　(f)　*gobbon* 85
　　　　　　(g)　*pluck* 85
　　　　　　(h)　*share* 86
　　　　　　(i)　*tear* 86
　3.2.2 Discussion 86
3.3 Reducing verbs 91
　3.3.1 The corpus 91
　　　3.3.1.1　*beat₁* 92
　　　3.3.1.2　*bray* 93
　　　3.3.1.3　*break₂* 94
　　　3.3.1.4　*bruise* 94
　　　3.3.1.5　*crumb* 95
　　　3.3.1.6　*grate* 95
　　　3.3.1.7　*grind* 96
　　　3.3.1.8　*mince* 98
　　　3.3.1.9　*powder₁* 100

   3.3.1.10 *press* 101
   3.3.1.11 *quest* 101
   3.3.1.12 *stamp* 102
  3.3.2 Discussion 102
 3.4 Removing verbs 105
  3.4.1 The corpus 105
   3.4.1.1 *blanch* and *whiten* 106
   3.4.1.2 *break₃* 108
   3.4.1.3 *cut₂ (away/off/out)* 109
   3.4.1.4 *flay, ⁺hild* and *skin* 109
   3.4.1.5 *pare* 110
   3.4.1.6 *peel, pill* and *pull* 111
   3.4.1.7 *pick (away/off/out)* 112
   3.4.1.8 *scrape* and *shave* 113
   3.4.1.9 *do₁ / take₂ (away/off/out)* 114
   3.4.1.10 Peripheral verbs 115
    (a) *bone* 115
    (b) *chop off* 115
    (c) *hull, shell and scale* 115
    (d) *smite off* 116
    (e) *strip* 116
  3.4.2 Discussion 116
 3.5 Penetrating verbs 118
  3.5.1 The corpus 118
   3.5.1.1 *break₄* 118
   3.5.1.2 *cut₃* 119
   3.5.1.3 *draw₄* 120
   3.5.1.4 *open* 120
   3.5.1.5 *slit₂* 120
  3.5.2 Discussion 121
 3.6 Conclusions 121

Chapter Four: Verbs of cooking 125
 4.1 Introduction 125
 4.2 Verbs of cooking in liquid 126
  4.2.1 The corpus 126
   4.2.1.1 *boil* 127
   4.2.1.2 *parboil* 130

7

			4.2.1.3	*scald*	131

                4.2.1.3   *scald* 131
                4.2.1.4   *seethe* 133
                4.2.1.5   *ouerstep 136
                4.2.1.6   *stew* 136
                4.2.1.7   *wall / well* 136
        4.2.2   Discussion 137
    4.3   Verbs of cooking with fat 143
        4.3.1   The corpus 143
                4.3.1.1   *bake* 144
                4.3.1.2   *broil* 145
                4.3.1.3   *fry* 145
                4.3.1.4   *roast* 147
        4.3.2   Discussion 149
    4.4   Verbs of cooking with any or no medium 152
    4.5   Conclusions 154

Chapter Five: Verbs of preparing 157
    5.1   Introduction 157
    5.2   Verbs of cleaning 158
    5.3   Verbs of adding and combining 159
        5.3.1   Verbs of combining 160
        5.3.2   Verbs of adding 163
        5.3.3   Verbs of stuffing 167
    5.4   Verbs of straining 169
    5.5   Verbs of seasoning 172
    5.6   Verbs of decoration 173
    5.7   Verbs of taking 177
    5.8   Verbs of serving 182
    5.9   Miscellaneous verbs 184
    5.10 Conclusions 185

Conclusion 187

References 191

Appendix 205

Index of verbs 207

List of Tables

Chapter One
Table 1: The size of the analyzed material 35

Chapter Two
Table 1: The ratio of fowl at different periods, drawn from the archaeological evidence (based on Serjeantson 2006) 41
Table 2: Types of grain crops and their uses in England in the period 1250–1540 (based on Stone 2006a) 47

Chapter Three
Table 1: Subdivision of the cutting verbs (Marttila 2009: 109) 68
Table 2: The number of occurrences of the 'dividing verbs' in the analyzed material. Relative normalized frequencies have been given in brackets [RNFs / 10,000 words] 71
Table 3: The number of occurrences of the 'dividing verbs' found in the analyzed material 88
Table 4: The number of occurrences (absolute frequencies) of the specifying phrases with particular general verbs 90
Table 5: The relative normalized frequencies of occurrence of the verbs formed by conversion and the corresponding nouns 90
Table 6: The number of occurrences of the 'reducing verbs' in the analyzed material. Relative normalized frequencies have been given in brackets 91
Table 7: The frequency of the occurrence of the 'reducing verbs' 103
Table 8: The number of occurrences of the 'removing verbs' in the analyzed material. Relative normalized frequencies have been given in brackets 106
Table 9: Number of occurrences of the 'removing verbs' found in the analyzed material 117
Table 10: The number of the 'penetrating verbs' found in the analyzed material 121

Chapter Four

Table 1: The number of occurrences of the 'verbs of cooking in liquid' in the analyzed material. Relative normalized frequencies have been given in brackets 127

Table 2: The number of occurrences of the 'verbs of cooking in liquid' found in the analyzed material 137

Table 3: The number of occurrences of the 'verbs of cooking in fat' in the analyzed material 143

Table 4: The number of occurrences of the 'verbs of cooking with fat' found in the analyzed material 150

Table 5: The most frequently occurring features of the 'verbs of cooking with fat'. In brackets ( ) the less frequent elements have been enumerated 151

Table 6: The number of occurrences of the 'verbs of cooking in fat' in the analyzed material 152

Chapter Five

Table 1: The number of occurrences of the 'cleaning verbs' in the analyzed material. Relative normalized frequencies have been given in brackets 158

Table 2: The number of occurrences of the 'combining verbs' in the analyzed material. Relative normalized frequencies have been given in brackets 160

Table 3: The number of occurrences of the 'straining verbs' in the analyzed material. The relative normalized frequencies have been given in brackets 169

Table 4: The number of occurrences of the 'seasoning verbs' in the 14th and 15th c. Relative normalized frequencies have been given in brackets 172

Table 5: The number of occurrences of the 'verbs of decoration' in the 14th and 15th c. The relative normalized frequencies have been given in brackets 174

Table 6: The number of occurrences of the particular colourants following the verb *colour*. Relative normalized frequencies have been given in brackets 175

Table 7: The number of occurrences of *take₁* and its synonyms in the analyzed material. Normalized relative frequencies have been given in brackets 178

Table 8: The number of occurrences of the 'serving verbs' in the analyzed material. Relative normalized frequencies have been given in brackets 183

Table 9: The number of occurrences of the verbs in the analyzed material. Relative normalized frequencies have been given in brackets 185

List of Figures

Chapter Three

Fig. 1: Types and tokens of particular verbal groups 70
Fig. 2: The ratio of occurrences of *break* with different senses 72
Fig. 3: The ratio of occurrences of *cut* with different senses in the 15th c. 76
Fig. 4: Distribution of the major specific 'dividing verbs' at
particular periods 87
Fig. 5: Distribution of the major general 'dividing verbs' at
particular periods 89
Fig. 6: The ratio of occurrences of *beat* with particular senses 92
Fig. 7: The ratio of foodstuffs ground in the 14th c. 97
Fig. 8: The ratio of foodstuffs ground in the 15th c. 97
Fig. 9: The percentage of products minced in the 14th and 15th c. 98
Fig. 10: Distribution of the major 'reducing verbs' at particular periods 103
Fig. 11: The ratio of the occurrence (%) of particular forms of *blanch*
in the analyzed centuries 107
Fig. 12: The ratio of the occurrence (%) of particular senses of *pick* in
the respective centuries 113

Chapter Four

Fig. 1: Types and tokens (RNFs / 1,000 words) of particular
verbal groups 126
Fig. 2: The percentage of forms of *boil* in the 14th and 15th centuries 129
Fig. 3: Foodstuffs scalded in the 15th c. 132
Fig. 4: The percentage of forms of *seethe* in the 14th and 15th centuries 134
Fig. 5: The ratio of ingredients seethed in the 14th c. 135
Fig. 6: The ratio of ingredients seethed in the 15th c. 135
Fig. 7: The distribution of the verbs at particular periods 138
Fig. 8: The hierarchy of the cooking verbs 140
Fig. 9: Foodstuffs boiled in the 14th c. 141
Fig. 10: Foodstuffs seethed in the 14th c. 141
Fig. 11: Foodstuffs boiled in the 15th c. 142
Fig. 12: Foodstuffs seethed in the 15th c. 142

Fig. 13: The percentage of particular forms of *roast* 147
Fig. 14: Distribution of the verbs at particular periods 150

Chapter Five

Fig. 1: Types and tokens (RNFs / 1,000 words) of particular verbal groups ... 157
Fig. 2: The ratio of occurrence of the particular particles
accompanying the verb cast in the 14th c. 163
Fig. 3: The ratio of occurrence of the particular particles
accompanying the verb *cast* in the 15th c. 164
Fig. 4: The ratio of occurrence of the particular particles
following the verb do_2 in the 14th c. 164
Fig. 5: The ratio of occurrence of the particular particles
following the verb do_2 in the 15th c. 165
Fig. 6: The percentage of the occurrence of the particular
senses of *draw* in the 14th and 15th centuries 166
Fig. 7: The number of recipes in the DS collection (14th c.)
containing the particular verbs 180
Fig. 8: The number of recipes in the Aus_Laud collection (15th c.)
containing the particular verbs 180
Fig. 9: The number of occurrences of the *take*-verbs
in recipe-initial position 181
Fig. 10: The ratio of occurrence of the verbs followed or not by *forth*. 183

Conclusion

Fig. 1: The ratio of the culinary verbs (types) of particular
origin, as found in the analyzed material 188

List of abbreviations

adj.	adjective
adv.	adverb
AF	Anglo-French
AN	Anglo-Norman
AND	*Anglo-Norman Dictionary*
ASD	*Anglo-Saxon Dictionary*
Aus	Austin
BK	*Boke of kokery*
BM	*Bake metis*
c.	century
cf.	confer
Com.Germ.	Common Germanic
Cosin	Historical menus
DC	*Diversa cibaria*
DS	*Diversa servisa*
Du	Dutch
e.g.	exempli gratia / for example
EDD	*English Dialect Dictionary*
esp.	especially
etc.	et cetera
FC	*Forme of Cury*
Fig.	Figure
Germ.	Germanic
GK	*Goud kokery*
GR	*Gathering of ME recipes*
Ht_Hrl	Hieatt: Harley MS
i.e.	id est / that is
intrans.	intransitive
L.	Latin
LALME	*Linguistic Atlas of Late Middle English*
LCC	*Liber cure cocorum*
LV	*Leche viaundez*

MAe	Hieatt: *Medium Aevum*
MDu	Middle Dutch
MED	*Middle English Dictionary*
MF	Midde French
MLG	Middle Low German
MS	manuscript
OCelt.	Old Celtic
ODEE	*Oxford Dictionary of English Etymology*
OE	Old English
OED	*Oxford English Dictionary*
OF	Old French
ON	Old Norse
OP	*Ordinance of pottage*
part.adj.	participial adjective
PD	*Potage diverse*
RNF	relative normalized frequency
s.v.	sub verbo
trans.	transitive
UC	*Utilis coquinario*
v.	verb
vs.	versus

Acknowledgements

I would like to take this opportunity and express my gratitude to several people for their support when working on the present study. In particular, I would like to thank my mentor, Professor Jacek Fisiak, for his constant encouragement to pursue my studies as well as his enormous trust and understanding. I am also indebted to some of my colleagues, from whom I would like to single out: Dr Anna Snarska, for her patient consultations on some syntactical issues concerning the medieval verbs; Dr Marta Sylwanowicz, for sharing some of the interesting books and articles on medieval recipes; and Mr Colin Phillips, for the hours spent on proofreading the manuscript.

Last but not least, my special thanks go to my relatives and friends for their patience and support. My biggest debt is to Walter for reminding me of what is really important as well as for the peace and quiet he provided me with. It is to him that I would like to dedicate this book.

Magdalena Bator   Poznań, April 2014

Chapter One: Introduction

1.1 Medieval recipes – an overview of the available sources

The earliest traces of English food vocabulary are probably those in Alexander Neckam's *De Utensilibus*, from the late 12th century. It was written in Latin and contained a few Anglo-Norman and English glosses. The recipes included there can also be found in fuller forms in some later collections. Our knowledge of the early Middle English food traditions comes from literary descriptions of feasts and banquets; however, they are not very helpful when it comes to linguistic research, as they are usually very scarce in detail and limited to the enumeration of the meats served, telling us nothing about the way of cooking or serving them. The earliest detailed menu description, *Treatise of Walter of Bibbesworth*, comes from the late 13th century. However, it was written in Anglo-Norman, thus, is of little use for a comprehensive study of the English culinary language of the period.[1]

Another source of information concerning the food eaten at particular periods is narrative texts and verse, e.g., Chaucer's *The Canterbury Tales* or *Morte d'Arthur*. However, as noticed by Shaw (1991: 8), these usually show extremes (either excess or default, gluttony or drunkenness, and frugality or starvation), and lead to moralizing, preaching or ridiculing rather than a realistic presentation of food habits of the time. Shaw enumerates the following reasons for writing about food and drink in the Medieval times:

> (…) for moralizing purposes, for characterization purposes, to illustrate and exult the wealth of a character or a social class, to satirise a determined estate or professional group, to reflect religious customs or the flouting thereof, to lend realism to a text, or, on the contrary, to add fantasy thereto, and thus to heighten its interest, or finally, to spark off further dramatic incident, in the fulfilling of all which functions, moreover,

---

1 It is not suggested, though, that the study of Anglo-Norman cannot help with the study of English. On the contribution of the study of French and Anglo-Norman to the study of English and vice versa, see for instance Durkin (2012), or Rothwell (2001). On a brief characteristics of Anglo-Norman, see for instance Trotter (2008).

humour, satire and irony will often be included to endow and enliven these manducatory and bibulatory episodes with a further literary dimension.
(Shaw 1991: 28)

The other sources of culinary tradition imply historical documents, such as *A collection of ordinances and regulations for the government of the Royal household, made in divers reigns. From King Edward III. to King William and Queen Mary. Also receipts in ancient cookery* (the recipes included here were later reprinted in the collection *Forme of Cury*); or are archaeological attestations – which may serve as evidence for the foods that were eaten at a particular period or the way of their preparation (see for instance Woolgar, Serajeantson and Waldron (eds.) (2009)); as well as medical recipes[2], which mostly contain recipes intended to cure rather than to dine (see for instance Taavitsainen, Pahta and Mäkinen (eds.) (2005)).

All these sources have contributed to the appearance of numerous cultural and sociological studies concerning food in Medieval England, such as Wilson's (1991) *Food and drink in Britain. From the Stone Age to the 19th c.*, three books by Hagen on the Anglo-Saxon food and drink (1994, 1995 and 2010), Hammond's (2005) *Food and feast in Medieval England*, and many others, including some special studies such as Lee's (2007) work on the role of food and drink in the burial rituals.[3] However, the most important source of information for a linguistic analysis is the manuscripts containing medieval recipes.

The present author is familiar with no extensive semantic analysis of the culinary language conducted so far.[4] Such a linguistic research requires a study of specific culinary recipes rather than materials included in the household

---

2   Unlike culinary recipes, the medical ones, which survived till present times, come from an earlier period. There are three major Old English medical texts: *The Leechbook of Bald, the Lacnunga* and *the Old English Herbarium* (Thomas 2011).
3   Additionally, for a brief sketch of studies on food seen from the historical perspective, see Super (2002) and Woolgar (2009).
4   Some studies dealing with a restricted area of the semantic field 'food', and/or restricted to a short period of time, were handled. For instance, Frantzen (2011) analyzed the culinary language in the Anglo-Saxon penitentials, Kornexl and Lenker (2011) dealt with lexical pairs within the culinary vocabulary, similarly, Weiss (2009) concentrated on lexical items referring to animals and their meat, Lehrer (2007) discussed wine vocabulary, and Bator (2013b) analyzed terms referring to herbs and spices in the 14th and 15th centuries. Bator (2011) conducted a general study on the food vocabulary in the 14th and 15th c. recipes. Additionally, a number of studies on more general topics dealt among others with food vocabulary, for instance, Baugh and Cable (2006), Lutz (2013).

accounts or provided by archaeological evidence. Thus, it has been decided to base the present study exclusively on the available editions of manuscripts containing Middle English culinary recipes. Unfortunately, the earliest culinary collections are Anglo-Norman records of menus of the upper class, which poses a number of restrictions concerning any linguistic research of the early culinary language. The earliest English material attested comes from the end of the 13th c. and is rather scarce. Thus, the author has no other choice but as to concentrate on the period of the late Middle Ages, i.e., the 14th and 15th centuries, from which a representative sample of recipes could be collected. Scully (1995: 5) calls the period "a hey-day for medieval cookery" due to the greater availability of culinary evidence comparing to the earlier times. It should be remembered that the available culinary material gives us an insight into the food habits of the upper classes only. The diet of the poor and middle classes can only be deduced from literary and archaeological material, since no recipe collections were created by peasants (see for instance Dyer 1988 or Carlin 2008). Black (1981: 54) suggests that "the poor lived mainly on porridgy gruels and salt bacon". However, she claims that their diet was definitely nutritious and healthy, full of fresh vegetables, fruit and herbs.

With time, more and more culinary evidence is being discovered. In 2002 Hieatt (2002: 19) wrote about more than forty known culinary manuscripts. Six years later she (2008: 11–20) enumerated 82 manuscripts, which, if not entirely devoted to culinary recipes, do contain at least single folios of them. When it comes to the availability of the edited material, Hieatt (1998) writes:

> By 1900 around thirteen culinary manuscripts of English provenance, whether Latin, Anglo-Norman or Middle English, had been edited and printed, in whole or in part, including those simply collated. The number of recipes printed from these manuscripts amounts to about 1850. Since 1900 (and almost *all* in the last decade or so), something like twenty-one additional manuscripts have been edited, in whole or in part – not counting those re-edited – giving us around 2075 recipes not previously printed, as well as a great many new (and often corrected) versions of some which had been edited before.
>
> (Hieatt 1998: 104–105)

Additionally, Hieatt (1998, 2008) noticed that almost 2000 recipes have not been edited yet.

The corpus for the present study has been based on the available editions of Middle English recipe collections coming from the 14th and 15th centuries.

1.1.1 The 14th-century collections

The earliest culinary collections were written in Anglo-Norman and found in two manuscripts, i.e., the MS Additional 32085, from the late 13th c., and the MS Royal 12.C.xii from the early 14th c. The latter was edited by Meyer in 1893. Later, both collections were published by Hieatt and Jones (1986: 859), who claim that these are the only two Anglo-Norman collections found so far: "No new Anglo-Norman collections have turned up since that time, although we have searched in a great number of libraries and their catalogues". All the recipes from the MS Royal as well as a great deal of those in the Additional MS were translated into Middle English and included in the collection *Diuersa cibaria* (= DC). The collection consists of recipes from the early 14th c. It was based on the MS Additional 46919, which was compiled under the direction and partly in the hand of William Herebert of Hereford. The manuscript has been dated to 1325 (Hieatt 2006) and includes 63 recipes. They are available in the edition by Hieatt and Butler (1985). A distinctive feature of these Anglo-Norman recipes is the use of fresh fruit and flowers, which were not found in any of the French recipes.

Other 14th-century recipe collections include:

Diuersa servicia (= DS), a collection of 92 recipes, dated to about 1381 and included in the MS Bodleian Douce 257. It was first published by Pegge (1780) under the title *Ancient Cookery*, as a supplement to his *Forme of Cury*. Later, the recipes were edited by Hieatt and Butler (1985).[5]

Utilis coquinario (= UC), edited from the MS B.L. Sloane 468 in Hieatt and Butler (1985), and dated to 1395. The collection consists of 37 recipes.

Probably the best known collection is the *Forme of Cury* (= FC), which, according to Hieatt has survived in six manuscripts (2006: xiv), and has been represented in at least eight collections (as a whole or partially) (1998: 108). The title has been recorded only in one manuscript, i.e., the MS B.L. Additional 5016 (the MS A). Following the head-note in the vellum scroll of the manuscript, it should:

> techiþ a man for to make commune potages and commune meetis for howshold as þey shold be made craftly and holsomly. Aftirward it techiþ for to make curious potages & meetes and sotiltees for alle maner of States bothe hye and lowe. And the techyng of the forme of making of potages & of meetes bothe of flessh and of fissh.
>
> (Pegge 1780: 2)

---

5   In the present study, the later edition has been used.

This note differs in the MS M (John Rylands University Library of Manchester) in that it is a collection of "curious metes for hy$_3$est astates" rather than for all men of both high and low social classes, as indicated in the MS A. The collection was compiled by the Chief Master Cook of Richard II. It was first edited by Samuel Pegge in 1780 and later copied by Richard Warner in 1791. In the present study the edition by Hieatt and Butler (1985) will be followed, together with later corrections and additions published in Hieatt (1988b). *The Forme of Cury* contains 205 recipes and has been dated to 1390 (Hieatt 2006).

Goud Kokery (= GK) is a collection of 25 miscellaneous recipes from various sources, dating from 1340 to 1480, and published in Hieatt and Butler (1985).

Hieatt and Butler's *Curye on Inglysch* also includes two menus for the banquet given for the English king in 1397 shortly after King Richard II's marriage to Isabella of France in 1396; as well as 7 other menus, which are rather general suggestions than historical records. They were all based on the MS Cosin V.III.11 (C), dated to the end of the 14th c. (= Cosin).

1.1.2 The 15th-century collections

The 15th c. presents us with a wider range of the culinary material than the previous century. Thus, the following collections are available:

A fifteenth century cookry boke published by Anderson (1962), with 153 recipes, divided into 11 groups: *fleysshe; fysshe; byrdys; mete pyes & tartes; daryoles & other tartes & frittours; mylke, eyroun & notys; frutes & flowres; potages dyuers; sauces pur diuerse viaundes; cakys, bredes & amydon; swetes*; and the recipe for *cokentrice*. The collection has been based on the MS Harleian 279 (1430), the MS Harleian 4010 (c. 1450), as well as the MS Ashmole 1429, the MS Laud 553 and the MS Douce 55, from c. 1450. The collection has been based on the same material as that used for Austin's (2000) collection, therefore it will not be included in the analysis in order not to duplicate the data.

An ordinance of pottage (= OP) edited by Hieatt (1988a) is one of the longest and most widely disseminated 15th-century culinary collections. It is based on the Yale University's MS Beinecke 163. The collection has also survived in the British Library Sloane MS 7 and 442 and in the Bodleian Library Oxford MS Rawlinson D 1222. It consists of 200 recipes, with a section of 8 'additional recipes' and 3 menus from the MS Sloane 442. Hieatt (2006) dated the collection to 1460, with the exception of the three menus, which are dated to 1475.

96 recipes, found in the MS Harley 5401, have been edited by Hieatt (1996) and published in the article "The Middle English culinary recipes in the MS Harley 5401: An edition and commentary"[6] (= Hrl). It is a collection of culinary recipes which were found in a fifteenth century manuscript devoted to medical matters. The culinary part of the manuscript has been signed by "Thomas Awkbarow", who according to Hieatt (1996) was a northerner. She also claims that the spelling used within the collection suggests that the author was from the east coast. Following *LALME*, the manuscript "appears to be in the language of NW Lincs". A number of recipes found in the MS Harley 5401 correspond to recipes in the *Forme of Cury* or Austin's collection but the majority of these constitute different versions of the dishes. Many recipes from the collection have not been found in any other medieval manuscript. A great deal of the recipes refer to the preparation of shellfish, which may indicate a coastal location as a place of origin of the collection. The collection is dated to c. 1490 (Hieatt 2006).

Probably the largest 15th c. collection has been edited by Austin (2000). The first of his *Two fifteenth-century cookery books* has been based on: the Harleian MS 279, which is composed of three parts: 'Potages dyuers' (= PD) with 153 recipes, 'Leche viaundez' (= LV) with 64 recipes and 'Bake metis' (= BM) with 41 recipes. The manuscript is dated to 1435. The second of the books (*A boke of kokery*) has been based on the Harleian MS 4016, from c.1450, and consists of 182 recipes (= BK). Austin's collection has been supplemented with 19 recipes for sauces, based on the Ashmole MS 1439, dated to c.1410 (= Ashm); 25 recipes based on the Laud MS 553 from 1430 (= Laud); and 12 recipes based on the Douce MS 55 from about 1450 (= Douce).

Additionally, Banham and Mason (2002) have edited 5 recipes for confectionery found in an early 15th-century manuscript in Lincolnshire, dated by Hieatt (2006) to 1420. They are probably the only surviving culinary recipes which come from an English monastic household. What is striking is that the recipes are written in Latin, "[t]hey have clearly been translated from English, since several English words survived the process" (Banham and Mason 2002: 48). No English equivalents of the recipes have been found.

In her article "The third 15th century cookery book: A newly identified group within a family"[7], Hieatt (2004) extracted 8 recipes which were included in a collection of recipes corresponding to those edited by Austin (2000) or Hieatt (1988a); however, the extracted eight mid-15th-century recipes were found in

---

6   Published in: *Medium Aevum* 65.1 (1996).
7   Published in: *Medium Aevum* 73.1 (2004).

neither. The recipes were found in the MS Douce 55 and collated with the MS Additional 5467 (= MAe).

In 2008 Hieatt published *A gathering of Medieval English recipes* (= GR), in which she included over 500 15th c.-recipes, 356 of which were either never published before or found in different forms than in the previously edited collections. The set has been based on three collections never edited before, i.e., the Bodleian MS Ashmole 1393, the MS e.Mus. 52 and the MS Welcome Western 5650, as well as several manuscripts which earlier might have been used for collation but which contain recipes not edited in any of the earlier collections, and a few recipes found in isolation. Altogether 82 manuscripts have been taken into account (Hieatt 2008: 12–20). The collection consists of the following parts:

- The MS Ashmole 1393: the extract contains 35 recipes, some of which are extremely short and seem incomplete. This leads to the conclusion that even though the manuscript comes from the 15th c. the character of the recipes indicates their earlier origin (e.g., lack of details, omissions, etc.); for the characteristics of medieval recipes see section 1.2. Thus, Hieatt (2008: 22) suggests that it is a later copy of the 14th c. material. However, the collection does not show any direct relation to any other compilation. It has been dated to 1410. (= GR_Ashm)
- The MS Ashmole 1439 (with variants from the MS Harley 279): the collection correlates with that edited by Austin (2000), thus the recipes have not been added to the present corpus in order not to duplicate the analyzed material.
- The MS Ashmole 1444: the recipes are dated to c. 1390. Most of them were also edited in Hieatt and Butler (1985); however, there are 5 recipes which either differ from the versions in Hieatt and Butler or have not been found there nor in any other collection, thus they have been added to the corpus used in the present study. The collection contains also a number of 16th century recipes, but the present study comprises the period until the end of the 15th c., hence, this part has been excluded from the database. (= GR_AshmB)
- The MS e. Mus. 52: the recipes represented in the manuscript are often early ones, corresponding not only to Austin's (2000) or Hieatt's (1988a) collections, but also to Hieatt and Butler's (1985). The manuscript has been dated to the end of the 15th c. The collection comprises 101 recipes and additional 26 entitled 'confectionary series'. Out of these, there are 35 recipes for which Hieatt (2008) finds no correspondence in any of the earlier editions or which correspond to familiar dishes; however, they differ in details and wording from the other collections. (= GR_eMus)

- The MS Rawlinson D 1222: the majority of these recipes correspond to Hieatt (1988a) or Austin (2000), but there are also a few recipes corresponding to *Noble book of cookery* or *Forme of Cury*. 85 of the recipes have not been found in any of the other editions. They have been dated to 1450. (= GR_Rwl)
- The MS Sloane 7 and Sloane 442: they consist of 23 recipes, either not mentioned in the other editions or representing such different variants that we have decided to include them in the present corpus. The collection has been dated to 1480. (= GR_Sl)
- The MS Sloane 1108: it is an early 15th c. manuscript in which for 11 recipes no parallels were found in any of the other editions. The collection has been dated to 1420. (= GR_Sl)
- The Cambridge University Library Ll.I.18: a late 15th c. manuscript, whose significant part corresponds to *An ordinance of pottage*. 68 recipes either have no parallels in the other editions or differ significantly from the versions found elsewhere. They have been dated to 1485. (= GR_CUL)
- The National Library of Wales MS Peniarth 394 D: contains 44 recipes which show no close resemblance to any of the recipes printed before. The collection has been dated to 1485. (= GR_Pen)
- The New York Public Library MS Whitney 1: this is an early 15th c. manuscript (from 1425). The majority of the recipes parallel those printed in other sources, but Hieatt identified 6 recipes which have not been found elsewhere. (= GR_Whit)
- The Society of Antiquaries MS 287: with 8 recipes not found elsewhere, dated to 1480. (= GR_SA)
- The Trinity College Cambridge MS 0.1.13: the collection corresponds to *An ordinance of pottage*, with the exception of 7 recipes which come from an unidentified source. They have been dated to 1465. (= GR_TC)
- The Wellcome Western MS 5650: the manuscript partly corresponds to the collection in *An ordinance of pottage*, with the exception of 19 recipes. The collection comes from 1470. (= GR_WW)
- The collection contains also a number of recipes found in isolation in various manuscripts, from various periods, i.e., altogether 13 recipes which either had not been edited before or differed from the previous versions considerably.

A collection of a different character than the above mentioned ones is *Liber cure cocorum* (= LCC). It is an early 15th-c. doggerel collection first edited by Richard

Morris in 1862. The poem is written in a north-western dialect of Lancashire[8] and contains 127 recipes dated to 1460 (Hieatt 2006).

Finally, we should not forget about the first cookery book published in English, i.e., *A noble boke of festes ryalle and cokery* published by Pynson in 1500. Following Hieatt (2006: xiv), "it survives only in a unique copy in Lord Bath's library at Longleat". However, an edition of the earlier manuscript of the same collection is known, i.e., Napier's edition of 1882, currently available online via www.medievalcookery.com [2008]. Napier's edition (= NBC) contains 253 recipes, which have been dated by Hieatt (2006) to 1475.

The last two collections, i.e., LCC and NBC have not been included in the corpus used for the present study. This can be accounted for by the different character of the former collection, i.e., vocabulary used in verse should be treated separately. The latter has been generally considered as an unreliable edition (see Hieatt 1988a).

The full list of collections and editions used for the present research can be found in the Appendix.

1.2 Medieval recipes – a brief look at their characteristics

The food habits of the upper class in medieval times were rather regular. The aristocracy usually ate twice a day. Meal times were determined by practical considerations, namely, cooking had to be conducted during daylight. Brears (2008: 369) claims that "[a]s a general rule, there were two meals each day, dinner served at 10 a.m. and supper at 4 p.m., although these could be moved an hour forward or back depending on the season, or the particular preference of the head of the household." Additionally, the more important members of the household might have been served breakfast in the morning, very often in their private chambers.

The late medieval recipes are a resource for the food habits at aristocratic households, feasts and banquets. (For information on the food habits of the other classes, see for instance Tannahill 1988 or Mennell 1996). The recipes give us fundamental evidence for actual ingredients, processes, final dishes, and the manner of serving them at table in the aristocratic households. Medieval feasts consisted of at least two courses, each composed of several dishes. The number of dishes depended on the occasion and on the financial situation of the host. The order of

---

8   See Wilson (1991: 205).

the dishes was not always the same. Definitely it was the soup which came first, followed by something more substantial, such as roasts of various kinds or pies. Then, lighter and/or richer dishes, such as tarts and fritters were served, then non-sweet delicacies, such as small game birds. Finally, something sweet was offered. Freedman (2007: 49), suggests that "[t]he courses were distinguished more by methods of preparation than by basic ingredients so that, partly for health reasons, boiled dishes came first, then roasts, and then fried foods." Brears (2008) agrees that the order of serving dishes depended on the way of cooking them; however, he suggests a slightly different sequence. Thus, first boiled, baked and fried foods were served, and only later roasted dishes were offered. As suggested by Henisch (2009), the cook was to entertain the master and his guests with a great variety of rich and luxurious dishes. At the end of each course a 'subtlety' might have been presented (see for instance Hammond 2005, Hieatt and Butler 1985). These were food decorations made to look like something else, e.g., birds with feathers or sugar sculptures. Their main function was to amuse or impress the guests as well as the host. Subtleties were usually made of sugar or marzipan, but in fact any material (often non-edible, such as wax, silk, plaster, wood, etc.) might have been involved in order to achieve the desired result. They might have been painted or gilded, and decorated with jewels, flowers, etc. Davidson (2006: 762) distinguishes two types of subtleties: the plain ones, "made of anything from pastry or butter to wood and canvas", and the elaborate ones, which included live participants. The subtleties were usually part of a spectacle taking place between courses. The entremets[9] involved a mixture of singing, acting, mechanics, and carpentry combined together in order to create an allegorical fantasy or a political message, etc.

Medieval recipes were very general in terms of instructions, especially in terms of specifying the quantities, temperatures or times. Their function was to consult rather than to teach. They were more like a list of ingredients defining the order of adding them and not detailed instructions guiding the cook step by step how to prepare a particular dish. Food historians, e.g., Hammond (2005) or Scully (1995), suggest that the recipes were intended as aids for the chief cook rather than for those working in the kitchen, who must have worked by memory and experience. The main aim of writing down medieval recipes might have been the estimation of the ingredients necessary to prepare a feast, so that when a menu was chosen, the recipes were used to prepare a 'shopping list'. The recipes might also have been memory aids for the cook in order not to forget about any ingredient or about the

---

9   A medieval course was referred to as 'met', thus, the activities which took place between courses were called 'entremets' (Davidson 2006).

order of adding particular ingredients. Additionally, many recipes do not instruct how to prepare a particular dish but instead give details of the sauce which should be served with the dish. This, according to Brears (2008), proves that the cook's memory had to be refreshed, i.e., they remembered the frequently prepared dishes, such as pastries or breads, and most basic processes, such as plain boiling or roasting, but details concerning foods which were not in everyday use might have been forgotten. On the other hand, Scully (1995) points out that recipes were not written *for* the cook, who was a professional and knew well enough how to prepare particular dishes, but *by* the cook (as some archival material). He writes:

> A recipe collection was compiled in manuscript form not for the cook in a noble or bourgeois household but for the master or mistress of that household. It served to document certain standards of an elite class. Occasionally revised with additions, deletions and modifications, occasionally copied, with the approval of the master or mistress in order to please a flattering friend or relative, a manuscript collection of recipes reposed in the household library, not in its kitchen.
> (Scully 1995: 8)

Scully notices that the majority of the surviving recipes are too clean to ever have been used in the kitchen. It is also possible, if we assume after Scully that recipes were written down by the cooks, that the most outstanding chefs were not willing to reveal details of their craft. For instance, Guillaume Tirel, one of the greatest chefs in the 14th c. France, the author of the *Viandier*,[10] explained the omission of instructions on how to cook some of the dishes included in his collection thus: "everyone knows how to do them. (…) as for tripe, which I have not put in my recipe book, it is common knowledge how it is to be prepared" (*The Viandier of Taillevent*, cited after Hennisch 2009: 19). On the other hand, the cook gives detailed descriptions of very complicated and sophisticated dishes, which only a master cook with a group of qualified assistants could stand a chance to prepare, which may be a way of boasting about his competence.

Comparing to their French counterparts, the English recipes were much less detailed. However, the character of recipes changed with time. The later a recipe,

---

10 Guillaume Tirel (also known as Taillevant) is believed to have lived from around 1312 to 1395. He served in a number of noble households. In 1373 he became the chief cook of Charles V and then of Charles VI. The *Viandier* is one of the best known French culinary collections. It was most probably compiled in the 1370's. It is a compilation of dishes gathered by Tirel from the earlier sources (Mennell 1996: 50). An edition of the *Viandier* with translation into English has been published by Scully (1997).

the more details it contains, although a few cases in which the 15th c. recipe is shorter than its 14th c. equivalent were also found (see examples (1a–b) below). Together with the length of the description, the nature of the recipes evolved too. Studies show that the same recipe changes over time in terms of the ingredients used for its preparation, way of cooking, or seasoning (e.g., Hammond 2005). Hence, following recipes with the same title but coming from different periods, one may come up with a different dish (see for instance Myers [Online]). Hieatt and Butler (1985: 9) explain the change of recipes over time in such a way: "these recipes were passed down through succeeding generations, however, there was a tendency to spell out procedures at greater and greater length and to add and/or vary ingredients."

Most of the recipes begin with a title, which depicts the cookbook's repository. The titles usually include the name of the dish or the main ingredient used for its preparation (Carroll 1999). The headings might also refer to a particular quality in the dish, such as the colour of the dish, the method of cooking or the type of the dish. "Recipe names sometimes reveal traditional influences and evolving patterns" (Laurioux 1999: 297). The English dish names very often reflect the French origin of the recipe. Even though the dish might have evolved into a different one than its French counterpart, not only in terms of the amount of details given in the recipe but also in the entire character of the dish; the recipe might even present a completely different dish than the one described in the French recipe of the same title (Hieatt and Butler 1985). Moreover, a number of recipes with a French looking title were never found in any of the French collections, e.g., 'Viaunde de Cypre' (DC_28), which suggests that the Anglo-Norman cooks developed their own recipes (see Hieatt and Butler 1985: 6).

(1a) 14th c.:

A tenche in syuee. Scalde þy tenche & atyre wel & boyle it; & tak þe same broth & myed bred & tempere it togedere, & tak good poudre / of canel & of clowes & do to þe sewe, & coloure it with safroun & salte it & lete hit boile. & tak myced onyounnes & frye hem in oyle dolyf or vynegre or in wyn or in þe same broth, & do hem in þat sewe & sesen it vp with vynegre or with eysel; & after þat lat it no more boyle.

(UC_9)

(1b) 15th c.:

Tenche in cyueye. Take a tenche, an skalde hym, roste hym, grynde Pepir an Safroun, Brede an Ale, & melle it to-gederys; take Oynonys, hake hem, an frye hem in Oyle, & do hem þer-to, and messe hem forth.

(PD_95)

1.3 The recipe as a text type

Probably the bane of research on the culinary medieval language conducted so far deals with the recipe as a text type[11]. Görlach (1992) shows that the recipe existed already in the Old English period, even though it was not distinguished as such – only when the lexeme 'receipt' was borrowed did the text type receive its name. However, no evidence concerning the Old English cooking recipe has been preserved[12]; all the conclusions referring to this period were drawn from the medical recipes. The medieval recipe, however, has been a more popular subject of scholarly studies. Nevertheless, most of the attention has been paid to the medical recipes, which were studied for instance by Carroll (2004), Görlach (1992), Mäkinen (2004), or Taavitsainen (2001a, b). A number of studies have been devoted to the particular features of the recipes, e.g., Massam and Roberge (1989), as well as Culy (1996) discuss the use of the null object in recipes.

Görlach (1992) considers the medical recipe to be formally identical to the cooking recipe. Apart from these, Schmidt (1994) enumerates also the general recipe. The main function of any culinary recipe has been defined by Görlach (1992: 745) as "the instruction on however to prepare a meal". In his later studies, the author (2004) describes the recipe as a category:

a) that is well-defined as far as function is concerned – the instruction on how to prepare a dish;
b) whose basic function has remained stable over the centuries – however much ingredients, utensils and the people involved in the process may have changed;
c) that has had an age-old name designating the particular text type (*recipe, receipt*);
d) that used to be collected in books of certain types (…); [from which] the proper *Cookery book*, restricted to a collection of recipes, developed rather late, mixed types surviving well into our times;
e) that has had similar types coexisting with it (the medical *recipe*) so that the history of contact/diversification can be followed up;
f) a text type that has had a vernacular tradition in Britain for a very long time, but also permits cross-cultural and interlinguistic comparisons (…).

(Görlach 2004: 123–4)

---

11   Görlach (2004: 105) defines a 'text type' as "a specific linguistic pattern in which formal/structural characteristics have been conventionalized in a specific culture for certain well-defined and standardized uses of language (…)".
12   Although, there were a number of attempts to recreate the recipes of the Anglo-Saxons, see for instance Savelli (2011).

The features which distinguish the recipe from other types of texts are: (a) the collection in which the text was found; (b) the terminology used in the title of the collection; (c) the language used (from the social perspective); (d) the addressee; (e) the linguistic features, such as the form of heading, the language style, the verbal forms, the use of possessive pronouns, the deletion of objects, the use of adverbs, the complexity of sentences, and the use of loanwords and genteel diction; (f) the specification (i.e., the use of quantifications); and (g) the standardized arrangement. (Görlach 1992, 2004, Carroll 1999).

The Middle English cooking recipes were definitely influenced by the French recipes, e.g., in terms of their frequent use of imperatives. Only at the end of the 15th c. did the written form of English recipes start to be popularized. Hardly ever did recipes take a rhymed form; one of the few examples is *Liber Cure Cocorum* (LCC) of the early 15th c. which is in the form of a doggerel. The research conducted by Carroll (1997, 1999) shows that medieval recipes contained a kind of technical language of cookery. She accounts for it by the fact that some of the vocabulary items were used in a more specific sense in the recipes than in other texts, e.g., the verbs *seethe*, *blanch*, etc.

Thus, the medieval cooking recipe can be characterized by:

a) the frequent use of imperative verb forms (additionally, forms with *shall* appear);
b) use of transitive verbs followed by an object rather than with a null object (which is typical of later recipes);
c) infrequent use of possessive pronouns;
d) the lack of complex sentences: simple, paratactic sentence structure, following the temporal sequence of instructions;
e) the lack of quantifications (lack of explicitness);
f) heading at the beginning (usually);
g) formulaic phrase at the end (frequently not always);
h) 'complete' sentences;
i) the existence of technical vocabulary;
j) being grouped into larger collections

(Görlach 1992, 2004; Carroll 1999).

Probably the most widely studied feature of the recipe as a text type concerns the use of non-overt objects. Culy (1996), who conducted a diachronic analysis of the English recipes, emphasizes that the use of zero anaphors as direct objects is a feature which distinguishes the English recipes from other text-types. The lack of an object has been accounted for by Massam and Roberge (1989: 135), who claim that "its [the object's] reference appears to be contextually defined". Horsey (1998) notices that null objects only appear in sentences without an overt subject such as imperatives. The studies show that "[t]he use of zeros in recipes has increased dramatically over time" (Culy 1996: 97). This has been accounted for by Fergusson (1994: 20), who suggested that "the language of cookbook recipes was at first not very different from other written varieties of English, [and] that it began to develop as the circulation of books increased" which resulted in the language taking a definitive form with the rise in literacy and in cookbooks' popularity. Fergusson also suggests a similarity of the English recipes to the French ones, in which the object omission also occurred. The use of zero anaphors could also be explained after Brown and Yule (1983: 175), who characterize the language of culinary books "as the elliptical written language".

1.4 An outline of the study

The present study has been based on the material found in various medieval culinary recipe collections. The first two chapters serve as a theoretical background to the topic. Chapter One brings closer the character of a medieval recipe and briefly discusses the recipe collections selected for the analytical part of the study. Chapter Two, in turn, focuses on the presentation of the medieval foodstuffs and culinary procedures, in order to make the reader familiar with the products the medieval recipes actually included, i.e., which ingredients were used and with what frequency, as well as with the cooking and preserving procedures which were at play in the medieval kitchen.

Chapters Three to Five constitute the practical part of the study and concentrate on the culinary verbs used in the recipe collections from the 14th and 15th centuries. The verbs have been divided into three main semantic groups, referring respectively to the subsequent chapters, i.e., verbs of cooking, cutting and preparing. All of them have been further subdivided into smaller groups. And thus, Chapter Three deals with the verbs of cutting. They have been subdivided into: (i) dividing verbs, i.e., verbs which refer to the division of foodstuffs into small but distinct (comparable) parts, such as *cut, dice, hack, hew, quarter*, etc.; (ii) reducing verbs, i.e., verbs which refer to the division of a foodstuff into small/minute particles which may not be perceptible in isolation but form a mass (or a pulp), such as *bray, grate, grind, powder*, etc.; (iii) removing verbs, i.e., verbs which refer to the separation of a part of a foodstuff from its main body, such as *blanch, hull, peel, shave, skin*, etc.; and (iv) penetrating verbs, i.e., verbs which either refer to cutting foodstuffs without dividing or removing anything

33

by the cut, such as *open* and *cut*, or to the action influencing the shape of the foodstuff, such as *break, burst*, etc. Chapter Four concentrates on the verbs of cooking, with the subdivision of the verbs with respect to the medium in which food is cooked. Thus, the particular sections are devoted to (i) verbs of cooking in liquid, e.g., *boil, parboil, seethe*, etc.; (ii) verbs of cooking in fat, e.g., *fry, bake*, etc.; and (iii) verbs of cooking in any or no medium, e.g., *heat, toast*, etc. A certain hierarchy of the verbs of cooking is being established. Chapter Five comprises the widely understood verbs of preparing, i.e., verbs which refer to any activities other than cooking and cutting which contribute to the process of food preparation and which have been enumerated or described in the analyzed recipes. The verbal groups which have been distinguished within this category are (i) verbs of cleaning, (ii) verbs of adding and combining, which have been put in one category due to the difficulty to distinguish between the senses of particular verbs in the context, (iii) verbs of straining, (iv) verbs of seasoning, (v) verbs of decoration, (vi) verbs of taking, which have been put into a separate category due to their frequency of usage within the analyzed material, and (vii) verbs of serving.

The first step in the analysis was to construct a corpus which would represent a broad sample of culinary instructions from the 14th and 15th centuries. The next step was to create an electronic database (to make automatic search possible), thus the recipes were scanned, labeled (for the sake of reference) and proofread. Altogether 1588 recipes were collected (431 and 1157 from the 14th and 15th centuries respectively). Due to the fact that the samples of material coming from particular periods are not of equal size (not only the number of recipes but also their length differ, see Table 1 below), the number of the occurrences of particular lexemes cannot be treated as a reliable indicator of the frequency of the lexemes. For instance, a higher number of records of a verb in the 15th c. does not necessarily mean that the verb was used more frequently at that time than in the 14th c. Thus, next to the absolute frequencies (i.e., the real number of occurrence of each verb), relative normalized frequencies will be given. The relative frequency is obtained by dividing the number of occurrences of the analyzed lexeme by the total number of words in the analyzed (part of the) corpus. The numbers will be then normalized to ten thousand words.[13]

---

13 For a detailed discussion on normalizing data, see for instance Römer and Wulff (2010).

Table 1: The size of the analyzed material

period	nr of recipes	nr of words
1st half of 14th c.	65	3,741
2nd half of 14th c.	366	25,282
1st half of 15th c.	650	57,147
2nd half of 15th c.	507	42,117

The strategies applied in the research are those of corpus linguistic studies and focus on the use of particular forms in context. The emphasis will be based on the quantitative rather than qualitative analysis. However, these two methods should be considered complementary. The texts included in the corpus will be examined in order to reveal the typical distributional patterns of particular verbs, focusing on the lexico-grammatical context. No comparison between the particular texts within the corpus will be made, mostly due to the fact that the single texts are rather scarce, and only an investigation of the corpus as a whole gives a sufficient picture. Additionally, the bottom-up approach will be adopted, in which "it is the linguistic element that is privileged" (Haan 2010: 103).[14]

A common feature throughout the analytical part of the study is the special attention put on the French influence[15] on the culinary language used in the analyzed recipe collections, as well as the existing parallels between vocabulary items of Germanic and Romance origin belonging to particular semantic categories, their frequency of use and possible shades of meaning. The particular subgroups of verbs will first be presented with respect to their etymology, denotation and frequency within the corpus. Next, we will proceed to the discussion on the synonymy, rivalry, and semantic changes, within the particular categories of verbs, depending on the specificity of the verbal subgroups.

---

[14] For a discussion on the bottom-up vs. top-down approaches, see also Biber, Connor and Upton (2007).

[15] Even though the early studies of the French influence on English enumerated a relatively poor stock of lexical items borrowed or influenced by French (see for instance Mettig 1910, Serjeantson 1962 [1935], or Scheler 1977), it is generally well known that the semantic field of food has been greatly influenced by French. The later studies are much richer in examples of borrowing within the domain of cookery (see for instance Miller 2012).

The study ends with the general conclusions, which review the characteristics of the analyzed groups of verbs and present the summary of the findings concerning the occurrences and the semantic behaviour of the verbs in question. Finally, the Appendix lists the recipe collections used for the study and serves as a reference point to the source of the recipes quoted within the text.

Chapter Two: Medieval food and drink

2.1 Medieval foodstuffs

After the Norman Conquest, the aristocracy enjoyed "a sophisticated cuisine based on that of Norman France, which had been inherited from the Roman era and modified through the centuries under Gothic and Frankish influence." (Wilson 1991: 237ff). However, food historians generally agree that medieval food did not differ much from what we eat today (see for instance Hammond 2005, Scully 1995). The variety of foodstuffs available in Medieval England comprised meat, such as beef, pork and lamb[16]; fish; fruit and vegetables; grain products such as bread or ale; and a wide range of spices.

Some foods served at the Medieval table, such as fruits and vegetables, were season dependent. Others, such as meat, fish and cereals, were present on a daily basis (Brears 2008). Even if some meats or fish were out of season, they were available in a preserved state (smoked, salted, dried, etc.). An important factor determining the food served at a particular time was religion; different dishes were served during Lent, for instance, when meat was forbidden, than at other times of the year. This has been reflected in the recipes, giving rise to dishes such as 'Leche frys in lentoun' (FC_166), 'Loseyns in fyssh day' (FC_132) or 'Hattes in lentyn' (OP_113), or including variants of a particular dish, e.g.:

> (…) and do þerto gode broth; and aray it as þou didest caboches.
> If þey be in fyssh day, make on the same manere with water
> and oyle, and if it be not in lent, alye it with 3olkes of eyren;
>
> (FC_9).

The recipes tell us a lot about the diet of the upper classes, but unfortunately the food habits of the other social classes are not so well documented. For the latter, scholars use the available archaeological evidence as well as a number of documents and accounts of payments paid to various workers in kind. The study conducted by Dyer (1988), for instance, dealing with the medieval diet of field workers in eastern and southern England, shows significant changes in their diet. Thus, in the 13th c. the

---

16   Details concerning meat consumption are among others known from the yields of slaughterhouses.

harvest workers' diet consisted mainly of bread and dairy products such as cheese and milk, with only a slight addition of ale, fish (usually smoked or salted) and meat (mostly bacon). In the early 15th c. the quality of their meals improved a lot. Not only were they given more meat rather than bread and dairy produce, but also the quality of the food improved. The bread was mainly baked of wheat rather than rye and maslin[17]. Similarly, the quality of ale was much better than in the 13th c. It's amount also rose. In those areas where in the earlier period cider was served, by the end of the 14th c. it was replaced by ale. Fresh beef was much more frequent than bacon or fish. Additionally, Dyer (1988) shows that in the 14th c. fresh mutton, and in the early 15th c. fresh (sea) fish, were incorporated into the field workers' diet. However, he also notices that the animals allotted for workers were usually those unsuitable for the lord's table (either too old or diseased).

2.1.1 Meat and fish

Cattle, sheep and pigs were the main meat-providing animals throughout the Middle Ages (see for instance Sykes 2006a, Albarella 2006). The data available from slaughterhouses' yields reveal that the demand for meat was great throughout the year (Scully 1995). In the aristocratic households, the finest meats were the most popular ones, especially after the Black Death, when meat consumption became considered an extraordinary excess (Woolgar 2006). However, it also became available for a wider range of the society (Mennell 1996, Montanari 1996).

The archaeological evidence shows that beef was the primary meat consumed throughout the Middle Ages (Laurioux 1999). Sykes (2006a) shows that mutton was dominant in the early Middle Ages, whilst the consumption of beef and veal increased from the second half of the 14th c. This has been accounted for by Lloyd (1977), who claims that a disease of sheep reduced the flocks in the 14th and 15th c. by up to two thirds. Following Darby (1936), in the 15th c. also the amount of wool trade decreased, which confirms a downward trend in sheep husbandry. However, Sykes (2006a) notices that in the aristocratic households the eating habits did not reflect the socio-economic situation, quite the contrary. For instance, before the sheep plague[18], the elite ate considerably less mutton than when the sheep population was lower.

---

17 Maslin is a combination of rye and barley.
18 The sheep plague, following Lloyd (1977), reduced the sheep flocks of the 14th and 15th centuries by up to two thirds.

Albarella (2006) writes that pigs were the third most popular animal after cattle and sheep, whilst Dyer (1998) places pork as the second most common meat in the aristocratic households, beef being the first. Swine were a good source of meat, since every part was suitable to eat. What is more, it could have been preserved by smoking or curing. However, in the later Middle Ages pork consumption was reduced in comparison to other types of meat (Albarella 2006: 73, Wilson 1991). Dyer (1998) explains this by the fact that eating pork went out of fashion. Albarella's study shows that the decreased popularity of pig husbandry was related to an increase in the number of sheep. Campbell (2000) as well as Wilson (1991) add problems with pannage[19] caused by the decreasing number of forests as contributing not only to the smaller number of pigs but also to a worse quality of their meat, due to worse feeding. As a result, by the end of the Middle Ages, aristocrats reduced consumption of pork drastically (Woolgar 1999), with only the meat of young swine perceived as appropriate for their refined tastes (Dyer 1998, Woolgar 2006). By the end of the 15th c. beef consumption retained its primary role (Woolgar 2006, Wilson 1991).

Generally, in the later Middle Ages, there was a tendency for lighter meats, such as piglets, calves, lambs and kids; as well as poultry, birds and game (Woolgar 1999). Of the domestic fowl, the recipes enumerate hens, cocks and roosters, chicks, chickens, pullets, cockerels and capons.

Apart from the domestic animals, game too was eaten. After the Norman Conquest hunting was the privilege of the upper classes of the society due to the forest law applied by the Norman kings[20]. It is difficult to estimate the amount of meat obtained by hunting. However, evidence shows a rising tendency after the Norman Conquest. The highest rate of venison eaten at aristocratic households was in the period from the middle of the 12th c. to the middle of the 14th c. (Sykes 2006b). The most often hunted game were deer and boar. Sykes's study (2006b) shows that in the early Norman period it was roe deer which constituted the largest amount of meat, while in the 12th c. the interest shifted to red deer as well as fallow deer, which is said to have been introduced to England from Sicily by the Normans. The Norman Conquest brought a number of changes not only in terms of the availability of the game exclusively to the upper classes, or the range of species hunted

---

19 Pannage was the right to exploit woodland for swine pasture.
20 Common people were sometimes granted occasional days when hunting was permitted (e.g., Henry III allowed to hunt on Easter day within 20 miles around London). Only after 1217 were the most restricted laws repealed; however, some restrictions still applied.

at a particular period, but also in terms of the techniques applied when hunting. The pre-Conquest hunting method, the so called 'drive', aimed at obtaining large amounts of meat. It involved large bands of people and consisted in driving deer to an enclosure and shooting them with arrows. Later, this method was replaced with the 'chase', in which a single deer was chased in the open. It was more a sport than a way of obtaining large quantities of meat. After killing the animal, a particular procedure was applied to skinning and disintegrating its meat. Additionally, a whole range of terminology was introduced from Norman French to describe the particular actions.

Birds were also an important element of the medieval diet, especially because their meat was permitted when animal meat was forbidden (e.g., in Benedictine houses, Harvey 1993: 40). Dyer (1998) estimates that one tenth of meat consumed before the Black Death in aristocratic and ecclesiastical households consisted of birds. Domestic fowl included chickens, capons, cocks, roosters, geese, ducks, doves, etc. Peafowl too were often domesticated and kept in captivity (Stone 2006b, Serjeantson 2006).

Wild fowl started to be eaten in the early Middle Ages (Serjeantson 2006). They included goose, duck, pigeon, dove, heron, cormorant, pheasant, partridge, quail, mallard, stork, crane, swan, bittern, teal, and the so called small birds (which comprised little, song birds, such as larks). Seabirds, which could have been preserved by salting and drying, were also captured for food, e.g., shearwater and gannet. Swan is said to have been the most expensive bird in the later medieval times, with crane, heron and bustard being costly too (Wilson 1991). In aristocratic households, a great deal of game fowl were caught by professional fowlers. Additionally, the nobles entertained themselves with hawking and falconry, especially popular after the Norman Conquest. A great variety of fowl served at a particular household indicated its high social status. Moreover, the young birds, which otherwise were kept either for eggs, feathers or for a greater amount of meat, were much more popular at the aristocratic tables.

Generally, in the Middle Ages chicken was the most popular fowl, but its consumption decreased in the later period in favour of wild fowl; the same tendency has been observed in terms of geese (see Table 1). Geese were, however, a seasonal dish. They were served in the autumn and winter, while during the summer some green geese (i.e., young geese) were consumed (Stone 2006b). The archaeological evidence agrees with the documents in that the later Middle Ages witness a higher consumption of fowl. For instance, young birds became more common. Small birds gained popularity, not so much due to the value of their meat (since they were too small for that) but rather due to health reasons. They were believed to bring health but also were an indicator of high status (Woolgar 1999). The increase in the consumption of small birds may account for the rise in the number of wild fowl eaten in the later period. Also some other birds gained popularity after the Black Death, e.g., pigeons, swans, herons, capons and peacocks (Stone 2006b). On the other hand, as suggested by Serjeantson (2006), some species became rarer in the 14th c., e.g., crane and partridge.

Table 1: *The ratio of fowl at different periods, drawn from the archaeological evidence (based on Serjeantson 2006)*

	chicken	goose	ducks, pigeons, wild fowl
Pre-Conquest	< 70%	> 20%	> 10%
11th–12th c.	> 70%	< 20%	> 10%
13th–e.14th c.	70%	20%	10%
l.14th c.–e.16th c.	60%	10%	> 30%

Little of a medieval animal or fowl was discarded. Such parts as giblets, offal, brains, tongue, a cock's comb, gizzard (throat), sweetbreads, lungs, entrails (including stomach, liver, kidneys and bladder), intestines, mesentery, marrow, udder, testicles, feet and tails were also eaten.

Meat was prepared by roasting, broiling on a gridiron, frying or stewing. It could have been also 'closed' in a pie and baked.

According to Wilson (1991), after the Norman Conquest a number of sausages were introduced into the English cuisine. Neckam mentions three types: 'aundulyes', 'saucistres' and 'pudingis'. They were all made at the time of killing hogs. "Andouilles were the large guts stuffed with the chopped entrails and well seasoned. Sausages were made from the lean pork; and black puddings from the animal's blood" (Wilson 1991: 309ff). The last type could have been prepared also at the time of the pig's slaughter, and soon became a delicacy. Sausages were eaten either boiled, grilled or fried in fat. In the 15th c. sausages were also made of other types of meat than pork. Puddings of other colours than black (made of different ingredients) were also introduced.

Fish were very important for the medieval diet, mainly due to fasting. According to Wilson (1991) the number of fasting days increased after the Norman Conquest. "It [fish] replaced meat every Friday, Saturday and, up to the early fifteenth century, Wednesdays too, as well as throughout Lent" (Brears 2008: 149). Following Wilson (1991), meat was forbidden altogether during about half of the days of the year. Both fresh water fish (e.g., eel, pike, trout, tench, carp) and sea fish (e.g., salmon, cod, herring) were eaten, as well as shellfish (e.g., oysters, cockles and mussels), which could be eaten even raw. Shellfish were gathered in great quantities, since they were easily available, and they were common not only in the diet of the rich but also of the peasants. On the other hand, whales, porpoise and sturgeon were typically an element of the royal and noble diet. Following Serjeantson and Woolgar (2006), marine fish were much more important in terms of diet; however, before the Norman Conquest river and inshore fishing were the most important ways for obtaining fish among the society. As Brears reports (2008: 247), most fish were prepared by removing the entrails and gills and boiling with spices and herbs. Sauces were probably poured over the fish just before serving. The most popular sauce served with fish was 'green sauce' (Wilson 1991). Already in the 12th c. Neckam noticed that fish should be boiled either in water or in water and wine. Additionally, it could be boiled in a mixture of water and ale (e.g., BK_162).

Archaeological evidence shows that herring was the dominant fish from the early times, cod being the second most abundant fish, especially in eastern England (London, York, Norwich). In the south-western parts of the country (Exeter, Bristol, Ilchester), hake was the dominant fish; in the south it was conger eel (Serjeantson and Woolgar 2006). Other fish gained popularity later, e.g., from the 13th and 14th c.: haddock, flatfish (flounder and plaice), gurnard, mullet, etc. Herring retained its popularity due to being cheap and available in large numbers. Fish eating declined towards the end of the 15th c.

Historical documents confirm a wide range of fish being eaten throughout the country in the Middle Ages, with cod and herring being the most frequent species. In the 15th c. the London market offered such fish as: flatfish, codling, whiting, mackerel, conger eel, herring, sole, plaice, turbot, mullet, shellfish, etc. By this time the fish trade was well regulated – for instance fresh fish could not be salted for reselling, preserved fish which were softened by soaking in water were banned from being sold, and shellfish could be sold only for a short time.

Fish could be prepared with or without their bones, in the latter case, the bones were crushed in a mortar. A similar procedure was applied to crustaceans. Even though sea fish could have been transported throughout the country within a short time, and fresh water fish were not transported to distant areas, many species of fish were usually preserved, e.g., herrings were dried or smoked.

The majority of meats and fish served in medieval households were available throughout the year, and even those which were seasonal were available in preserved forms (see section 2.2.4).

Fish were served in a variety of forms, and they could have been eaten hot or cold. They were used for cooking pottage, in baking pies and crusts, jellies, etc. In a great number of recipes meat and fish were interchangeable; however, there were some dishes in which only fish was allowed, for instance pikes and eels in 'balloc broth' (e.g., OP_15 or Gr_WW 62).

2.1.2 Fruit and vegetables

As reported by Hieatt (1988a: 19), people in the Middle Ages ate "whatever green salads and fresh fruits might be in season". However, culinary recipes mention fruit only in a cooked form. Neither the available cookbooks nor historical documents say how much fresh fruit or vegetables were eaten in the medieval times. Scully (1995: 71) notices that "[i]t is likely (...) [that] vegetables and fruits were so commonly served at mealtimes, and in a fairly plain state, that medieval recipes books remain relatively silent about them." On the other hand, eaten raw, horticultural products were thought to be dangerous for health and difficult to digest. For instance, Russell warns his readers:

> beware of saladis, grene metis, & of frutes rawe
> for þey make many a man haue a feble mawe.
> þerfore, of suche fresch lustes set not an hawe,
> For suche wantoun appetites ar not worth a strawe.
>
> (Russell: 8)

Additionally, Clark (1975) notices that in the French aristocratic cuisine fresh fruit and vegetables replaced dried and otherwise preserved ones only in the late 16th c. And taking into account that the English medieval recipes are largely influenced by the French cuisine, its highly improbable that the use of fresh fruit and vegetables was different than on the other side of the Channel. According to Wilson (1991), raw fruit, vegetables and nuts were allowed but only as an appetizer before the meal proper. After a meal, they were recommended, but in a cooked form (usually roasted), as suggested by Freedman (2007), mainly due to the fact that they were believed to rot in the stomach and thus were considered dangerous.

Dyer (2006: 27) accounts for the scarcity of material on fruit and vegetables by saying that they were treated by historians as marginal and trivial. The fact that garden work was conducted by members of a household rather than by hired workers also contributed to the scarce evidence in historical records. However, he assures that "gardens were an integral part of the English economy in the later Middle Ages, and that they reflected the social hierarchy: some aristocratic houses had large, well-stocked, and professionally managed gardens, while almost all peasants and a considerable number of urban households had access to smaller parcels of garden ground" (Dyer 2006: 33).

Vegetables were rarely mentioned in feast menus. However, culinary recipes of the time enumerate such vegetables as: onion, radish, leek, cabbage, turnip, etc.; as well as fruit, e.g., pears[21], apples[22], cherries, peaches, quinces and gooseberries. Many fruits and nuts were imported from the Mediterranean, very often in a dried or otherwise preserved form, e.g., raisins[23], currants, figs, dates and almonds. Hammond (2005) adds oranges, pomegranates and lemons. He notices that they were imported in especially large amounts in the later Middle Ages. Some vegetables were also imported, e.g., onions, garlic or cabbage. Leeks were very popular during Lent. Parsley was mainly eaten in the leaf, but the flavoursome root was also used for cooking.

Fruit seem to have become more popular in the later Middle Ages. As stated by Cortonesi (1999), from the 13th c. an increase in the cultivation of fruit trees has been documented. Both fruit and nuts are especially well documented archaeologically, due to the preservation of fruit stones and nutshells. Following Moffett (2006), the most popular were: plums, walnuts, cherries, pears, apples, strawberries, grapes and figs. Fruit (fresh or dried) were often used to decorate meat dishes. Dried fruit and nuts were added to batter and fried in oil.

Pulses, such as peas and beans, were the most documented crops in England. For instance, at the end of the 14th c. and throughout the 15th c. peas constituted 30% of vegetable gardens at Leicester Abbey, and beans were reported as one of the most important crops in the 13th c. in Sedgemoor, a district in Somerset (Cortonesi 1999: 270). Probably the greatest advantage of the pulses was the fact that they could have been dried and kept throughout the year. They were used mainly for cooking pottages.

And finally, almonds were very popular in the medieval kitchen. According to Brears (2008), the royal household used almost 13 tons of almonds during one year at the end of the 13th c. Wilson (1991) calculates that it was 28,500 pounds in 1286 and almost 20,000 a year later. They were believed to help digestion. They

---

21 A common type of pears were warden pears, they were much bigger and harder than other pears, thus they were often treated as a separate type of fruit, and hence, phrases such as 'wardens and pears' can be frequently found in the available recipes.
22 Similarly, 'costards' were such a distinctive type of apple (much bigger) that they were treated as a separate kind of fruit, thus, phrases such as 'apples and costards' can be frequently found in the recipes.
23 'Raisins of Corinth' were especially common. For more on the name, see Rothwell (1998).

might have been used in their whole form, blanched, fried, scattered over a dish, or powdered. However, the most common use of almonds was in the form of almond milk (see section 2.1.3 and 2.1.6). Additionally, almond butter or cream could have been extracted, and formed a substitute for animal dairy products at the time of fasting. Almonds were also used to produce marzipan (by mixing almonds with sugar), often used in subtleties.

2.1.3 Dairy products

Domestic animals were an important source not only of meat but also of dairy products: milk, cheese, butter, etc. Not only cows and sheep were a good source of milk, but as Wilson (1991) reports, also goats, especially in the south-west of England, where they were especially numerous in the later Middle Ages. The amount of sheep's milk available diminished after the 13th c. due to the concentration of sheep husbandry on wool production. Thus, cattle dairy products became more widespread in the 14th and 15th c. (Woolgar 2006). Hammond (2005: 9) reports that "the annual milk yield per cow in the fourteenth century has been calculated as 120–150 gallons". Wilson (1991: 155) claims that by the end of the medieval period cow milk ousted sheep and goats as milk suppliers. However, animal milk, due to the scarcity of winter feed, was seasonal and most of the milk was obtained in the summer[24].

Most of the milk was processed to form the so called 'white meats', i.e., cream, butter, whey, curds, cheese, etc. rather than drunk fresh or used for cookery. Cream and butter were produced mainly from cow's milk. Additionally, a little butter was obtained from ewe's milk. Often cream was preferred to milk in the process of enriching cooked dishes. Butter was either made in large open bowls or later in the churn. The first skimming gave the best quality butter, a few hours later the second skimming gave butter of inferior quality. The worst butter was obtained from the curds, which rose on the whey after the full cream milk had been drained for cheese. Different kinds of butter were used for different purposes. Sweet butter was beaten in fresh water in order to separate it from buttermilk, then it was salted and served for consumption. Salt butter could have been kept longer; it was prepared by working out the buttermilk alone (without water), with later salt or brine beaten into it. Clarified butter was used for cooking.

---

24 Although, following Wilson (1991: 155), "cows were milked at all times of year".

Cheese was obtained from cows', goats' and ewes' milk. Medieval cheeses were classified according to their texture rather than their place of production. Boorde (in Furnivall 1870: 266) distinguishes four types of medieval cheese: green, soft, hard cheese and 'spermyse'. Green cheese was the fresh and moist cheese. A special type of green cheese was the so called 'junket', originating in Normandy. It was a rich delicacy prepared of pure cream curdled with rennet. 'Spermyse' was a soft type of cheese made with the addition of herbs. Hard cheese was probably low fat cheese, made of skimmed milk; and soft cheese – made of whole or semi-skimmed milk. Apart from these, Boorde enumerates 'rewene cheese', which is said to be the best of all. According to Brears (2008: 84), cottage cheese was also eaten. It was made "by adding rennet to warm milk" (e.g., LV_14). The curds were used as a refreshing drink (e.g., GK_23) or for making various cheesecakes.

Eggs were a commonly available product not only at noble households but also among the lower classes. They could have been eaten during fasting days except for Lent. There were a number of ways of cooking eggs: boiling, roasting in their shells, or frying in butter or lard. Eggs were also a very popular ingredient of more complex dishes. They functioned as a thickener added to various sauces and soups, were used for making various batters and pastry, and were mixed with wine or ale to produce a common drink served warm for breakfast or at bedtime. Additionally, in the late 14th c. a precursor of the modern omelette was recorded (e.g., FC_180).

Moreover, almond milk should be mentioned here. It predominated over animal milk in aristocratic households. The reason was very practical: almonds could be stored and milk extracted at any time whilst animal milk had to be used within a short period. Thus, cow's milk, for instance, was more often used for the production of dairy products such as butter and cheese (which were easier to preserve) rather than used in everyday cooking (Scully 1995: 14ff). Moreover, almond milk was an alternative to animal milk in the time of fasting (Brears 2008). Its production involved shelling and blanching almonds (usually in boiling water), then grinding them with a liquid such as wine or water. It could be either sweet or savoury, depending on how it was prepared.

According to Woolgar (2006), the amount of dairy produce served at noble households was small in the 13th and 14th c. They were given especially to young and sick people. He also notices that in the households headed by women, milk and cheese were more popular than elsewhere. In the 15th c. an increase in the use of dairy products can be seen in aristocratic households, which can be accounted for by the wider variety at meals and greater interest in desserts.

2.1.4 Grains

Not only historical documents (e.g., Stone 2006a) but also archaeobotanical evidence from the Middle Ages (see Moffett 2006) show that grain exceeded any other foodstuff in Medieval Britain, although, as Stone (2006a) writes, cereal consumption varied throughout the country. "It has been estimated that at the start of the fourteenth century grain accounted for up to 80 per cent of a harvest worker's calories and 78 per cent of a soldier's; even among the lay nobility of medieval England, grain provided 65–70 per cent of their energy intake" (Stone, after Murphy 1998: 120). The main crops planted were wheat (wheat bread was more desired than any other), rye, barley and oats. In the 15th c. farmers concentrated on barley and oats since these gave higher yields. The former was a source of bread as well as ale. The latter was often used to feed horses but also in the kitchen (for thickening meals as well as for 'gruel', i.e., a kind of an oatmeal porridge). Rye was eaten mostly by the peasants. Mixtures of grains were also grown, e.g., 'dredge' (barley + oats), 'berevechicorn' (dredge + vetch); 'maslin' (rye + wheat), 'pulse' (beans + peas), 'bollymong' (oats + peas + vetches / buckwheat), etc. Rye and wheat were sown after the autumn ploughing, the rest in early spring. Table 2 shows Stone's (2006a) summary of the major types of grain crops cultivated in England in the period 1250–1540 and their uses.

Table 2: Types of grain crops and their uses in England in the period 1250–1540 (based on Stone 2006a)

grain:	its use:
wheat	bread, ale
rye	bread, thatch, fodder
winter barley	ale, bread, fodder
wheat + rye	bread
wheat + winter barley	bread, ale
oats	pottage, fodder, ale, thatch, bread
spring barley	ale, bread, pottage, fodder
beans, peas, vetches	fodder, nitrogen-fixing, pottage, bread, vegetables
spring barley + oats	ale
oats + beans + peas	fodder, nitrogen-fixing, pottage
oats + legumes	fodder, nitrogen-fixing, pottage

The most common use of grains was grinding for flour, which in turn was used for making bread. In the Middle Ages bread was a staple food for all the social classes. It was available throughout the year, and was present at every meal. Moreover, as Brears (2008) notices bread corn could have been stored from one year to the next. Following Scully (1995), the range of grains ground into flour and used for the production of bread was wide. Grains, such as wheat, millet or barley, could have been used alone, while others, such as oats or rye, were usually used in a mixture. Additionally, rice, peas, beans, lentils, chestnuts, etc. were ground and used for baking bread. 'Paindemayn' (or 'white bread') was considered to be the best quality white bread. It was made of wheat flour alone. Hieatt and Butler (1985) suggest that the best quality flour was called 'mayne' and thus the name of the bread (meaning 'bread made of mayne flour'). Darker bread was made of wheat and rye; the cheap bread was baked from barley and oats; whilst the cheapest bread was made of ground peas and beans. Bread was usually baked in bakeries rather than in aristocratic kitchens. The largest houses had their own bakeries and bread ovens. It was a very common, everyday procedure, which may account for the fact that it is hardly ever mentioned in medieval documents. Wilson, however, claims that the techniques of bread making "formed a secret lore, learned by the housewife from her mother and by the baker from the master craftsmen who were his seniors in the 'mistery'." (1991: 241). For methods of baking bread see for instance Brears (2008). One of the available recipes for making bread comes from the beginning of the 15th c.:

> Take fayre Flowre, & þe whyte of Eyroun, & þe 3olke, a lytel; þan take Warme Berme, & putte al þes to-gederys, & bete hem to-gederys with þin hond tyl it be schort & þikke y-now, & caste Sugre y-now þer-to, & þenne lat reste a whyle; þan kaste in a fayre place in þe oven, & late bake y-now; & þen with a knyf cutte yt round a-boue in maner of a crowne, & kepe þe cruste þat þou kyttyst; & þan pyke al þe cromys with-ynne to-gederys, an pike hem smal with þin knyf, & saue þe sydys & al þe cruste hole with-owte; & þan caste þer-in clarifiyd Boter, & Mille þe crome3 & þe botere to-gedere3, & keuere it a-3en with þe cruste, þat þou kyttest a-way; þan putte it in þe ovyn a3en a lytil tyme; & þan take it out, & serue it forth.
>
> (BM_25)

The amount of bread consumed at particular households varied. Stone (2006a) suggests that greater amounts of bread were eaten on Lent days. After the Black Death, not only did the amount of bread eaten rise, but also its quality improved. Except from the 'pure' version, breadcrumbs were used as a thickener for pottages and sauces. Moreover, a precursor of toast was available in the medieval cookery.

"Pieces of white bread were browned on the gridiron, soaked in wine, reheated and crisped, and then served with almond milk" (Wilson 1991: 248).

Following Scully (1995), apart from being ground into flour, small grained cereals were also boiled (soups and porridges) or roasted; however, boiling or roasting grains were the basic operations and thus these procedures were hardly ever described in the culinary collections. A number of cereal pottages were cooked. Their type depended on the corn available in a particular district. A very popular dish consisting of boiled cereal grains is 'frumenty' (e.g., PD_8, PD_59, BK_7). The simplest form of such a pottage was served as a dish in itself. However, it was often involved in the preparation of other 'more complicated' dishes, e.g., venison (FC_1, DS_1) or porpoise (FC_70, FC_119). According to Brears (2008: 273ff), in England frumenty "has probably been made continuously for some 12,000 years, for some families in North and East Yorkshire still prepare a batch every Christmas. (…) Medieval cooks preferred to place the wheat in a stone mortar, sprinkle it with a little water, and pound it with a wooden pestle to remove the bran, but still leave the grains intact." Then, the grain was rinsed, boiled (until bursting), simmered with milk, flavoured, coloured and finally thickened.

Stone (2006a) adds ale as being, after flour and pottage (which was especially relevant to the lower classes' diet), the most important product of grain. Barley was thought to be the best grain for ale production. Additionally, oats and dredge (a mixture of barley and oats) were used for lower quality ale.

Flour was also used for making cakes, pies, tarts, lozenges and wafers. Pies come from the Roman times. These are various dishes made of flour and oil paste with stuffing (of various kinds) closed inside the pastry. Open pies were also baked. Wafers were introduced by the Normans. They were often used as layers of a crust or a pie. Otherwise, they were served spiced, savoury or sweet, always hot and crispy.

In the early Middle Ages, rice was cultivated in Spain and Sicily, but by the end on the 15th c. it was also grown on a large scale in northern Italy, from where it was imported to England (Adamson 2004). It was perceived as a high quality food (Brears 2008: 275ff), with the price depending on the colour of the rice (white rice being the most precious). Rice was used mainly for various pottages. Additionally, rice flour was commonly used to thicken a dish. A similar effect was obtained by adding starch. Rice was also used for stuffings or as a side dish. It was perceived as a healthy food, especially when cooked with milk.

"[M]edieval pastry was essentially a mouldable substance in which very quickly-cooked delicate foods could be enclosed while being briefly baked in the oven" (Brears 2008: 125). Some pastries were made with self, free-standing crusts, others were made in traps. There were two types of pastries: the richer one with eggs used in the process of preparation, and the poorer variety consisting of flour, salt and water. Pastries could have been coloured with some colourants such as saffron (see section 2.2.3). Unlike bread, pastries were prepared in aristocratic kitchens. The medieval pastries included tarts, custards, darioles, doucets, flampoints, flans, pies, pasties, etc. They usually differed in terms of their type of filling, or appearance, etc. For instance, flans were wider than doucets. The pastries could have been open or closed.

Additionally, grains were used to produce malt, which was made by roasting germinated grain in order to convert the grain starch into sugar. As reported by Moffett (2006: 52ff), any kind of cereals might have been used for malting.

2.1.5 Herbs and spices[25]

Redgrove (1933) distinguishes between spices and herbs by saying that the former are the dried parts of aromatic plants, whilst the latter are the herbaceous parts of the plants. He also defines 'condiments' as spices or other flavourings added to food at the table. Davidson (2006: 380) suggests that herbs can be used both in dried and fresh form, whilst spices are always dried.

Spices were very popular already in Antiquity, which is evidenced in the collection compiled in the 4th c. by Apicus (see for instance, Grig [Online]). They were imported from India and the Far East.[26] However, following Flandrin (1999), at no other period in history did they play as great a role as from the 14th to the 16th centuries. They were used in a great variety, amount and with a high frequency. Freedman (2007: 50) reports:

> Spices were omnipresent in medieval gastronomy. Something on the order of 75% of medieval recipes involves spices. In their updated compendium of medieval dishes adapted to modern techniques, *Pleyn Delit*, Constance Hieatt and Sharon Butler collected 131 medieval recipes of which 92 involve exotic spices. A Catalan cookbook compiled for the king of Naples in 1500 contains approximately 200 recipes and of these no less than 154 call for sugar. Cinnamon is used in 125 of the recipes and ginger is mentioned in 76.
>
> (Freedman 2007: 50)

---

25 For an analysis of vocabulary belonging to the semantic field 'herbs and spices' in the 14th and 15th centuries, see Bator 2013b.
26 For a discussion on the medieval records of the major English ports, see Rothwell 1999.

Also, the use of particular spices had changed from the times of Apicus, e.g., the most important spice in Apicus's collection, i.e. pepper,[27] had lost its favour (see Laurioux 1985). As Laurioux (1999) suggests, in the Middle Ages it was replaced by such spices as ginger or grains of paradise, to regain its popularity in the 18th c.

Various reasons for such popularity of spices were suggested (see for instance Scully 1995, Laurioux 1985, Flandrin 1999). For instance, they were used to preserve meat and fish from decay. However, it should be borne in mind that meat and fish were usually salted, dried or smoked (see section 2.2.4). Another reason for the use of spices was to show one's social position. Spices, most of which were imported, were generally very expensive. Thus, the more of them were added to dishes, the better the financial situation of the host. The medical properties of spices seem to be the most convincing factor for their use.[28] Laurioux (1985) claims that spices were first imported as medicine and only later incorporated as seasoning, thus, making the food more tasty as well as healthier.

The medieval dishes were much spicier than today. The range of various spices added to food was enormous: ginger, cinnamon, cloves, grains of paradise (seeds of gingery flavour), long pepper, mace, spikenard, round (or black and white) pepper, saffron (which was also used as a colourant, giving a reddish yellow colour), galingale, nutmeg, cumin, sugar, etc. Saffron was probably the most expensive spice (Hammond 2005). There were also a few native spices, such as mustard.

Among herbs popular in the Middle Ages, there were: dill, fennel, coriander, celery, black mustard, borage, briar, clary, parsley[29], avens, anise, sage, cress, mallow, nettles, mint, primrose, thyme, violet and opium poppy (Moffett 2006). The last one was frequently used as a flavouring for bread and cakes. Additionally, savory, hyssop, marjoram, etc. were used. Brears (2008: 259) reports that various pottages made of mixed green herbs were very popular. They were usually prepared by parboiling, draining, chopping and then simmering in some liquid, and thus, the strongest tastes were soothed.

With time, dishes became sweeter and spicier. The amount of spices added to particular dishes is very often disputed. However, they were definitely used in a great variety. Abram (1913: 136) even suggests that "Medieval cooks flavoured some of their dishes so highly that it must have been impossible to tell whether

---

27 See: Soyer 2004: 277.
28 However, on the positive and negative effects of using spices, see Sherman and Hash (2001).
29 According to Adamson (2004), parsley was the most popular herb across medieval Europe, used especially for herb omelettes, green sauces, etc. but also for ornaments.

they were made of fish or meat". The mixtures of herbs and spices were either prepared by the cook or bought ready-made, e.g., *powdour douce* (e.g., FC_6, Gr_Rwl 90), *powdour fort* (e.g., FC_15) or *powdour marchant* (e.g., FC_116). Flavours were often mixed, e.g., salt with sugar.

According to Laurioux (1999), medieval cooking involved three main tastes: sweet, sour and pungent. Montanari (2012) enumerates four possible flavours: sweet, bitter, sour and salty.[30] Sweet spices, especially sugar[31], were much more important in England than in France. Laurioux (1999) even claims that sugar gained popularity in France as an influence of the English recipes and customs. According to Brears (2008: 343), "[sugar] was first experienced by English people during their first major incursion into the Mediterranean as part of the First Crusade of 1096–9. Within a few years, small quantities were being imported as an expensive luxury, the amounts then being gradually increased to several tons by the late thirteenth century." As Scully reports it was increasingly common on the 14th c. markets. He adds that "[d]uring the fifteenth century European householders seem almost to have become addicted to the flavour that sugar lent their foods. Recipe collections of the time attest to the increasing reliance upon sugar in dishes that were concocted for the wealthy" (1995: 52). Sugar was imported from all over the Mediterranean in large amounts, the most popular was probably 'sugur cypre' (from Cyprus) (e.g., FC_43) and 'sugre of Alisaunder' (from Alexandria) (e.g., LV_27). Hammond (2005) reports that in 1480 a single ship carried almost 10 tons of the sweetener. It was imported in various forms, e.g., refined conical loaves, 'black' (muscovado) sugar, etc. Sugar mixed with various flower petals (e.g., violet or rose sugar) was believed to cure colds and other health problems. However, much as the use of sugar was popular, purely sweet tastes were rare. Sweet spices were usually mixed with sour or spicy ingredients.

Honey was used next to sugar as a sweetener, mainly for preserving and for gingerbreads[32]. It was much cheaper than the imported sugar; very often beehives were kept in the gardens of a particular household. However, sugar was preferred for the finer processes of confectionary. Similarly to sugar, honey was believed to have healing properties. "There are many excellent qualities to be found in honey.

---

30   Aristotle, on the other hand, recognized eight flavours: sweet, oily, harsh, pungent, astringent, acid, saline and bitter (see Johansen 2007).
31   Sugar was considered to be a spice in the Middle Ages.
32   Medieval gingerbread was "a chewy but fairly hard candy, a confection resembling toffee, made of nothing more than honey and spices" (Hieatt 1998: 104), rather than what we understand as gingerbread in its modern sense.

(…) it cleanses the chest and the stomach; it purges the abdomen; it keeps the humours of the flesh and the mouth from decaying. It heats the blood and is suited to those with cold, moist temperaments, and to the elderly." (Spencer 1984: 26).

Sour tastes were achieved by the use of such ingredients as vinegar or verjuice. The former was usually obtained from grapes or apples; the latter from crabapples and sour grapes or other unripe fruit. Verjuice was produced in medieval English vineyards. It was a common ingredient in cooking, due to its acidic qualities. One of its most frequent uses was as a sauce served with veal and bacon.

A pungent taste was very often achieved by using vegetables of the onion tribe, but also ginger, mustard, etc. They were not only used as spices but also constituted the main ingredients of sauces. Ginger sauce was typically served with lamb, kid, piglet or fawn, but also partridge and pheasant. Mustard was probably the cheapest spice grown in Britain. It was used to make sauces, typically served with brawn, beef or salted mutton, as well as fresh fish and stockfish. They were very practical due to being easy to store. Additionally, garlic was brought regularly from the continent (Wilson 1991).

The most frequently used spice was saffron. It was very difficult to yield, though it was grown over much of south-east England (Dyer 2006: 39). It is suggested that saffron, which is not only a valuable spice but also a dye (see section 2.2.3), was cultivated as a result of there being little interest in staple crops at the local markets.

Very often opposite tastes, such as bitter and sweet, were combined together, e.g., we find mixtures of vinegar and sugar or other sweet ingredients such as raisins or currants, e.g.:

(…) nym vineger & þe þredde perty of sugur

(DS_60)

Next to their culinary use, herbs and spices were also known for their healing properties. The cook often consulted the daily menu with the doctor, and adjusted the choice of herbs and vegetables to the physical condition of the members of the household[33] (see for instance Scully 2008). In many of the households, at least some of the herbs were grown. Following Wilson (1991: 288), coriander, fennel, cumin, dill and peony were the favourite herbs planted in medieval British households. Herbs and spices were thought of as varieties of drugs (Scully 1995: 30). Spices were believed to enhance digestion:

---

33   This was connected to the theory of the four humours. For details, see Henisch 2009.

spiciness held a position of singular prestige during the Middle Ages for dietary reasons. (…) the heat afforded by spiciness (and in particular by spices) was considered a cure-all for enhancing the process of metabolism.

(Montanari 2012: 87–88)

Additionally, flower petals were often used, not only as colourants or garnishing, but also for making pottages, e.g., rose, primrose, violet, or hawthorn pottage.

2.1.6 Grease

There were two types of cooking oils: animal and vegetable oils. Animal fats were turned into oil or grease. They were used as both an ingredient and a cooking medium. Vegetable oils were obtained from olives, nuts, almonds, etc.

Almond oil is frequently referred to as 'almond milk', but it was not diluted with water or broth. It was hardly ever used as a frying medium, but foods were often boiled in it or in almond milk (proper).

Olive oil was commonly used for fish frying. Another medium used for frying was clarified butter. However, its use was limited. It was forbidden during Lent (except for children and the elderly). Moreover, only meatless dishes were prepared with the use of butter, e.g., pancakes or eggs (Laurioux 1999).

Animal fat (grease) and lard (refined animal fat) were obtained as a by-product of domestic animals' slaughter.

2.1.7 Beverages and liquids

Water did not play an important role as a beverage, but it was used for cooking. The major problem with the water used in the kitchen was its (im)purity. Water from a well or from a river was heavily polluted, as a result of the disposing of the wastes of butchering. Only spring- or fountain-water could be trusted (under certain conditions). In fact, physicians advised against drinking water at meals as it was believed to be harmful for digestion (Scully 1995). Instead, alcoholic drinks (even if weak) were claimed to be easily digestible, pure and healthy. For instance, already in the 2nd half of the 12th c., the king of England was advised to drink good wine instead of water:

(…) the monarch is advised against drinking water exclusively, for it is said to cause intestinal upsets and block digestion; wine is deemed the best drink, especially sweet white wine. The criteria for selecting a good wine, according to the Italian diet specialists, are smell, taste, color, and transparency – in that order.

(Riera-Melis 1999: 258)

However, water was an essential element for every kitchen. It was used as a cooking medium and a cleaning agent. Boorde (in Furnivall 1870: 252) enumerates the best sources of water supply. Thus, rain water was the best (clean and pure), then running water (esp. if it runs from the east to the west), the third source of water to be used was river or brook water. Standing or well water, i.e., water which is not exposed to the sun, was not recommended.

Wine was the most popular drink accompanying meals. As reported by Brears (2008), medieval culinary wines were heavy and sweet. They were partly produced in England, partly imported. The best wines were those whose juice was pressed from grapes in the most natural way. The more forceful the pressing of the grapes, the lower the quality of the wine. Depending on the grapes, there were white and red wines. The level of alcohol could have been reduced by watering the wine. Additionally, spiced wines (also called 'mulled wines') and reduced wines were drunk. The former, e.g., 'hipocras', 'claret' or 'piment', depended on the invention of the cook. Thus, hipocras was usually a red wine with a mixture of ginger, cinnamon, galingale and sugar. Sometimes also nutmeg, cloves, grains of paradise, mace and spikenard were added (see for instance GK_5). The drink was usually served at the beginning or at the end of a feast, but it was also used as an ingredient to prepare some dishes. Another very popular spiced wine, i.e., 'claret' was made of cinnamon, galingale, grains of paradise, pepper and honey mixed with white wine (FC_205). The reduced wine was a kind of wine syrup, often referred to as 'boiled wine'. It was obtained by boiling wine, and available after two thirds of it had evaporated.

Beer and ale were served in England as regular table beverages. They were described by Andrew Boorde, who wrote:

> Ale is made of malte and water; and they which do put any other thynge to ale than is rehersed, except yest, barme, or godesgood, doth sofystical theyr ale. Ale for an Englysshe man is a naturall drinke. Ale must have these propertyes: it must be fresshe and cleare, it muste not be ropy nor smoky, nor it must have no weft nor tayle. Ale shuld not be dronke vnder v. days olde. Newe ale is vnholsome for all men. And sowre ale, and deade ale the which doth stoned a tylt, is good for no man. Barly malte maketh better ale then oten malte or any other corne doth: it doth ingendre grose humoures; but yette it maketh a man stronge.
>
> Bere is made of malte, of hoppes, and water; it is the naturall drynke for a Dutche man, and nowe of late dayes it is moche vsed in Englande to the detrymont of many Englysshe people;
>
> (Boorde, in Bickerdyke 1889: 6).

A separate chamber was usually allotted for ale production. It was the brewer who decided which type of malt to use, and frequently mixtures of malt were used. Similarly to wine, ale could have been seasoned with spices (e.g., ale hoof or ground ivy); it was then referred to as *braggot*[34] (e.g., FC_205). As Wilson (1991) reports, the favourite spice added to ale seems to have been long pepper; but nutmeg, cinnamon and grains of paradise were also frequent. Following Stone (2006a), ale went off easily, and thus was brewed regularly rather than kept in stock. Various qualities of ale were prepared. The amount of ale drunk at a particular household differed depending on the time of the year, rising significantly during Christmas. After the Black Death, mostly due to a stronger position of barley, the quality and strength of ale improved, as well as the amount of its consumption, and production, although in some areas of the country, e.g., in Cornwall and Devon, oat and rye ale was still malted, as suggested by Fox (1991: 303), out of preference rather than due to any limitations, such as soil or climatic conditions. "Hopped beer also began to appear in the later Middle Ages" (Stone 2006a: 23). It could have been kept for a longer period, due to being boiled with hops before fermenting. It also had a different (bitter) taste. It became more and more popular in the 15th c., but it did not threaten the popularity and consumption of ale. Brewing seems to have been a regular everyday process, which accounts for the fact that none of the surviving culinary collections records its methods (Brears 2008).

As Dyer (2006: 36) reports (after Myers 1959), "[r]eally wealthy aristocrats would not usually have drunk anything but wine and ale".

Mead was obtained by boiling honey with water. In the late medieval cookery mead was not very popular, and drunk in small quantities. Sometimes spiced mead was drunk, so called 'metheglin'. Brears describes the process of making mead in this way:

> Around midsummer, the bees were killed off or driven from their hives, so that the combs could be crushed and the honey wrung out into bowls. The residue was then put into a tub of water, which absorbed the honey, and left the wax ready for clarification ready for making candles or for modelling into various subtleties. The sweetened water was then fermented to produce a rather dry, honey-flavoured long drink called mead or metheglin, each hive producing around 3 gallons.
>
> (Brears 2008: 107)

---

34 Braggot is an "ancient celebratory drink". Its name derives from OCelt. *bracata*, which is 'a kind of cereal grain'. It was made of strong ale or a mixture of strong and middle ale, after they had been cleared for three or four days (Brears 2008: 103). Various kinds of braggot were especially popular during festive days.

Fruit juices were made of any fruit available at a particular time. Juices were drunk either fresh or after fermentation, in the form of, for instance, cider. Drinking cider and perry was recorded from the 13th c. It was made by pressing apples and pears, respectively.

Liquids and beverages were also used in cooking. The major four liquids used for cooking were made of grapes, i.e., wine, vinegar, verjuice and must. Verjuice, for instance, was a sharp flavoured juice, first made of a particularly tart variety of grape; later it was made of crab apples. The liquids were usually used for broths and sauces. Wine and vinegar were also used for cooking.

Milk was rarely drunk by the aristocrats, as it was considered to be the food of the poor. More often it was used for cooking (see section 2.1.3). However, sometimes a drink called 'posset' was produced. It consisted of milk heated with ale or wine, and in noble households a certain amount of various herbs and spices was added to make it more luxurious (Henisch 2009, Wilson 1991).

'Caudle' was another refreshing drink, made of egg yolks cooked in ale, with the addition of some oatmeal or breadcrumbs to thicken the drink. Additional ingredients could have been added depending on the available resources of the household.

2.2 Food preparation

A medieval meal must have been prepared in such a way as to allow the diners to eat it by means of a knife, a spoon or one's fingers. Thus, the meals could not have been too thin. For instance, depending on the consistency, a number of types of pottage can be distinguished: "A running pottage is usually one that is only moderately thick, like a modern cream soup, whereas a 'standing' pottage is one that is thickened to the consistency of a thick porridge." (Hieatt 1998: 111); while jelly was a pottage thicker than 'standing pottage'. The consistency of meals depended not only on the way of cooking but also on how particular ingredients were cut up. Thus, we have distinguished two main operations conducted in the kitchen: cutting and cooking. Additionally, the way of serving was also important, since the dishes had to be 'interesting', thus, they were richly ornamented. In what follows, we will also briefly discuss the possible ways of food preservation.

2.2.1 Cutting

The preparation of ingredients to be cooked requires various ways of cutting. According to Adamson (2004), chopping was one of the basic culinary operations performed in the kitchen. The wide range of cutting methods were referred to by a variety of names, especially after the Norman Conquest, due to the introduction of numerous vocabulary items denoting the actions of cutting food, e.g., dicing, chopping, slicing, carving, mincing, leaching, etc. The category 'cutting verbs' has been defined by Levin (1993: 157) as verbs which involve "notions of motion, contact and effect (...) [and] a 'separation in material integrity', but it also includes some specification concerning the instrument or means used to bring this result about". Marttila (2009: 108) distinguishes three types of cutting operations:

(i) Dividing cuts – the division of foodstuffs into homogenous pieces of various size with the use of a bladed instrument, e.g., *slice, mince, chop*;
(ii) Removing cuts – the removal of unwanted parts of foodstuffs with the use of a bladed instrument, e.g., *peel, bone*;
(iii) Penetrating cuts – the cutting of foodstuffs with a bladed instrument "for either aesthetic or functional purposes, without dividing it or removing anything from it", e.g., *open, score*.

We could add one more category, i.e., reducing (or crushing), containing verbs such as *powder, break*[35], *grind*, etc. in which case the structure of the foodstuff changes (the instrument does not have to be specified, thus, a mortar, grinder or even a stone could have been used). These operations were extremely frequent, possibly due to the common belief that "a foodstuff in granular or powder form will exert the fullest possible influence when in contact with another substance" (Adamson 2004: 62). For a detailed discussion of the verbs of cutting found in the analyzed corpus, see Chapter Three.

2.2.2 Cooking

Cooking[36] is a way of transforming food chemically and physically by subjecting it to heat. Scully (1995) enumerates four main types of cooking in the Middle Ages: boiling, frying, roasting and baking, of which, as Tannahill (1988: 13)

---

35 This verb has been categorized by Marttila as a 'dividing cut'; however, it is believed that it calls for a separate category.
36 Lehrer (1969) indicates that 'cooking' is the most general activity, referring to (i) the act of the preparation of a meal. However, the verb *cook* can have more specific senses as well, i.e., (ii) $cook_2$ 'to prepare foodstuffs other that those which are baked', and (iii) $cook_3$ 'to apply heat and so to produce an irreversible change in the food cooked'. Each of the senses of *cook* involves a number of sets of verbs/activities.

suggests, roasting must have been the first method, discovered by accident. The main difference between the four types of cooking is the source of heat and the medium in which the procedure was performed. The cooking techniques depended on the type of food, and they were applied in such a way as to make the food more digestible. The chosen technique had to be in agreement with the theory of the four humours (see for instance Henisch 2009). For instance, the best way to cook dry food was by boiling, whilst fat foodstuffs would rather be roasted.

Boiling, was the basic cooking procedure in the Middle Ages (see Hagen 1994). It served as a way to make food tender. Boiling involves a medium such as water, wine, milk or other liquid and a vessel such as a pot or a pan and it takes place over heat. Lehrer (1969) distinguishes two senses of the verb *boil*: the general and the specific (= 'full boil'). Following Beck et al. (1961: 8), technically boiling involves "seething, rolling and sending up bubbles". In practice, they distinguish slow boiling (= simmering[37], i.e., cooking just below the boiling point), medium (= shivering), and fast boiling. The last one agrees with Lehrer's 'full boil' (i.e., the specific reference of *boil*, which implies vigorous action with the rolling bubbles). Throughout the medieval period boiling was often applied to the preparation of tough meats, e.g., beef, thus, to make it softer several boilings or parboiling were applied before the proper frying or roasting. Hagen (1994) explains this by the fact that in such a way meat juices could have been preserved. Boiling was also recommended with wild game, e.g., hares, due to the fact that the meat was usually dry (Adamson 2004). **Parboiling** denoted the action of the partial cooking of solid foods in boiling water. Following Lehrer (1969), the process was relatively short (in contrast to stewing).

Stewing involved cooking in a small amount of water, milk, butter or other liquid. Lehrer (1969: 42) defines it as "a long slow method of cooking (…) in a liquid which is kept at simmering point". It was applied especially to salted meats, which otherwise would have become hard, but also to vegetables and fruit. Additionally, Lehrer distinguishes **poaching**[38], which is synonymous to stewing, but the purpose of both actions differs. Stewing is to soften the food, whilst poaching is supposed to retain the shape of the cooked food. Both activities are applied to solid foods.

As reported by Wilson (1991: 86), by the 15th c. the process of **braising** had developed: "To make 'a dry stew for beef', the flesh with minced onions, cloves,

---

37 According to the etymological dictionary, *simmer* was borrowed into English only in the 17th c. (Hoad: s.v. *simmer*).
38 Following Hoad's etymological dictionary, *poach* entered English in the 15th c. and refers exclusively to cooking eggs (s.v. *poach*[1]).

maces and currants was enclosed in a glass vessel which was suspended inside a cauldron of boiling water over a low fire". Lehrer (1969) defines the action as a sequence of 'browning' (in a little fat) and 'stewing' (in a little liquid, in a closed vessel). The former implies an action undertaken under the grill or in a hot oven, as a result of which food is given a golden brown colour. It is related to **toasting**, which refers to 'browning by broiling (direct heat)'. Following Wilson (1991), toast was present in the English diet in the later medieval times. She writes: "It has been suggested that toast was an English invention for freshening up stale bread. But in fact trencher-bread was preferred at least four days old, when it was easier to slice and square, and was drier and more absorbent." (Wilson 1991: 248). And she finds the origins of toast in browning pieces of white bread on the gridiron, the pieces then being "soaked in wine, reheated and crisped, and then served with almond milk" (ibid).

Frying, categorized by Levi-Strauss (in Leach 1972) as a way of boiling which uses fat instead of water, involved heating in a hot liquid (usually oil, butter or animal fat), and usually took place in a (frying)-pan. Fried foods should be moistened while being exposed to moderate heating. The major advantage of frying was that it involved a short period of time. Brears (2008: 321ff) distinguishes two types of frying: shallow frying (of pancakes, bacon, omelette or vegetables) and deep frying (used for fritters, lozenges, etc.). In the former, fat or oil were used to prevent food from sticking to the pan rather than as the cooking medium, as in the latter. Deep frying involved a lower temperature since the food was to be cooked through. Battered dishes and pastries were very often the subject of deep frying. To make them more attractive, fried pastries were frequently stuffed.

Roasting and **baking** are dry types of cooking, with no medium involved, in which the heat is transmitted through the air. Leaf (1971) notices that the difference between the two may lie in the exposure to fire: the former is conducted in a 'closed' form of a hearth, and the latter in an 'open' one. However, he sums up that the real choice between roasting and baking depends on the food involved and is determined etymologically. Thus, if the foodstuff is named with a lexeme of Germanic origin – it is baked (since the verb is also of Germanic origin), whilst if food is named with a word of Romance origin – it is roasted (since the verb is a borrowing from French). This has been contradicted by the other scholars dealing with cooking techniques, e.g., Sihler (1973). They agree that the difference between roasting and baking is functional rather than cultural (as suggested by Leaf (1971)), i.e., roasting consists in the exposure to fire and baking involves hot air. According to Sihler (1973), in the Middle English cookery books almost everything cooked had a name of French origin (1973: 1723). Thus, he suggests that "meat which was cooked before an open fire is always *rosted*, and preparations requiring more even heat (or being too delicate to turn before a fire) are always called *bake, bakyn*" (ibid.) (from this categorization he excluded boiled or stewed dishes). Similarly, Lehrer (1969: 44) notices that for baking "the heat acts 'by conduction and not by radiation' (…) [and] the source of heat is indirect". Depending on the foodstuff, the intensity of the heat varies.

Roasting was a very popular way of cooking, usually applied to meat and fish. "[I]t was prepared by threading the pieces, either boiled or raw but always well seasoned, onto a skewer that was then rotated over the fire on the hearth" (Riera-Melis 1999: 259). And, as suggested by Sykes (2006a), it was especially beneficiary for young animal flesh, e.g., veal, lamb and kid. Brears (2008) adds the tender meat of game and poultry. Roasting was conducted on various kinds of spits and grills. The latter were used with foods which were too flat to mount them on a spit. Roasting was the procedure which dried food the most, thus it was often applied to pork and water fowl rather than to dry meats (Scully 1995). It was a very demanding procedure, the meat could not have been exposed too much to the fire[39] since it would burn, thus, it involved constant turning, which made the procedure long lasting. Moreover, the meat required some preparation in order not to dry out while being roasted, e.g., venison, veal or rabbits might have been first parboiled, game and birds – larded, etc. The fact that fuel was expensive and the procedure itself time consuming, meant the consumption of roasted meats indicated high status, and peasants hardly ever (if at all) consumed roasted meat. However, Brown (2002) presents archaeological evidence for the rising popularity of roasting from the second half of the 12th c onwards.

Baking took place in an oven, usually made of stone, heated by a fire inside it. After heating the inside of the oven, the coals or wood are moved to another chamber and the dish to be baked is placed inside (e.g., Adamson 2004). According to Hagen (1994), in the Anglo-Saxon times baking was usually applied to meat and bread. Later, it was extended to more complex dishes, e.g., "a '*soutil brouet d'Angleterre*': chestnuts, hard-boiled egg yolks, and pork liver ground up and made into a paste cooked with spices and saffron" (Hagen 1994: 62).

A number of minor cooking methods were also used, e.g., vegetables were usually simmered or steamed, meats could have been broiled or grilled. Thus, broiling has been defined by Lehrer (1969: 44) as a process of "cook[ing] directly under a heating unit or directly over an open fire" and the source of heat is usually hot coals. It is more specific than grilling, which in turn refers to broiling on an open

---

39 "(…) meat was always roasted in front of the fire, never over it" (Brears 2008: 306).

grill or a griddle. Additionally, the verb *charcoal* started to be used in the 14th c. (Hoad: s.v. *charcoal*). It is synonymous with *barbecue*, but the process does not require any sauce, as in the case of barbecuing.

Usually, when a meal was being prepared, the food was exposed to a sequence of cooking procedures. For instance,

> When starting a pottage, for example, the meat might be prepared by <u>roasting, frying or parboiling</u>. Not only did this set the texture and flavour of the meat before it was finished by <u>simmering</u> in richly-flavoured stocks, but it also enabled the cooks to transform in a matter of minutes the many plain spit-roast and pot-boiled joints into a range of quite different, individual dishes just before they were to be served. Such pre-cooking could enrich basic flavours too, (…). It might also add to the efficiency of the kitchen, enabling left-over cooked but unbroken joints to reappear in hashed form at succeeding meals.
>
> (Brears 2008: 225ff; underlining mine)

The 'multiple cooking' was "to cleanse and firm the flesh, perhaps also to make sure the meat was well done by the time it left the roasting spit" (Adamson 2004: 62). However, multiple cooking was also done to make food more attractive, for instance different parts of fish were prepared in different ways and served with different sauces.

The order of adding particular ingredients seems to have been very important in the process of cooking too, for instance due to the significance of the colour of particular dishes. Some colourants lost their intensity if cooked too long, but on the other hand, the other ingredients had to be soft.

2.2.3 Serving

Not only was the taste of dishes important but also the way they looked. Medieval cooking attached great significance to the colour of food. To make it look more attractive, food was often dyed (red and gold were the most attractive colours). A wide variety of products were employed to achieve a wide range of colours: roots, plants, woods, minerals, foodstuffs. They were used alone or in combinations. A very popular way to colour a dish was to paint it with egg yolks (also mixed with some spices) and to cook it until a golden crust was obtained. Yellow was also the favourite colour, obtained by the use of saffron. Green was achieved with the addition of some herbs, e.g., mint, parsley, vine sprouts, currants, newly sprouted wheat or sage. Sandalwood, sanders and root of borage gave a red colour; mulberries – blue; indigo, turnsole and heliotrope gave a purple colour; alkanet was used to retain the rosy colour of salmon; whilst black or brown dye resulted from adding some blood or burnt breadcrumbs. Additionally, Adamson (2004) enumerates cooked chicken liver, dark raisins and prunes as good colourants giving food a black colour. Some dishes were dyed with a few colours. Following Henisch (2009: 156), "[s]trong colour contrasts added visual excitement to any dish". A variation of colours was also introduced within the same dish, e.g., rice was divided into three portions: one was left white, the second one green (with the use of herbs) and the third one yellow (with saffron).

Another way of decorating food was to cover it with gold or silver foil. Gold was another popular colour chosen by cooks to catch the host's (and guests') eye. Meat and fish jellies were often given a colour different from their own.

Flowers were often used both for colouring and decoration, e.g., violets were used to colour milk pudding, similarly roses, primroses and hawthorn.

Some dishes were often thickened before serving (e.g., pottages). The main thickeners were: flour, egg yolks, starch (amydon) or breadcrumbs, but meals were also made thicker by the appropriate cutting of particular ingredients or by pounding them in a mortar.

Meats were also glazed. Glazing was obtained by coating meat in honey or wine caramel, or by sprinkling the surface with ground spices or sugar.

2.2.4 Preserving

A great variety of foodstuffs, even though short-lived, such as meats and fish, dairy or some fruit, did not have to be consumed fresh, but could have been preserved by salting, pickling in brine, smoking or drying. Long term methods of preservation were required especially in the time of the autumn to ensure enough food for the winter. Short term preservation was to protect food from hot weather.

2.2.4.1 Salting and pickling

Salt was probably the most frequent substance used for food preservation, due to its properties of drying food. According to Wilson (1991), the amount of salt produced in Britain was not enough and by the 13th c. it had to be imported from France. Soon, two varieties of salt were distinguished: 'Bay salt' (imported) and white salt. The former was used for food preservation, the latter for the table.

Salting was applied mainly to meat and fish. Tannahill (1988) distinguishes two ways of salting food: dry-curing, in which meat/fish was placed in granulated salt with the addition of some spices or herbs; and brining (or pickling in brine), which consisted in placing the food in a strong solution of salt and water. For the former, a servant known as 'the powderer' was responsible. Dry-salting was much more time consuming, as the process of pounding salt into fine crystals which were to surround the meat/fish closely was difficult, but it seems to have been more effective, since the powdered salt penetrated meat better and had a better drying effect. Brining was used for both short- and long-term preservation. If meat was to be kept for only several days, it was placed in the brine overnight. Longer preservation required much longer soaking in the liquid, and had to be followed by drying and smoking of the meat.

The operation of pickling, as Scully (1995) reports, was commonly known and practiced. Salt brine ensured that the meat could have been preserved over a relatively long period. For shorter preservation, jelly (gelatin) was used. Gelatin was obtained from some animals, e.g., sheep's feet; or fish, e.g., pike, tench, carp, eel, etc., and was usually used to preserve pork or chicken. Sometimes, a spiced gelatin was used, so called 'galentine'. Also, a mixture of spices which enhanced the preserving effect of the gelatin was used.

Only the best quality meat could have been preserved. When it comes to salting fish, herring was the most popular, as Tannahill (1988) says, because it was very oily and so had to be preserved soon after being caught. Its entrails were removed, then it was soaked in brine (for up to fifteen hours) and placed in barrels with salt layers without air access (Wilson 1991).

Another product which was very short-lived was animal milk. Its by-products, such as butter or cheese, were also preserved by adding salt. For instance, heavily salted butter could have been kept for a considerably long time. Before serving it, cooks de-salted it so that it was again fit for consumption. De-salting usually consisted in soaking food in a few changes of water.

Pickling could have consisted in the impregnation of food in acidic liquids, such as vinegar, or in alcohol. Brears (2008) reports that brawn was often pickled in ale, wine, cider, vinegar and salt, a method, known in the 14th c., which has not survived into modern times.

Additionally, fruits and nuts were often preserved in sugar or honey. Wilson (1991) notices that a method of preserving meats in honey was also known, which is reflected in some recipes, e.g.,

> Yf þou wylle kepe þe tayle of a dere
> Fresshe in seson over þo 3ere,
> Or oþer venesone yf þat hit nede,
> þus schalt þu do, I wot in dede;

Presse oute þo blode, for anythyng
þat is cause for grete rotyng;
In erþyne pot þou shalt hit pyt
And feyre hony do into hit;
To þo hony stoned over þo flesshe
Too fyngurs thyke for harde or nesshe;
With leder þo mouthe þen schalt þou bynde,
Kepe hit fro ayre, son or wynde,
In cofer, or huche or seler merke.

(LCC_83)

However, honey was much more expensive than other preservatives, thus, the method was applied sporadically.

2.2.4.2 Drying

Drying was the second most common way of preserving food. It was important already in the Anglo-Saxon times (see Hagen 1994). A great variety of foodstuffs could have been preserved in such a way, e.g., herbs, cereal crops, legumes. It was also applied to fruit, such as figs, grapes, and dates, as well as fish, in which case only the most oily fish (such as herring or mackerel) could not be dried. It was a cheap and relatively easy method. Whilst fruit were exposed to sun or heat, meat might have been first beaten to remove juices and thus precipitate the process of drying. Mushroom and fungi could be dried by hanging on a string. A number of methods were applied for drying: in the open air, by the fire, in an oven, etc.

2.2.4.3 Smoking

Smoking was a good way of preserving meats and fish which were particularly oily. Leach (1972) defines it as "a process of slow but complete cooking; it is accomplished without the mediation of any cultural apparatus, but with the mediation of air" (1972: (c) no indication of page). The most popular foods preserved by smoking were probably bacon, ham[40] and red herring[41]. Additionally, cheese could have been preserved in such a way. They were first put in a brine pot to soak and after a while hung near a fire to dry and smoke. Wood smoke saturated them. The type of wood used depended on the food to be preserved, e.g., birch

---

40   Pig meat was extremely suitable for long-term preserving.
41   Herring started to be preserved in such a way only in the late 13th c. (Wilson 1991).

wood for herrings and hams (Hagen 1994). Archaeological evidence shows that after the Norman Conquest, cattle meat was preserved by hot-smoking much more frequently than in the earlier period (Sykes 2006a). Smoking preserved meat for a shorter time than brining; however, smoked meats were more flavoursome than salted. Sometimes, a combination of salting and smoking was applied.

Chapter Three: Verbs of cutting

3.1 Introduction

In the *Boke of Keruynge* (signed by Wynkyn de Worde) from 1508, its author gives a list of verbs of cutting together with the foodstuff they referred to. Even though the quote below comes from the beginning of the 16th c., i.e., the period shortly later than the analyzed material, it nicely presents the great variety of verbs belonging to the semantic field under investigation. It should be borne in mind that the verbs must have been present in the language earlier than the date of the composition of the *Boke*, thus, they must have been used at least in spoken form in the period analyzed.

Breke that dere	tyere that egge
lesche the brawne	chynne that samon
rere that goose	strynge that lampraye
lyfte that swanne	splatte that pyke
sauce that capon	sauce that place
spoyle that henne	sauce that tenche
fruche that chekyn	splaye that breme
unbrace that malarde	syde that haddocke
unlace that conye	tuske that berbell
dysmembre that heron	culpon that troute
dysplaye that crane	fyne that cheuen
dysfygure that pecocke	traffene that ele
unioynt that bytture	traunche that sturgyon
untache that curlewe	undertraunche that purpos
alaye that fesande	tayme that crabbe
wynge that partryche	barbe that lopster
wynge that quayle	
mynce that plouer	
thye that pygyon	
border that pasty	
thye that woodcocke	
thye all maner small byrdes	
tymbre that fyre	

(*Boke of Keruynge*: 'Termes of a keruer')

So far, 'verbs of cutting' have been analyzed diachronically in a short article by Marttila (2009) and synchronically in the Present Day English in a more general work on verbs by Levin (1993). The former based his study on a small sample of recipes from the late 14th to the 19th c. He divided verbs of cutting into nine categories: (i) dividing and specific; (ii) dividing and general; (iii) dividing and generic; (iv) removing and specific; (v) removing and general; (vi) removing and generic; (vii) penetrating and specific; (viii) penetrating and general; and (ix) penetrating and generic. For the examples of verbs belonging to each category, see Table 1 below.

Table 1: Subdivision of the cutting verbs (Marttila 2009: 109)

	Specific verbs	General verbs	Generic verbs
Dividing cuts	dice, fillet, halve, leach, mince, shred, slice	carve, chop, cleave, clip, cut, hack, hew	break, divide, part, reduce, separate, split
Removing cuts	beard, bone, core, draw, flay, cut, scale, stone	chop off, cut out, pare away, scrape off	clean, clear off, detach from, remove, take out
Penetrating cuts	crimp, lace, notch, score, scotch, splat	cut, incise, pierce, scrape, stab	break, open, split, thrust

In the period analyzed in the present study, Marttila found the following verbs:

(i) Dividing cuts: *break, carve, chine, chop, cleave, culpon, cut, dice, dismember, gobbet, hack, hew, leach, mince, part, quarter, shred, slice*;
(ii) Removing cuts: *chop off, core, cut* (+ adv.), *do away, draw, flay, make* (+ adj.), *pare, peel, pick* (+ adv.), *scale, scrape* (+ adv.), *shell, skin*;
(iii) Penetrating cuts: *break, cut, make, open, splat*.

The latter study by Levin (1993) was more general and synchronic. She found the following cutting verbs in the Present Day English (1993: 156–158):

(i) Cut verbs: *chip, clip, cut, hack, hew, saw, scrape, scratch, slash, snip*;
(ii) Carve verbs: *bore, bruise, carve, chip* (potatoes), *chop, crop, crush, cube, dent, dice, drill, file, fillet, gash, gouge, grate, grind, mangle, mash, mince, mow, nick, notch, perforate, pulverize, punch* (paper), *prune, shred, slice, slit, spear, squash, squish*;

Additionally, she distinguishes such categories as 'separating and disassembling verbs', e.g., *break, cut, detach, disconnect, divide, part, split*, etc.; and 'removing verbs', e.g., *debone, dehair, remove, separate*, etc.

The present chapter deals with the verbs of cutting found in the 14th and 15th c. material. This category was extremely rich in terms of the types of verbs, but the number of tokens of most of them was rather insignificant (see Fig. 1). This shows that, despite a great variety, many of the verbs were recorded sporadically. The verbs of cutting have been divided into four major groups. The division has been based on Marttila's (2009) categorization; however, an additional group of 'reducing verbs' has been added. It includes verbs referring to pulverizing and crushing (absent from Marttila's grouping). Thus, in what follows, we will differentiate the following categories:

(i) Dividing verbs, i.e., verbs which refer to the division of foodstuffs into small but distinct (comparable) parts, such as: *bard, break₁, carve, chop₁, cleave, culpon, cut₁, (de)part, dice, dismember, gobbon, hack, hew, leach, pare₁, pluck, quarter, share, shred, slit₁, smite, tear* and *tease*;

(ii) Reducing verbs, i.e., verbs which refer to the division of a foodstuff into small / minute particles which may not be perceptible in isolation but form a mass (or a pulp), such as: *beat₁, bray, break₂, bruise, grate, grind, mince, powder₁, quest, stamp*;

(iii) Removing verbs, i.e., verbs which refer to the separation of a part of a foodstuff from its main body, such as: *blanch, bone, break₃, chop₂ off, cut₂, do₁ (away/off/out), flay, ⁺hild, hull, pare₂, peel/pill/pull, pick (away/off/out), scale, scrape, shave, shell, skin, smite off, strip, take₂ (away/off/out), whiten*;

(iv) Penetrating verbs, i.e., verbs which refer to the action of separating foodstuffs without dividing or removing anything by the cut, such as *open, cut₃* and *slit₂*; these are also verbs which refer to the action of reshaping foodstuffs without the use of any instrument, such as: *break₄*, etc.

Additionally, phrases such as *make something on little parts* (i), *do powder* (ii) and *make white* (iii) can be added to the particular groups respectively.

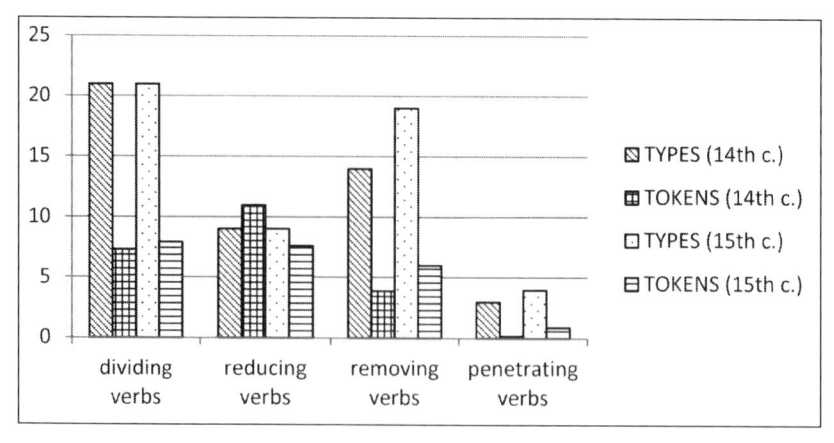

Fig. 1: *Types and tokens of particular verbal groups. For the latter, RNFs have been given [per 1,000 words]*

In the following sections devoted to the particular groups of verbs, each verb will be presented in terms of its etymology, the time of the first occurrence of the borrowed verbs in English, the number of records in the analyzed material, as well as the possible senses with which the verbs were found in the culinary recipes. Then, the collected data will be discussed with reference to the synonymity of the particular lexemes, possible rivalry, shades of meaning or contextual constraints for the use of the verbs.

3.2 Dividing verbs

3.2.1 The corpus

This group includes verbs which refer to the division of foodstuffs into small and distinct parts, usually with a tool such as a knife. However, in the analyzed corpus the tool was hardly ever specified. Altogether, 23 verbs belong to this category (see Table 2 below). Additionally, phrases such as *make something on little parts* were also used; however, they occurred sporadically and only in the 14th c. material.

Table 2: The number of occurrences of the 'dividing verbs' in the analyzed material. Relative normalized frequencies have been given in brackets [RNFs / 10,000 words]

verb:	14th c.	15th c.	verb	14th c.	15th c.
bard	0	5 [0.5]	hack	21 [7.2]	26 [2.6]
break₁	1 [0.3]	12 [1.2]	hew	57 [19.6]	163 [16.4]
carve	45 [15.5]	16 [1.6]	leach	10 [3.4]	89 [9]
chine	0	8 [0.8]	pluck	1 [0.3]	0
chop₁	1 [0.3]	102 [10.3]	quarter	7 [2.4]	5 [0.5]
cut₁	13 [4.5]	230 [23.2]	share	3 [1]	3 [0.3]
cleave	2 [0.7]	14 [1.4]	shred	3 [1]	20 [2]
culpon	1 [0.3]	3 [0.3]	slit₁	4 [1.4]	3 [0.3]
(de)part	3 [1]	16 [1.6]	smite	23 [7.9]	34 [3.4]
dice	8 [2.7]	18 [1.8]	tear	1 [0.3]	0
dismember	3 [1]	1 [0.1]	tease	3 [1]	12 [1.2]
gobbon	1 [0.3]	3 [0.3]			

3.2.1.1 break₁

Break developed from the Old English verb *brekan*, of such a general denotation that even the *OED* states: "Many of the uses of this verb are so contextual, that it is difficult, if not impossible, to find places for them in a general scheme of signification …" (*OED*: s.v. *break*, v.). In general, the verb refers to the action of severing into distinct parts, either by the application of force or violence. Its reference to cooking (as found in the *OED*) indicates the following senses:

(i) 'to cut up (a deer)[42]; to tear in pieces (a fox); to carve (a fowl)' – its first attestation comes from 1330. (*OED*: s.v. *break*, v. I.2.b);
(ii) 'to burst. Of an abscess or boil: To burst the surface, so that the contents escape' – with the first record dating to 1398. (*OED*: s.v. *break*, v. I.4).

---

42 The sense has been reflected in the *Boke of Keruynge* (see section 3.1).

Levin (1993) enumerates *break* neither among the verbs of cutting[43] nor the verbs of carving[44]. Instead, she categorizes it as a 'split verb' (together with *blow, cut, draw, hack, hew, kick, knock, pry, pull, push, rip, roll, saw, shove, slip, split, tear, tug* and *yank*). We have classified *break* into four categories, i.e., as a 'dividing', 'reducing', 'removing' and 'penetrating verb'. Due to the fact that the verb has a number of references, for the matter of clarity it will be specified in what follows respectively as:

$break_1$: dividing verb
$break_2$: reducing verb
$break_3$: removing verb
$break_4$: penetrating verb

For the discussion of $break_{2,3}$ and $_4$, see sections 3.3.1.3, 3.4.1.2 and 3.5.1.1, respectively. For the ratio of the occurrences of *break* with the specific senses, see Fig. 2 below.

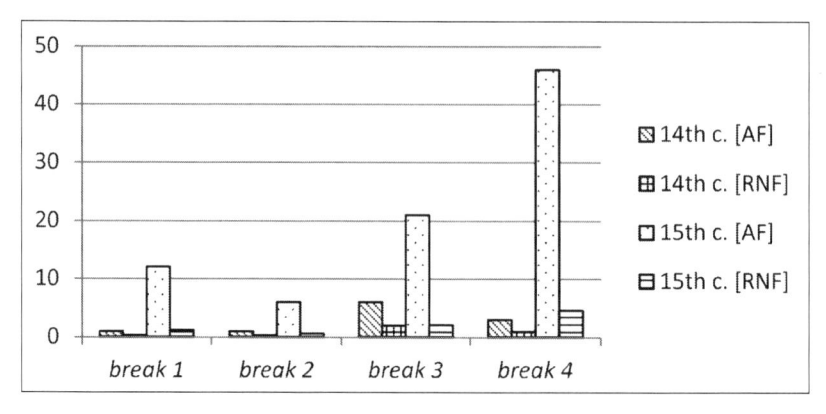

Fig. 2: *The ratio of occurrences of* break *with different senses.* [AF = absolute frequency; RNF = relative normalized frequency (per 10,000 words)]

---

43 She finds the following 'cut verbs': *chip, clip, cut, hack, hew, say, scrape, scratch, slash* and *snip* (Levin 1993: 72).
44 Her 'carve verbs' include: *bore, bruise, carve, chip* (potatoes), *chop, crop, crush, cube, dent, dice, drill, file, fillet, gash, gouge, grate, grind, mangle, mash, mince, mow, nick, notch, perforate, pulverize, punch* (paper), *prune, shred, slice, slit, spear, squash* and *squish* (Levin 1993: 72).

Most of the records of *break* were found in the 15th c., they referred usually to the category of penetrating or removing verbs. The other two categories were rather insignificant. In the present section, *break₁* will be discussed. It was found only once [RNF: 0.3] in the 14th c. (= 6.7% of all the 14th-century records of the lexeme), and 12 times [RNF: 1.2] in the 15th c. (= 12.9% of all its 15th c. records). It was applied mostly to herbs which were to be 'broken in hands', e.g., (1), but also to bread, and meat, which was to be 'broken in gobbets', e.g., (2). However, the majority of records do not specify how the foodstuff should be broken.

(1) Take parcelly, Sauge, Isoppe, Rose Mary, and tyme, and **breke** hit bitwen thi hondes,

(BK_19)

(2) (…) **breke** þe hennes in gobetes. Do þem in dysshes;

(GR_Rwl_171)

3.2.1.2 *carve*

Carve is a Common Germanic verb, cognate with the Greek γράφ-ειν 'to write', which originally referred to the sense 'scratch, engrave' (*OED*: s.v. *carve*, v.). It was the main verb used with reference to cutting in the early English. The *OED* enumerates the following cutting senses of *carve:*

(i) 'to cut' – used as the common verb for this action in Old English;
(ii) 'to castrate (a cock)' – used from the 15th c. until the 17th c.;
(iii) 'to cut (artistically or ornamentally)' – used from the Old English period;
(iv) 'to cut up meat at table' (= 'to serve') – used from the 14th c.

The verb was found 45 times [RNF: 15.5] in the 14th c. and only 15 times [RNF: 1.5] in the 15th c. In four of the 14th c. records it was followed by the particle 'out' and referred to 'cutting out certain shapes in paste', e.g., (3).

(3) And whan it is colde, **kerue out** with a knyf smale pecys of þe gretnesse and of þe length of a litel fyngur, (…)

(FC_196)

Carve referred to various foodstuffs, such as fruits and vegetables, meat and fish, eggs, paste, cheese, etc. (see (4)). It is suggested that it was used with the most general sense, i.e., 'to cut'. When some specific kind of cutting was required, the verb was accompanied by a specifying phrase, such as: 'in quarters', 'in two', 'to gobbets', 'to dice', etc. (see (5)–(7)). Apparently, 'carving to powder' was also possible (one record in the 15th c.), see (8). Hardly ever was the tool for carving mentioned (if it was then it was a knife), see (3) above; and seldom was the process of carving followed by further cutting procedures.

(4) (...) & mak it boyle & do þerto wit of <u>egges</u> **coruyn** smal. & tak fat <u>chese</u> & **kerf** þerto wan þe licour is boylyd.

(DS_78)

(5) Take a sausage & **kerf** hym <u>to gobetes</u>, and cast it in a possynet, (...)

(FC_169)

(6) (...) & after tak a chese & **kerf** yt <u>on fowre pertis</u> & cast in þe water. (...) & **kerf** þy chese <u>in lytyl schyuis</u> [= slices] & do hem in þe sewe wyþ eggys,

(DS_38)

(7) (...) & dresse vppe-on a cloþe, & **kerue** þer-of <u>smal lechys</u> [= slices],

(LV_7)

(8) (...) nym appelis & **kerue** hem <u>as small as douste</u>,

(Aus_Laud_14)

The corpus clearly shows the drop in frequency of the verb. In the 15th c. only one tenth of its 14th c. records were found (see its RNFs).

3.2.1.3 *chop₁*

Chop, of uncertain etymology, appeared in the 14th c. with the meaning 'to cut with a blow', and later 'to cut into pieces'. It has been compared to some Germanic languages, such as Middle Dutch, Low German, Swedish or Danish; its relation to the French *couper* 'to cut' (see *AND*: s.v. *couper₃*) has also been suggested.

In the analyzed material only one record [RNF: 0.3] was found in the 14th c. (see (9)), comparing to 102 [RNF: 10.3] in the following century. In the 15th c. the verb was not only much more numerous, but it also referred to a greater variety of foodstuffs, e.g., meat and fish, fruits and vegetables, eggs, herbs, etc. The tool for chopping was not mentioned. Sometimes the way of chopping was specified, e.g., 'in pieces', 'in quarters', 'in culpons', 'in gobettes', or simply 'small/great', (see (10)–(12)). Additionally, *chop* with the particle 'off' started to be used as a removing verb in the 15th c. (see section 3.4.1.9.b). Contrary to *carve*, discussed in the previous section, *chop₁* became highly popular in the 15th c. as a general cutting verb.

(9) Take kydde oþer chikens oþer flesh, & **choppe** hem small and seeþ hem.

(FC_138)

(10) Take an Henne, and rost hure almoste y-now, an **choppe** hyre <u>in fayre pecys</u>,

(PD_41)

(11) Take eles, and fle hem, and **choppe** hem in faire colpons,

(BK_101)

(12) Take a pygge, scalde hym ande **chop** in iiij quarters.

(GR_CUL_77)

3.2.1.4 cut_1

The verb *cut* was first found in the written sources at the end of the 13th c., and since the 14th c. it has been in common use as the proper word for the action of 'dividing into two or more parts with a sharp-edged instrument' (*OED*: s.v. *cut*, v. II.7a). Before its introduction, the action was referred to with the Old English verbs *snīðan* 'to cut, make an incision' and *ceorfan* 'to cut, cut down, hew, rend, tear, carve, engrave' *(ASD)*. The former was used in the Middle English period with the sense 'to slaughter (an animal), sacrifice' (*MED*: s.v. *snīthen*, v.), and later, with its original sense 'to cut', became restricted to the dialects of the North Country, Westmoreland, Yorkshire, Lincolnshire, Leicestershire, and Northampton; however, it was accompanied by the particle 'off' (*EDD*: s.v. *snithe*, v.). The latter synonym, *carve*, remained in use until the Present Day English, but with a narrowed meaning, see sections 3.2.1.2 and 3.2.2.

The etymology of *cut* is uncertain, its origin has been searched for in the Scandinavian languages, but no convincing explanation has been offered so far.

The number of records of *cut* found in the 14th c. proves that at that time the verb was only just entering English. We have found only 13 occurrences [RNF: 4.5], all of them referred to the sense 'to divide into smaller parts'. The meaning was general, since in most of the cases the way of cutting was specified, e.g., 'in pieces', 'in gobbets', 'in length', etc. In the 15th c., on the other hand, the verb seems to have become a significant member of the semantic field. Not only did the number of its records increase, but also the number of senses with which it was found extended. Thus, we have classified the verb into three sub-fields: (a) 'dividing verb' with 230 records [RNF: 23.2]), (b) 'removing verb' (= cut_2) with 78 records [RNF: 7.9] (see section 3.4.1.3), and (c) 'penetrating verb' (= cut_3) with 18 records [RNF: 1.8] (see section 3.5.1.2). The following senses of *cut* were found in the 15th c. corpus:

cut_1 > dividing verb

(i) 'to divide into smaller parts', e.g., (13);
(ii) 'to cut sth in', e.g., (14);

cut_2 > removing verb

(iii) 'to cut off', e.g., (15);
(iv) 'to cut sth out', e.g., (16);
(v) 'to dig sth out', e.g., (17)
(vi) 'to incise; to slit (e.g., throat)' in order to remove blood or guts, e.g., (18);

cut_3 > penetrating verb

(vii) 'to incise; to slit (e.g., throat)' in order to shape fish, e.g., (19).

Fig. 3 below shows the ratio of the occurrences of particular senses of *cut* in the 15th c. material.

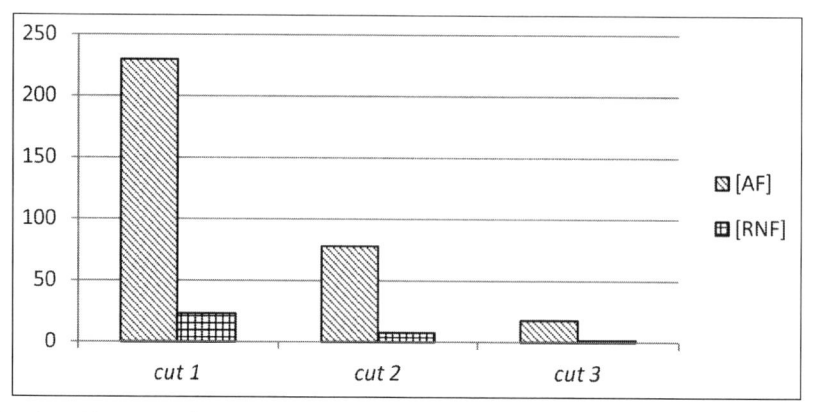

Fig. 3: *The ratio of occurrences of* cut *with different senses in the 15th c. [AF = absolute frequency; RNF = relative normalized frequency (per 10,000 words)]*

The most general use of cut_1, i.e., with the sense 'to divide into smaller parts' was the most numerous one. Frequently, the way of cutting was specified with such phrases as: 'in gobbets', 'in leaches', 'in round pieces', 'in quarters', 'like lozenges', 'in culpons', 'in slices', etc., e.g., (20)–(21).

(13) þan take Datys, & **kytte** hem, & cast þer-to;

(BM_16)

(14) (…) mell anysing of capons and yokes of eggs and **kytt** thame in and sette by side.

(GR_WW_64)

(15) And cast him [chick] in faire water, and wassh him; and þen **kutte of** þe hede and nek,

(BK_70)

(16) And couer hit ayen with þe cruste that þou **kuttest** awey;

(BK_138)

(17) Make an hole depe in the ground and **cut** out a lode of turfe, and let the hole be depe and large so that the flesch may hang theryn not touching the erth on no side upon a staf.

(GR_SA_1)

(18) Take a swanne and **cut** the rofe of his mouth in to the braynwarde endlonges and lete hym blede to deth

(MAe_106)

(19) Yff þu wylt hafe hym [= trout] rounde, **cutte** hym over þe bake syde in iij or iiij places, but not through.

(GR_CUL_164)

(20) Take elys, and fle hem, and **kutte** hem in colpons,

(BK_102)

(21) **Cut** venson yn longe leches & frye hem or rost hem with poudyres;

(OP_47)

The study shows not only that *cut* became much more frequent in the 15th c. but also that its meaning broadened: in the 14th c. it referred only to the group of dividing verbs, whilst a century later it represented a much wider range of senses, which classify the verb not only as a dividing verb but also as removing and penetrating. This may serve as evidence for the verb gaining dominance in the semantic field due to it being the most general, i.e., it was allowed in many more contexts than the other verbs, as for instance *chop*. For the discussion on the relation between particular dividing verbs see section 3.2.2.

3.2.1.5 *(de)part*

Part, from AN *partir, partier, parter* and OF/MF *partir* 'to divide or share into several pieces; to share in, partake of, to leave, separate', was used in the analyzed recipes with the sense (recorded from the 14th c. on) 'to put apart, make a separation between (two or more persons or things); to bring about, effect a separation of (a thing) from another' (*OED*: s.v. *part*, v. 4). The related form, i.e., *depart*, derived from OF *departir*[45] 'to divide', was used with the general sense 'to divide into parts' from the 13th c. Due to a small number of occurrences, the two forms will be discussed together.

The verbs occurred only 3 times [RNF: 1] in the 14th and 16 [RNF: 1.6] in the 15th c. All the records referred to the separation of various foodstuffs, but without the use of any instrument, thus for instance, they might have referred to the division into parts or into two vessels as in (22).

(22) (…) than **deperte** þe stuffe in two partes

(GR_Sl7_11)

3.2.1.6 *dice*

This verb was formed from the plural number of the noun *die* (= 'a small cube'). It was derived from OF *de* (pl. *dés*). In Middle English the form was changed into *dȳ* and *dȳs* (*dyse, dyce, dice*), respectively. Moreover, the originally plural form *dice* has been used both as singular and plural in English. According to the *OED*, the culinary sense of the verb, i.e., 'to cut into dice or cubes', has been recorded from the 14th c.

The analyzed corpus contained only 8 occurrences [RNF: 2.7] of the verb in the 14th c. and 18 [RNF: 1.8] in the 15th c. Additionally, 5 [RNF: 1.7] and 1 [RNF: 0.1] nominal records which specify the more general cutting verbs were found in the respective centuries, e.g., *carve to dice, quarter to dice* (see (23)). Dicing was applied to various foodstuffs, such as meat and fish, eggs, herbs, bread, etc. Sporadically (and only in the 15th c.) was the action of dicing specified with such phrases as: *dice small, dice into morsels, dice to small gobbets* (see (24)–(25)).

(23) Take the noumbles of calf, swine, or of shepe; perboile hem and **kerue** hem **to dyce**.

(FC_14)

(24) **Dyce** payndemayn in smale morcells

(GR_Rwl_262)

(25) Make a steff mylke of almonds blanched; **dyse** the brawn smal, do it therto in a pot with sugar and salt.

(OP_A7)

---

45 It is a Romance compound of *de-* + *partīre*.

3.2.1.7 *hack*

Hack, from OE **haccian*, denoted 'to cut with heavy blows in an irregular or random fashion; to cut notches or nicks in; to mangle or mutilate by jagged cuts' and 'to make rough cuts, to deal cutting blows' (*OED*: s.v. *hack*, v.[1]). In the culinary corpus, the verb was found 21 times [RNF: 7.2] in the 14th c. and 26 times [RNF: 2.6] in the 15th c. In most cases it was specified with the adjective 'small', e.g., (26), but also 'well', 'gentle' and the phrase 'to gobbets'. Hacking was applied to such foodstuffs as meat and fish, herbs, eggs and cheese.

(26) (…) & grynd peper & safroun & temper vp wyþ swete mylk, & boyle it; & **hakke** chese smal & cast þeryn,

(DS_23)

3.2.1.8 *hew*

Hew is a Common Germanic verb (OE *héawan*) which referred to cutting. Among its senses there are: (i) 'to strike, or deal blows, with a cutting weapon', (ii) 'to strike forcibly with a cutting tool; to chop, hack, gash', and (iii) 'to divide with cutting blows; to chop into pieces' (*OED*).

In the analyzed material, *hew* was found with sense (iii). The verb was relatively more frequent in the 14th c. (57 records [RNF: 19.6], comparing to 163 records [RNF: 16.4] in the 15th c.). The 14th c. occurrences of *hew* applied to meat, herbs, eggs, sometimes also fish and seafood. The action of hewing was usually specified with phrases such as 'small', 'to gobbets', 'to pieces', 'to morsels', 'in quarters', 'in (two/many) parts', etc. A few records suggest that hewing might have involved the element of mixing, e.g., (27). Hewing was sometimes preceded by various cooking procedures (boiling, seething, parboiling, etc.), and followed by further cooking (boiling, frying, seething) or cutting (usually grinding or braying), e.g., (28)–(29).

(27) Tak whyte lekys & perboyle hem & **hewe** hem smale with oynouns.

(FC_2)

(28) Take the lyre of hennes and of þe pork and **hewe** it small, and grinde it al to doust;

(FC_46)

(29) Take clene pork and boile it tender, þenne **hewe** it small, and bray it smal in a morter.

(FC_116)

The 15th c. occurrences of *hew* referred mostly to meat and fish (esp. pork), herbs, and eggs (yolks). The action was often preceded by boiling or seething and followed by further cutting, esp. grinding but also braying. Sporadically, hewing was preceded by other cutting procedures such as hacking or chopping, which suggests a certain hierarchy of the cutting procedures, depending on the size of the received pieces (for the discussion of the hierarchy of cutting verbs, see section 3.6). Occasionally, it might have been an option to grinding, e.g., (30). Similarly to the 14th c. material, in the 15th c. hewing might have involved some mixing, e.g., (31)–(32).

>   (30) Perboyle hem [herbs] welle yn water. Presse out the watyr; **hew** hem right smalle, or grynd hem.
>
>   (OP_8)
>
>   (31) þan take raw percely, & Oynonys smal y-scredde, & 3olkys of Eyroun soþe hard, & Marow or swette, & **hew** alle þes to-geder smal;
>
>   (LV_30)
>
>   (32) And then take yolkes of yren, sodde hard, and **hewe** the yolkes and the parcel small togidre;
>
>   (BK_84)

3.2.1.9 *leach*

This verb originates from the noun *leach* (from AN / OF *lesche*) 'slice (of bread)' and 'a dish prepared from various ingredients cut into strips or slices' (*AND*: s.v. *lesche*₁). According to the *OED*, the verb (with the sense 'to slice') was in use from the end of the 14th c. until the 19th c.

In the analyzed corpus *leach* occurs 10 times [RNF: 3.4] in the 14th c. and 89 times [RNF: 9] in the 15th c. Only a few records refer to cutting single ingredients (e.g., pork, onions); leaching was usually applied to the completed dish (see (33)), and the action of leaching was applied by or just before serving a particular dish. As a result, hardly ever is it followed by any other action, such as cooking or further cutting. Sometimes the action is specified with phrases such as 'in thin / broad / thick slices / pieces', 'in gobbets', etc., e.g., (34)–(35).

A number of recipes containing this lexeme refer to dishes which have nothing to do with cutting/slicing, e.g., (36). These occurrences of the lexeme have been interpreted as an integral part of the proper name of the dish, and thus they have not been counted in the present study. On the other hand, sometimes *leche* when included in the heading, indicates that the dish consists of sliced ingredients, as in (37). These occurrences of the lexeme have been included in the corpus.

(33) Take ayren and wryng hem thurgh a straynour, and do þerto cowe mylke, with butter and safroun and salt. Seeþ it wel; **leshe** it,

(FC_83)

(34) **leshe** it in liknesse of a peskodde [= pea pod]

(FC_66)

(35) And then take faire dates, and y-take oute the stones, and **leche** hem in faire gobettes al thyn,

(BK_97)

(36) **LECHE** FRYS[46] OF FISCHE DAYE Take god chese & dyse hit; medel þerwyt 3olkes of eyren rawe. Cast þerto poudur of gynger, sugur and salt. Make a cophyn of þe heghte of þi lyte fingur, and do þi fars þerin & bake hyt as tartes. Set þerin flower of canel & clowes.

(FC_165)

(37) **LECHE** LUMBARD Take rawe pork and pulle of the skyn, (…), and lat it seeþ til it be ynowh3. And whan it is ynowh, kerf it; **leshe** it in liknesse of a peskodde [= pea pod];

(FC_66)

Apart from the verb, nominal phrases, such as 'carve small leaches', 'cut in broad leaches' occur. They are typical of the 15th c. material. In the 14th c. only one [RNF: 0.3] noun was found, comparing to 67 [RNF: 6.7] in the next century.

3.2.1.10 *quarter*

This verb, derived from AN *quartrer*, was found only 7 times [RNF: 2.4] in the 14th and 5 times [RNF: 0.5] in the 15th c.-recipes. It referred mostly to fruit and vegetables (pears, figs, dates, radishes), e.g., (38), but also to meat (capon, pig, partridge). Additionally, it should be noted that phrases with the noun *quarter* which specified the way of cutting (see (39)–(40)), or in which *quarter* was used as a quantifier, were more frequent.

(38) Pare peris & **quarter** them;

(GR_Sl7_10)

(39) Soþþen nim þe hole alemauns & corf heom to quartes;

(DC_56)

(40) tak pertriches & chikenes rosted & hew hem in quarteres.

(UC_22)

---

46 Following Hieatt and Butler (1985: 198), *leche frys* are "tarts of cheese, butter and egg yolk baked in a pastry shell, again neither sliced nor fried".

81

3.2.1.11 shred

Shred (from OE *scréadian*) in its culinary reference denoted:

(i) 'to cut into shreds or small thin strips or slices' – used from the 14th c.;
(ii) 'to cut or hack in pieces; to cut down' – used from the 13th c. until the 17th c. when it became obsolete.

In the analyzed corpus, we have found only three records of *shred* [RNF: 1] in the 14th c. and 20 [RNF: 2] in the 15th c. Most of the occurrences refer to fruit and vegetables (pears, onions, leeks, parsley), but also to almonds and dates. The way of cutting, except for phrases such as 'small' or 'not too small', e.g., (41), is hardly ever specified.

(41) þen take Perys, & sethe hem a lytil; þen reke hem on þe cloys tyl þey ben tendyr; þan smale **schrede** hem rounde;

(PD_129)

3.2.1.12 slit$_1$

Slit, "obscurely related to Old English *slítan*", denoted 'to cut into, or cut open, by means of a sharp instrument or weapon; to divide or sever by making a long straight cut or fissure' (*OED*: s.v. *slit*, v.). It has been categorized into the groups of 'dividing' and 'penetrating verbs' (as *slit$_1$* and *slit$_2$*, respectively). The former group contains 4 records [RNF: 1.4] in the 14th c. (all the records refer to leeks, e.g., (42)). In the 15th c. there were only 3 occurrences of the verb [RNF: 0.3]. The latter group was more numerous (at least in the 15th c.), with 1 record in the 14th c. and 18 in the 15th c. For the discussion of *slit$_2$*, see section 3.5.1.4. There is the possibility that in the 15th c. the verb shifted from the category of 'dividing' to 'penetrating' verbs. However, the number of records is too scarce to state anything for certain.

(42) Take white of lekes and **slyt** hem

(FC_82)

3.2.1.13 smite

Smite (OE *smítan*) originally denoted 'to blemish, pollute' and 'to smear on something'. Only in Middle English did the cutting sense, i.e., 'to hew, cut, chop, or break in pieces', replace the original one. In the analyzed corpus 23 records [RNF: 7.9] were found in the 14th c. and 34 [RNF: 3.4] in the 15th c. Smiting was applied only to meat and fish and was always accompanied by some cooking procedure, either preceding or following it (or both). However, this can be accounted for by the fact that the ingredients submitted for smiting were never eaten raw. The way of cutting was always specified by phrases such as 'to (fair / little / etc.) pieces', 'in two', 'in quarters' or 'to gobbets', which proves the general meaning of *smite*. In the 15th c. *smite* started to be used with the preposition 'off' and thus its meaning extended to 'to cut off', putting the verb also in the group of 'removing verbs' [RNF: 0.2], see for instance (43) and section 3.4.1.9.d.

> (43) Take a pigge, Draw him, **smyte of** his hede, kutte him in iiij quarters, boyle him til he be ynow, (…)
>
> (BK_16)

3.2.1.14 *tease*

Tease (from OE *tæsan*), which according to the *OED* meant 'to separate or pull asunder the fibres of; to comb or card (wool, flax, etc.) in preparation for spinning; to open out by pulling asunder; to shred', was found only 3 times [RNF: 1] in the 14th c. and 12 times [RNF: 1.2] in the 15th c. All of its records referred to brawn (except two 15th c. occurrences which referred to fish). The way of cutting was never specified otherwise than by stating 'tease small'.

3.2.1.15 Peripheral verbs

The present section presents those verbs which have been classified as 'dividing' (at least with one of their senses) but which were too rare to devote separate sections to their presentation, i.e., their relative normalized frequency was equal to or lower than 1 in both the analyzed centuries.

(a) bard / baud

Following Austin (2000: 120), this verb was borrowed from French *barder* and denotes 'to cut in thin slices'. It has not been recorded in the *AND*, whilst in the *OED* records, the form *bard* appears only from the middle of the 16th c., with the sense (i) 'to arm or caparison with bards'. From the middle of the 17th c. the sense (ii) 'to cover with slices of bacon' was found. The latter may suggest a relation to the French meaning (cf. Austin).

Even though the *OED* dates the verb to the 16th c., we have found it already in the 15th c. material, with 5 occurrences [RNF: 0.5], which refer to cutting. The action was applied to meat and fish and was always preceded by seething and followed by further cutting, e.g., leaching, hewing or grinding (see (44)). No mention of the shape of the cut pieces has been made. What is more, the fact that the action is often followed by further cutting, usually with the use of a more specific verb, suggests that the verb is general in meaning. And this, in turn, suggests that the original (French) meaning, i.e., 'to cut into thin slices', has been extended to 'to cut (in general)'.

> (44) and þen take a porpeys, and chyne him as a Samon, And seth him in faire water. And whan hit is ynowe, **baude** hit, and leche hit in faire peces,
>
> (BK_174)

(b) chine

According to the *OED*, the verb *chine*, related to French *echiner*, was used from the 16th c. with the sense 'to cut up (fish)'. A century later the sense 'to cut along or across the chine or backbone; to cut the chine-piece' was added. (*OED*: s.v. *chine*, v.²). The analyzed corpus contains 8 records [RNF: 0.8] of *chine*. This shows that the verb was in use earlier than stated in the dictionary. All the records were found in the 15th c. material. They refer to cutting fish.

(c) cleave

Cleave is a Common Germanic verb, which referred to cutting in two of its senses:

(i) 'to part or divide by a cutting blow; to hew asunder; to split. Properly used of parting wood, or the like, 'along the grain', i.e. between its parallel fibres; hence, of dividing anything in the direction of its length, height, or depth; also, of dividing slate or crystals along their cleavage planes, and other things at their joints';

(ii) 'to separate or sever by dividing or splitting'

(*OED*: s.v. *cleave*, v.¹).

The verb played a marginal role in the analyzed semantic field, with only 2 records [RNF: 0.7] in the 14th c. It was used with the sense 'to cut (into a number of parts)', e.g., (45). In the 15th c. material, the lexeme *cleave* was found 14 times, but only four of these records [RNF: 0.4] referred to cutting. The other occurrences represented the homonym denoting 'to stick fast or adhere, as by a glutinous surface' (*OED*: s.v. *cleave* v.²), see for instance (46).

> (45) Take 3olkes of ayren harde ysode and **cleeue** a two and plauntede with flour of canell, (…)
>
> (FC_63)
>
> (46) Take fayr clene hony iclaryfyede, (…) & di of saunders, & þe quantite of half a lofe of brede igrattede, & boyll hem wele to þey begyne to cleve to þe pott in þe maner of a lofe; but stere hem well fro brynnyng to þe potte,
>
> (GR_eMus_76)

(d) culpon

This verb, formed by conversion from the noun *culpon* (from OF *colpon, coulpon, copon*), was found only once in the 14th and three times in the 15th c. This disagrees with the *OED*, according to which, the verb, with the sense 'to cut into pieces, cut up, slice' surfaced only in the 15th c. In the corpus the earlier record refers to venison, the later ones to fish (eels).

(e) dismember

Dismember, from OF *desmembrer*, entered English in the 13th c. with the sense: (i) 'to deprive of limbs or members; to cut off the limbs or members of; to tear or divide limb from limb'. In the 14th c. the sense (ii) 'to divide into parts or sections, so as to destroy integrity; to cut up to pieces' was added (*OED*: s.v. *dismember*, v.). The collected data show only sense (ii). The verb was found only 3 times [RNF: 1] in the 14th and once [RNF: 0.1] in the 15th c. It always referred to cutting meat into parts.

(f) gobbon

This verb was formed by conversion, out of the noun *gobbon* (from OF *gobon, related to *gobbe* and *gobet*), meaning 'gobbet, (cut) strip' (*OED, AND*). Following the *OED*, the verb, with the sense 'to cut into gobbets', was recorded only in the 15th and 16th centuries. The analyzed corpus contains one record of the verb in the 14th c. and 3 in the 15th c., hence, the verb was found earlier than stated in the *OED*. Additionally, the 14th c. material contains 26 occurrences [RNF: 9] of the noun *gobbet*, which is used to specify the way of cutting various foodstuffs. It accompanies a wide range of verbs, suggesting their general meaning, e.g., *smite, hack, hew, cut, carve*. Similarly, in the 15th c. 45 nominal records of *gobbet* [RNF: 4.5] were found, 26 of which [RNF: 2.6] accompanied some general cutting verbs to specify their meaning.

(g) pluck

Pluck is cognate with some Germanic languages but it might also be related to Romance languages. It was found only once in the 14th c. It referred to tearing herbs into smaller parts with one's hands (see (47)). No 15th c. occurrences were found in the analyzed corpus.

> (47) Take persel, sawge, grene garlic, chibolles, oynouns, leek, borage, myntes, porrettes, fenel, and toun cressis, rew, rosemarye, purslarye (...). **Pluk** hem small wiþ þyn honde
>
> (FC_78)

(h) share

Following the *OED*, *share*, which is a variant of the Common Germanic *shear* (OE *sceran*) 'to cut with a sharp instrument', started to be used only in the 16th c. However, the analyzed recipes contain 6 occurrences of the verb (3 in each century, i.e., [RNF: 1] and [RNF: 0.3], respectively). The verb referred to cutting onions, pears, and fish. In all the cases the way of cutting was specified, for instance, 'on slices', 'as dice', or 'in big pieces'. This indicates the general sense of the verb *share*.

(i) tear

Only one instance of the verb *tear* was found in the 14th c. It referred to cutting capon into smaller parts, see (48). According to the *OED* (s.v. *tear*, v.[1] I.1a), *tear* (from OE *teran*) was used from the 14th c. on, with the sense 'to pull asunder by force (a body or substance, now esp. one of thin and flexible consistence, as cloth or paper), usually so as to leave ragged or irregular edges; to rend'.

(48) þanne take þe brawn of þe capouns, **teere** it small and do þerto.

(FC_38)

3.2.2 Discussion

The group of 'dividing verbs' is definitely the most numerous in terms of types of all the verbal groups analyzed in the present study. It consists of 23 verbs. However, numerous as it is, a number of verbs were rather peripheral due to their rare occurrence, e.g., *bard, chine, cleave, culpon, gobbon, pluck* or *tear*. Table 3 shows the frequencies of particular verbs (both absolute and normalized) in the two analyzed centuries. (See also Fig. 1 at the beginning of the chapter.)

Etymologically, the verbs may be divided into: the Germanic ones: *break$_1$, carve, cleave, hack, hew, pluck, share, shred, slit$_1$, smite, tear* and *tease*; and those of French origin: *bard, chine, culpon, (de)part, dice, dismember, gobbon, leach* and *quarter*. Two of the verbs are of uncertain etymology, i.e., *cut* and *chop*. The former might be related to Scandinavian languages (*OED*). The latter has been compared to some Germanic languages; however, its relation to French has also been suggested (*OED*).

The verbs represent a clear cut division, with reference to meaning, into general and specific. The former consist of: *break$_1$, carve, chop$_1$, cut$_1$, cleave, (de)part, dismember, hack, hew, pluck, share, shred, slit$_1$, smite, tear* and *tease*. The latter, i.e., *bard, chine, culpon, dice, gobbon, leach* and *quarter*, specify the way of cutting. Thus, each of the specific verbs gives a particular shape of the cut foodstuff or refers to one type of food only (e.g., *chine* referred only to fish). *Culpon, gobbon* and *leach* seem to correlate, since all of the three activities refer to cutting into slices or strips. *Gobbon* and *culpon* were extremely infrequent, while *leach* gained popularity in the 15th c. (see Fig. 4), only to become obsolete in the 19th c. (*OED*), presumably due to its rivalry with the verb *slice*, which, following the *OED* (s.v. *slice*, v.[1]), entered English at the end of the 15th c.; however, it was not found in the analyzed corpus. What should be noted here is the fact that all the specific verbs were borrowed from French.

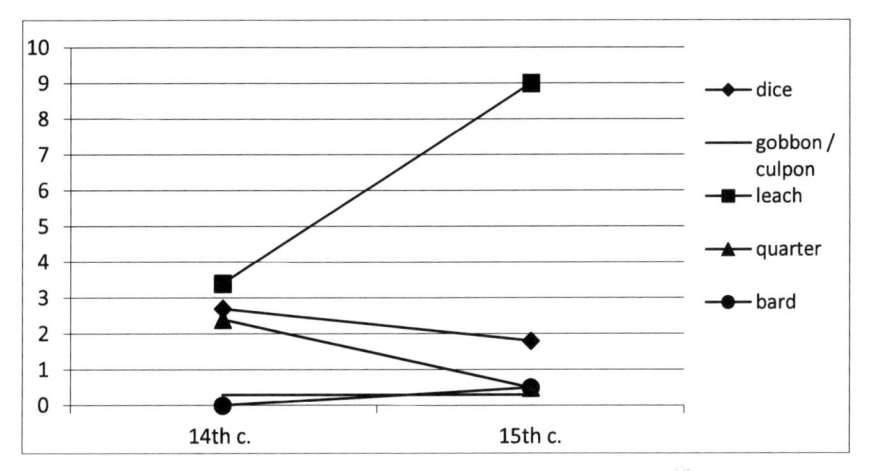

Fig. 4: Distribution of the major specific 'dividing verbs' at particular periods (RNFs / 10,000 words)

The group of general verbs was more numerous and comprised verbs of various etymology, but the French borrowings belonging to this group were peripheral. The most prominent of the verbs were: *carve, chop₁, cut₁, hack* and *hew*. What is interesting, the verbs which continued their presence from the Old English period tend to decrease in frequency, whilst the two verbs of dubious etymology, i.e., *chop₁* and *cut₁*, which surfaced in the 14th and late 13th c. respectively, take up dominance over the semantic field (see Fig. 5). *Hew*, which despite its drop in frequency is still popular in the 15th c., loses its culinary reference in the late 15th c. (see *OED*: s.v. *hew*, v. II.6a; or Marttila 2009: 116). Thus, the analyzed period not only introduced a number of French verbs which referred to specific ways of cutting, i.e., carried meanings which earlier had to be expressed with the use of specifying nominal phrases (still present in the 14th and 15th c.), such as *carve in leaches; cut in gobbets*, etc., but also the general domain was dominated by the newly introduced vocabulary (*cut₁* and *chop₁*). This shows a general tendency towards the replacement of 'the old' vocabulary with 'the new', 'the new' being not necessarily French.

Table 3: The number of occurrences of the 'dividing verbs' found in the analyzed material

	verb	14th c.	15th c.		verb	14th c.	15th c.
	bard	0	5		bard	0	0.5
	break₁	1	12		break₁	0.3	1.2
	carve	45	16		carve	15.5	1.6
	chine	0	8		chine	0	0.8
	chop₁	1	102		chop₁	0.3	10.3
	cleave	2	4		cleave	0.7	0.4
	culpon	1	3		culpon	0.3	0.3
	cut₁	13	230		cut₁	4.5	23.2
3a. Absolute frequencies:	(de)part	3	16	3b. Normalized frequencies (to 10,000 words):	(de)part	1	1.6
	dice	8	18		dice	2.7	1.8
	dismember	3	1		dismember	1	0.1
	gobbon	1	3		gobbon	0.3	0.3
	hack	21	26		hack	7.2	2.6
	hew	57	163		hew	19.6	16.4
	leach	10	89		leach	3.4	9
	pluck	1	0		pluck	0.3	0
	quarter	7	5		quarter	2.4	0.5
	share	3	3		share	1	0.3
	shred	3	20		shred	1	2
	slit₁	4	3		slit₁	1.4	0.3
	smite	23	34		smite	7.9	3.4
	tear	1	0		tear	0.3	0
	tease	3	12		tease	1	1.2

The meaning of the general verbs might have been specified by being followed by a nominal phrase describing the way of cutting. Table 4 shows the frequency of particular phrases. Additionally, phrases composed of general verbs and referring to cutting, such as *draw small, make on little parts, make to gobbets*, etc. were also used. These were, however, rare and occurred only in the 14th c. material [RNF: 1.4].

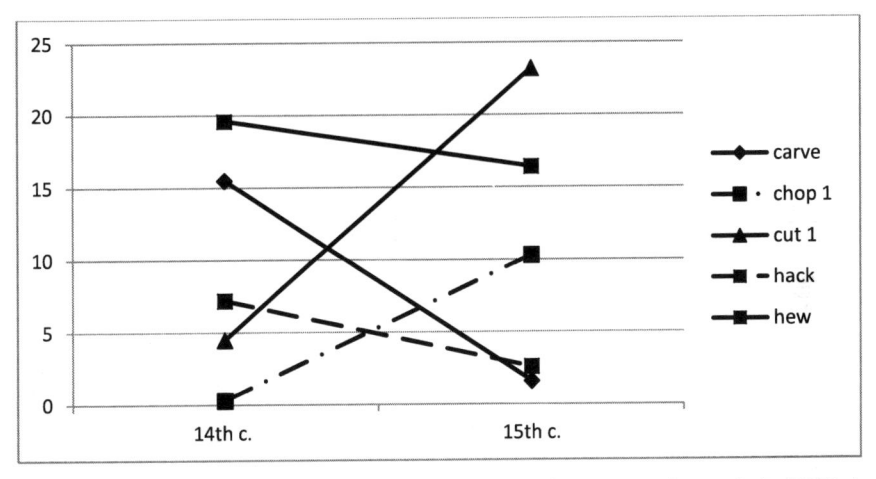

Fig. 5: Distribution of the major general 'dividing verbs' at particular periods (RNFs / 10,000 words)

Another interesting fact is that six of the specific verbs (all of French etymology) were formed by conversion (i.e., *chine, culpon, dice, gobbon, leach* and *quarter*). Hence, what comes to mind is that the verbs were created out of nouns due to the need for specific verbs which would express the shape of the cut foodstuff. The corresponding nouns were also present in the analyzed corpus. Only three of the nouns (*chine, gobbon* and *quarter*) were more frequently used than the corresponding verbs (see Table 5). The three pairs differ from the others only in the fact that the period between the first attestation of the noun and the verb was longer than in case of the other pairs (*OED*). Thus, the nouns *chine, gobbon* and *quarter* were better rooted in English than the respective verbs, hence, they were used more often than their verbal counterparts.

Table 4: The number of occurrences (absolute frequencies) of the specifying phrases with particular general verbs

shape \ verb	*carve*	*chop₁*	*cut₁*	*hack*	*hew*	*break₁*	*cleave*	*(de)part*	*share*	*smite*	**TOTAL**
14th c.											
gobbets	4		3	2	10					6	25
quarters	4				1		1				6
slices	2								2		4
morsels	2				5						7
dice	4		1						1		6
halves	1				1		1	1			4
powder	1										1
15th c.											
gobbets	1	2	8	4	6	1				4	26
quarters		1	6					1		1	9
slices	1		8						1		10
morsels	1		2								3
halves	2		10					3		4	19
leaches	2		17								19
powder	1										1
culpons			1								1
round			9								9
lozenges			8								8

Table 5: The relative normalized frequencies of occurrence of the verbs formed by conversion and the corresponding nouns

lexeme	14th c. noun	14th c. verb	15th c. noun	15th c. verb
chine	0.3	0	2	0.8
culpon	0	0.3	0.1	0.2
dice	2	2.8	0.2	1.8

lexeme	14th c. noun	14th c. verb	15th c. noun	15th c. verb
gobbon	9.3	0.3	1.9	0.3
leach	0.3	3.4	6.7	8.9
quarter	4.8	2.4	3.7	0.5

3.3 Reducing verbs

3.3.1 The corpus

This group of verbs could as well be included in the previous section on 'dividing verbs', but due to the fact that the number of verbs referring to pulverizing and crushing found in the analyzed material is pretty high, it has been decided to form a separate subgroup of 'reducing verbs'. 12 verbs have been classified as 'reducing' (see Table 6). The procedure usually requires a mortar or a similar tool and results in the reduction of foodstuffs into small / minute particles which may not be perceptible in isolation but form a mass (a powder or a pulp).

Table 6: *The number of occurrences of the 'reducing verbs' in the analyzed material. Relative normalized frequencies have been given in brackets [RNFs / 10,000 words]*

verb:	14th c.	15th c.
beat$_1$	4 [1.4]	2 [0.2]
bray	66 [22.7]	104 [10.5]
break$_2$	1 [0.3]	6 [0.6]
bruise	1 [0.3]	8 [0.8]
crum	0	3 [0.3]
grate	14 [4.8]	69 [7]
grind	164 [56.5]	356 [35.9]
mince	63 [21.7]	186 [18.7]
powder$_1$	0	3 [0.3]
press	8 [2.8]	53 [5.3]
quest	1 [0.3]	0
stamp	6 [2]	20 [2]

3.3.1.1 beat₁

Beat is a verb of Germanic origin (OE *beatan*) denoting 'to strike repeatedly'. According to the *OED*, it refers to cooking with the senses (i) 'to make into powder, or paste, by repeated blows; to pound, pulverize', and (ii) 'to mix (liquids) by beating with a stick or other instrument; to make into a batter; to switch or whip (an egg, etc.)'. The former was first recorded at the beginning of the 15th c., the latter in the 2nd half of the 15th c. (*OED*: s.v. *beat*, v.¹). Only sense (i) qualifies *beat* as a reducing verb, thus, sense (ii) will be discussed in section 5.3.1, and the verb will be presented as *beat*₁ and ₂, respectively. The total number of records of *beat* were 8 [RNF: 2.8] and 23 [RNF: 2.3] in the respective centuries. Fig. 6 shows the ratio of occurrence of *beat* with particular senses.

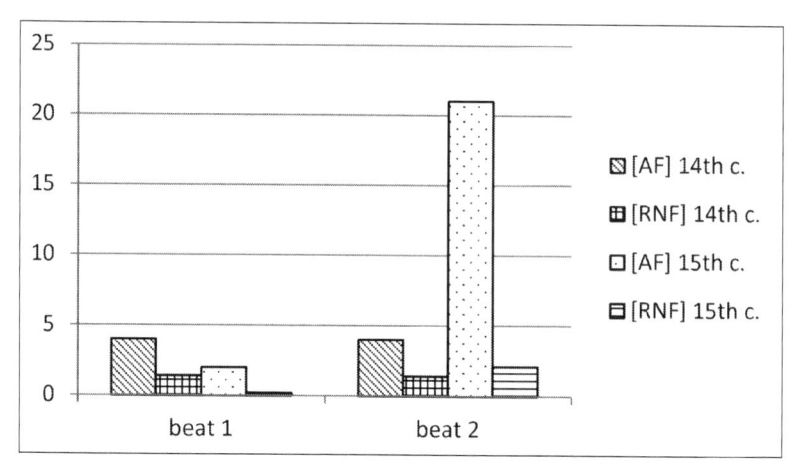

Fig. 6:   The ratio of occurrences of beat *with particular senses [AF = absolute frequency; RNF = relative normalized frequency]*

Beating in order to pulverize foodstuffs was rather infrequent, with only four records [RNF: 1.4] in the 14th c. and two [RNF: 0.2] a century later, see (49) and (50) for the respective centuries. The presence of *beat*₁ in the 14th c. material proves an earlier use of the sense than indicated in the *OED*. The action always took place in a mortar and was applied to such foods as wheat, rice, nuts and dried fruits, see examples below.

(49) Take clene whete and **bete** it small in a morter and fanne out clene the doust;
(FC_119)

(50) Tak <u>rys</u> and pyke hem clene and wasshe hem, and þenne druye hem a lyte ageyn þe sonne, and affter **bete** hem in a morter small and þen sarse hem, and þenne druye hem wel agayn þe sonne

(GR_TCC_115)

3.3.1.2 *bray*

The verb *bray* is of French origin. It first occurred in Anglo-Norman in the form *braier*, from OF *breier* 'to crush small', in the 14th c. Following the *ODEE*, it refers semantically to OE *break* (Germ. **brekan*). It was used with the sense 'to beat small; to bruise, pound, crush to powder; usually in a mortar' (*OED*: s.v. *bray*, v.[2]).

The analyzed corpus contains 66 occurrences [RNF: 22.7] of *bray* in the 14th c. and 104 [RNF: 10.5] in the 15th c. material. The only tool used for braying was the mortar. The operation was usually conducted in order to obtain a powder or, by the addition of some liquid or a moisturizing product, such as wine, broth, ale or yolks of eggs, to produce a pulp. Such products were brayed as grains (rice, wheat), bread, pulses, herbs and spices (ginger, galingale, cloves), various meats (such as pork, veal, beef, poultry, partridge, etc.) – the meat was usually first cut into smaller pieces – fish (e.g., salmon, oysters, etc.), as well as almonds (for instance to obtain almond milk), nuts, dates and cheese.

Braying was applied most of all to make a product prone to mixing with other foodstuffs, but also (sporadically) to remove the hulls, e.g., (51). Sometimes braying was preceded by cooking procedures, such as frying, boiling, roasting, scalding and seething, e.g., (52)–(53); or cutting operations, such as chopping, grating, hewing, hacking, mincing and pressing, e.g., (54)–(55). Usually, braying was not the final procedure applied to food, brayed foods were mixed with other foodstuffs and then cooked, e.g., boiled, baked, fried or seethed. Braying itself might also have involved mixing (see (55)).

(51) Tak clene qhete & **bray** it in a morter þat <u>þe hulles gon of</u>

(GR_AshmB_1)

(52) Tak þe braun of capounes or of hennes <u>ysoþe or rosted</u> & **bray** it in a morter smal as myed bred

(UC_21)

(53) Take wardouns perys & <u>seth</u> hem tender, & **bray** hem & temper hem with wyne.

(GR_eMus_47)

(54) tak pertrichis wit longe filettis of pork al raw & hak hem wel smale, and after **bray** hem in a morter.

(DS_59)

(55) Thenne take a litell tansey mynced and parseley and **bray** theym togeder,

(GR_SA_7)

3.3.1.3 *break₂*

This verb has already been discussed in section 3.2.1.1. Although the 'reducing' sense of *break* was rather peripheral, it should be mentioned here as well. There is one recorded use in the 14th c. and six records in the 15th c. material (i.e., [RNF: 0.3] and [RNF: 0.6] for the respective centuries). It referred to pulverizing spices or almonds, e.g., (56). For the ratio of particular senses of the verb see Fig. 2 in section 3.2.1.1.

(56) Take qwhyte suger; **breke** it in a morter, draw it through a streynour with saffren (…)

(GR_Sl7_21)

3.3.1.4 *bruise*

The verb *bruise* goes back to the OE *brȳsan*, and after coalescence with the OF *bruisier*, it gave rise to the AN *bruser*, meaning (i) 'to break, smash; violate', (ii) 'to destroy', (iii) 'to bruise', and (iv) 'to charge' (*AND*: s.v. *briser*). Its culinary reference, i.e., 'to beat small, pound, crush, bray, grind down' (*OED*), originated in the 14th c.

The verb was extremely rare in the analyzed material: with only one occurrence [RNF: 0.3] in the 14th c. (see (57)) and seven [RNF: 0.7] in the 15th c. The number of records is so insignificant that hardly any conclusions can be drawn.

The earliest record of *bruise* comes from the first half of the 14th c. and refers to the preparation of starch (GK_3). In the recipe, bruising is applied to wheat (dipped in water); it takes place in a mortar and is followed by seething and straining. In the 15th c. material the verb was used mostly in the names of dishes recorded in menus, e.g., 'bruised Viand' or 'bruised brawn', but detailed recipes for these dishes were not attached. In the 15th c. material, there is no mention of the tool used for bruising. Moreover, two occurrences of the verb seem ambiguous, see (58)–(59):

(57) Tak whete and step it ix daies, & eueri dai change þe water. And **bruse** it wel in a morter ri3t smal.

(GK_3)

(58) **Bruse** fygges on brede; cut þem in quarters

(GR_Rwl_256)

(59) blawnch almondes, & grinde þam (…) **bruse** it with a sawcer tyll it be als softe as 3e haue it

(Ht_Hrl_49)

In the former (58), *bruise* seems to be closer in meaning to the verb *spread*, giving the sentence the following sense 'spread bruised figs on bread and cut the bread in quarters', since crushed figs cannot be cut into four parts. The latter recipe (59) refers to making almond cream, after processing and boiling the almonds, water should be drained, and what is left should be mixed with white wine and 'bruised with a saucer till it is soft enough'. We are willing to assume that the action of bruising should take place 'in a saucer' rather than 'with it' and refers to mixing or stirring rather than crushing, especially in that at the beginning of the recipe the cook is instructed to grind the almonds.

3.3.1.5 *crumb*

Crumb is a verb of little importance in terms of its frequency in the analyzed corpus. However, it was used with the sense 'to break down into crumbs or small fragments, reduce to crumbs', thus it should be mentioned in the present section. The verb was derived from the Old English noun *crumb*. We have found only 3 records [RNF: 0.3] of this verb, all of them come from the 15th c. material. They referred to yolks of eggs or marrow.

3.3.1.6 *grate*

Following the *OED*, *grate* (from OF *grater*), with the culinary sense, was used from the 15th c. on, meaning 'to reduce to small particles by rasping or rubbing against a rough or indented surface; to pulverize by means of a grater' (s.v. *grate*, v.[1]). We have found it already in the 14th c. material, with 14 records [RNF: 4.8]. It referred either to bread or cheese (with 7 records each).

In the 15th c., the verb was more frequent, with 69 occurrences [RNF: 7]. All the records, except three, were used with reference to bread. The others referred to cheese, figs and raisins, and fish (one record each). This might suggest some narrowing of meaning of the verb.

3.3.1.7 *grind*

Grind is a native Germanic term denoting 'to reduce to small particles or powder by crushing between two hard surfaces; esp. to make (grain) into meal or flour in a mill', 'to produce by grinding' (*OED*: s.v. *grind*, v.[1]).

It was found 164 times [RNF: 56.5] in the 14th c. and 356 times [RNF: 35.9] in the next century. It was applied mostly to a) nuts and fruit; b) herbs and spices; and c) meat (see Fig. 7 and 8 for the ratio of foodstuffs ground in the respective centuries). In the majority of cases the action took place in a mortar (60) and was applied in order to pulverize a particular foodstuff ((61)–(62)) which was further processed. However, grinding was also applied in order to colour something, e.g., (63)–(64). Very often grinding was preceded by seething, boiling, frying, and other cooking procedures, e.g., (65). Moreover, foodstuffs such as meat or fish were first cut, hewed or hacked and only then were they ground ((66)–(67)). Grinding very often involved mixing various ingredients, e.g., (65). Additionally, in the 15th c., grinding involved straining food through a sieve or a cloth, for instance in order to remove hulls or dirt, e.g., (68), or to obtain juice.

(60) and take grete raysouns and **grynde** hem in a morter.

(FC_66)

(61) Take almandes blaunched and **grynde** hem al to doust;

(FC_140)

(62) (…) & do gingere, peyuere in an morter, & a lute bred, & **grind** wel togedre al to poudre,

(DC_39)

(63) & **grynd** egges and safroun or sandres togedere þat it be colourd

(DS_34)

(64) & **grind** egges & saferon togider so þat it be 3alow,

(Ht_Hrl_16)

(65) Take brede and frye it in grece oþer in oyle. Take it vp and lay it in rede wyne; **grynde** it with raisouns.

(FC_60)

(66) Take boylid Porke, & hew yt an **grynd** it;

(LV_7)

The usual instruction for grinding was 'to grind small', but also (less frequently) 'to grind to dust' (61) or 'to grind to powder' (62). However, it did not necessarily involve pulverizing but also 'cutting into small parts'. For instance, beef is to be ground 'not too small', e.g., (67). Additionally, the sequence of cutting procedures (as in (69)–(70)) suggests some hierarchy of cutting, depending on the size of the pieces resulting from a particular cutting procedure (see section 3.6).

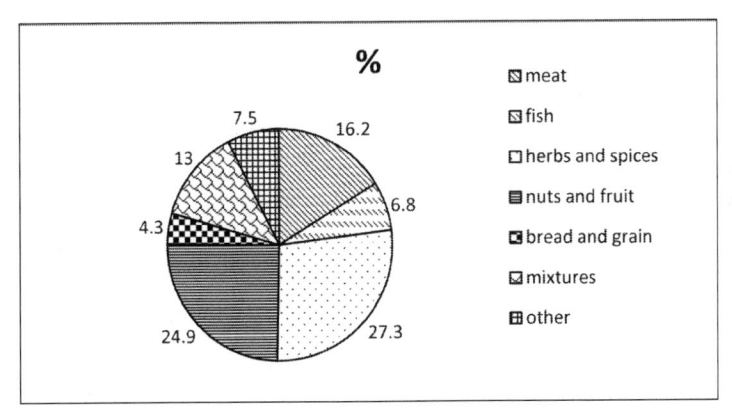

(67) tak buff & hewe yt smal al raw, & cast yt in a morter & **grynd** yt no3t to smal.
(DS_42)

(68) And take Almondes, and blaunche hem, and **grynde** hem thorgh a Streynour into stuffe mylke
(BK_12)

(69) Take persel, myntes, sauerey & sauge, tansy, veruayn, clarry, rewe, ditayn, fenel, southrenwode; hewe hem & **grinde** hem smale.
(FC_180)

(70) Nym þe lyre of þe hennyn & þe porke and hake small, & **grynd** hit al to dust,
(DS_5)

Fig. 7: *The ratio of foodstuffs ground in the 14th c*

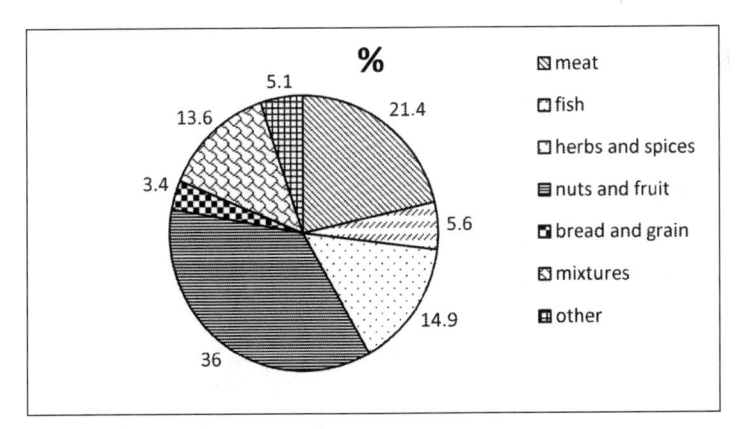

Fig. 8: *The ratio of foodstuffs ground in the 15th c*

97

3.3.1.8 mince

Mince derives from the Anglo-Norman *mincer, mincier* 'to chop into small pieces' (*AND*: s.v. *mincer*). The *OED* records it first in the 14th c. with the sense 'to cut up or grind (food, esp. meat) into very small pieces, now typically in a machine with revolving blades'. It was also found in the forms *myce* 'to cut into small pieces, to dice (food, ingredients)' and *mye* 'to crumble or grate (bread, etc.)'. However, the former became obsolete in the 16th c., and the latter in the 15th century[47]. According to the *AND*, *mye* corresponds to the Anglo-Norman noun *mie* (i) 'crumb, soft part of bread', (ii) 'crumb', (iii) 'morsel, tiny piece', (iv) 'fragment', (v) 'a small quantity', and (vi) 'scrap' (*AND*: s.v. *mie₁*). In the analyzed corpus it was found in the form of the Past Participle *mied*, and with the exception of one record always referred to bread.

The absolute frequencies of occurrence of the verb in the analyzed database equal: 63 in the 14th c. and 186 in the 15th c., i.e., [RNF: 21.7] and [RNF: 18.7] for the respective centuries. In the 14th c. the most frequently minced products were onions and bread; but also dates, herbs and meat/fish. In the 15th c. mincing was the most popular cutting procedure for dates, almonds and fruits as well as onions (for details see Fig. 9).

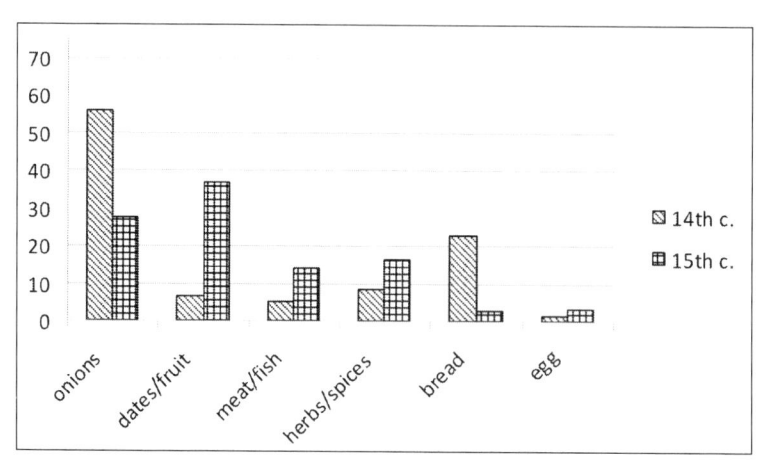

Fig. 9: *The percentage of products minced in the 14th and 15th c*

---

47 This is supported by the fact that only two records of the form were found in the 15th c. corpus.

It is suggested that *mince*, apart from its basic meaning, was also used with reference to mixing, see for instance (71)–(72):

(71) Take datys and pyke hem clene with apples and peeres, & **mince** hem with prunes damysyns; take out þe stones out of þe prunes, & kerue the prunes a two.

(FC_166)

(72) (…) his sauce is to be **mynced** with pouder of ginger, vynegre, & Mustard.

(BK_45)

In both cases, the context seems to call for 'mixing' rather than any form of 'cutting'. In (71) the fruits are first minced and only later are the stones taken out of the prunes before they are cut into two parts. In (72) by no means can we cut sauce.

The verb is also used as part of the phrase *myse bread* referring to crumbs of bread, see (73). Especially common in the phrase was the form *mie* (which disappeared from the language in the 15th c.). Its occurrence in the 14th c. contributed to the high score of bread as the referent of the verb (see Fig. 9 above).

(73) Nym eyryn wyþ al þe wyte & **myse bred** & schepys talwe as gret as dysys.

(DS_15)

Some of the occurrences of *mince* might be classified as belonging to the group 'dividing verbs' (e.g., (74)–(75)); however, since hardly any mention of the size of the received foodstuffs has been made, it is assumed that the verb referred to an action resulting in finely chopped ingredients. Minced foodstuffs might have been further cut, e.g., brayed (76) or ground (77).

(74) And þen **myce** þe lyuers in faire pecys; And whan the paunche hath wel y-boyled in þe licour, caste þe lyuers thereto, and lete boyle a while;

(BK_123)

(75) Take a gode quantyte of Oynonys, an **mynse** hem not to smale, an seethe in fayre Water;

(PD_33)

(76) and make a lyre of white crustes and oynouns **ymynced**. Bray it in a morter

(FC_118)

(77) Take Porke y-sode, & **mencyd** Datys, and grynd hem smal to-gederys;

(BM_8)

3.3.1.9 powder₁

The verb *powder* refers to the Anglo-Norman *pudrer, poudrer* and Middle French *poudrer*, meaning 'to (dust with) powder', 'to strew, scatter', 'to pulverize', 'to ornament (with small patterns or devices' and 'to salt' (*AND*: s.v. *pudrer*). It has been attested in the *OED* with the following senses (only senses related to the semantic field 'cookery' have been chosen):

(i) 'to reduce to powder; to pulverize' (1400-).
(ii) 'to sprinkle powder or a powdery substance on; to sprinkle or cover with or as with some powdery substance' (1325-);
(iii) 'to sprinkle (food) with a powdery condiment; to season, spice' (1300–1450; obs.); 'to mix with some qualifying or modifying ingredient; to season' (1425–1790; obs.);
(iv) 'to sprinkle (meat, etc.) with salt or powdered spice, esp. for preserving; to salt; to corn or cure' (1425-; in later use dialectal[48]);

Due to the fact that only sense (i) refers to the category 'reducing verbs', the other senses will be discussed in Chapter Five (see section 5.5), and the verb will be referred to as *powder₁* (= 'reducing verb') and *powder₂* (= 'verb of seasoning').

The only record of the verb *powder* found in the 14th c. refers to an action of either decorating or seasoning the dish, thus it carries sense (ii) or (iii), see (78).

(78) Coloure it with saffferoun; **powdur** yt with pouder douce.

(FC_2)

Out of the 12 records of the verb found in the 15th c., only 3 [RNF: 0.3] refer to pulverizing (see (79)), while the other occurrences categorize the verb as 'preparing' and thus will be discussed in section 5.5.

(79) (…) & than take halfe a quartron of gynger **powderd** & **bete** it with the yolkes,

(GR_S17_2)

The extremely rare occurrence of *powder₁* can be accounted for by the fact that pulverizing herbs was rather a basic operation in the medieval kitchen, as herbs were added to almost every dish; thus it is assumed that the action of turning herbs into powder did not have to be indicated in the recipes. Additionally, phrases such as 'make/do powder' or 'turn to powder' were used, e.g., (80)–(81).

---

48 The *EDD* records the verb with the sense 'to sprinkle, esp. to sprinkle butter or meat with salt; to cure meat for immediate use' in the dialects of Scotland and Suffolk; and in the form of a Past Participle: in Scotland, Cornwall, Sussex and Hampshire.

(80) Take þe rote of enula campana dry, ii unc, and galingale, longe peper, notemuges, greynes, clowes: of eche, i quarter of a unc. Rosemaryn, baye leuys, ysope, mynte, sauge, vi penywey3te drye; and **make pouder**, and put þerto.

(GK_17)

(81) Make a battur of þyk mylk of almondes & pared flour, & **turne þe frutur in powdres** & sumwhat of salt.

(GR_Rwl_256)

On the other hand, the noun *powder* was extremely frequent in both periods. On the discussion of the noun, see Bator (2013b).

3.3.1.10 *press*

The verb *press* was used as a reducing verb with the sense 'to subject to pressure so as to reduce to a particular shape, consistency, smoothness, thinness, or bulk, or so as to extract juice, etc., from; to compress, squeeze' (*OED*: s.v. *press*, v.¹ 2). The verb was formed from the noun *press* (AN *pres*). We have found it 8 times [RNF: 2.8] in the 14th c. and 53 times [RNF: 5.3] in the 15th c. In the corpus *press* referred to liquid or liquid-like products, and the action was always conducted in order to remove the liquid from the solid.

3.3.1.11 *quest*

The etymology of this verb is uncertain. The *OED* (s.v. *quest*, v.²) states:

> Origin uncertain; perhaps < an unattested metathetic variant of either Dutch *kwetsen, †quetsen* (Old Dutch *quezzen* to strike, Middle Dutch *quetsen, quessen*) or German *quetschen, †quetsen* (Middle High German *quetzen, quetschen*; compare Middle Low German *quessen, quetsen, quetten*), both in sense 'to crush, pound, bruise, squeeze', and of uncertain origin, perhaps imitative; or perhaps < either Middle Low German *questen* to beat, thrash (a person, especially as punishment) or early modern German (now regional: central, east central) *questen* to beat, scourge (late 15th cent.), which are derived respectively < Middle Low German *quast, quest* and early modern German *quast, quaste, quest, queste* (Middle High German *queste*; now *Quaste*) tassel, twig, branch.
>
> (*OED*: s.v. *quest*, v.²).

According to the dictionary, the verb appeared in English in the 17th c. However, we have found one occurrence of the verb in the early 14th c. (see (82)).

(82) Nim þe rote & vache out þe grapes, & do in an morter wiþ a lute salt, & **quest wel þe grapes**, & soþþen vach out þe ius,

(DC_39)

Additionally, the *AND* records the verb *casser* (also spelt *quessir, queissir, queissier, queisser, quaisser, quaser, quacer, quassir*), with the senses 'to shake', 'to break, shatter', 'to subdue, suppress' and 'to shatter, crush' (*AND*: s.v. *casser*). Thus, it is suggested that the form found in the corpus is rather an earlier French introduction, which later became obsolete.

3.3.1.12 *stamp*

Stamp is an early Middle English verb of Germanic origin (?OE **stampian*). However, it was influenced by Old French *estamper*, giving it the meaning 'to bray in a mortar; to beat to a pulp or powder; to pound' (*OED*: s.v. *stamp*, v.). Although, according to the *OED*, the verb was present in English from the late 12th c., we have found only 6 records [RNF: 2] of *stamp* in the 14th c. and 20 [RNF: 2] in the 15th c. The action was applied mostly to grains, herbs and spices, almonds and fruit, and took place in a mortar. It is believed that stamping consisted in beating foodstuffs coarsely since in a number of recipes the action was followed by grinding to powder, e.g., (83)–(84)

> (83) And put in þi morter a half lb. suger and ii unc gynger, were paryd, and **stampe** euermore smartly with þi pestell till it begynne to flye leke mele. And whan it begynnys so to flye, stampe it no more bue euermore grynde it wyth 3oure pestell be þe bothum,
>
> (GK_16)

> (84) Take Almaunde Mylke, & Floure of Rys, Sugre, an gode pouder Gyngere, Galyngale, Canel, & gode Erbys, and **stampe** hem & grynd hem þorw a cloþe,
>
> (PD_70)

3.3.2 Discussion

Out of the twelve verbs categorized as 'reducing', only four were of Germanic origin, i.e., *beat$_1$, break$_2$, crumb,* and *grind*. However, the first three were rather peripheral (*beat$_1$* = RNF: 1.4 and 0.2, and *break$_2$* = RNF: 0.3 and 0.6, and *crumb* = RNF: 0 and 0.4, in the respective centuries). All the other verbs were either borrowed from or influenced by French. Table 7 shows the absolute as well as relative normalized frequencies of the occurrence of the verbs (see also Fig. 10 for the distribution of the most prominent reducing verbs).

Table 7: The frequency of the occurrence of the 'reducing verbs'

<table>
<tr><td rowspan="12">6a. Absolute frequencies:</td><td>verb</td><td>14th c.</td><td>15th c.</td></tr>
<tr><td>beat₁</td><td>4</td><td>2</td></tr>
<tr><td>bray</td><td>66</td><td>104</td></tr>
<tr><td>break₂</td><td>1</td><td>6</td></tr>
<tr><td>bruise</td><td>1</td><td>8</td></tr>
<tr><td>crumb</td><td>0</td><td>4</td></tr>
<tr><td>grate</td><td>14</td><td>69</td></tr>
<tr><td>grind</td><td>164</td><td>356</td></tr>
<tr><td>mince</td><td>63</td><td>186</td></tr>
<tr><td>powder₁</td><td>0</td><td>3</td></tr>
<tr><td>press</td><td>8</td><td>53</td></tr>
<tr><td>quest</td><td>1</td><td>0</td></tr>
<tr><td>stamp</td><td>6</td><td>20</td></tr>
</table>

<table>
<tr><td rowspan="12">6b. Normalized frequencies:</td><td>verb</td><td>14th c.</td><td>15th c.</td></tr>
<tr><td>beat₁</td><td>1.4</td><td>0.2</td></tr>
<tr><td>bray</td><td>22.7</td><td>10.5</td></tr>
<tr><td>break₂</td><td>0.3</td><td>0.6</td></tr>
<tr><td>bruise</td><td>0.3</td><td>0.8</td></tr>
<tr><td>crumb</td><td>0</td><td>0.4</td></tr>
<tr><td>grate</td><td>4.8</td><td>7</td></tr>
<tr><td>grind</td><td>56.5</td><td>35.9</td></tr>
<tr><td>mince</td><td>21.7</td><td>18.7</td></tr>
<tr><td>powder₁</td><td>0</td><td>0.3</td></tr>
<tr><td>press</td><td>2.8</td><td>5.3</td></tr>
<tr><td>quest</td><td>0.3</td><td>0</td></tr>
<tr><td>stamp</td><td>2</td><td>2</td></tr>
</table>

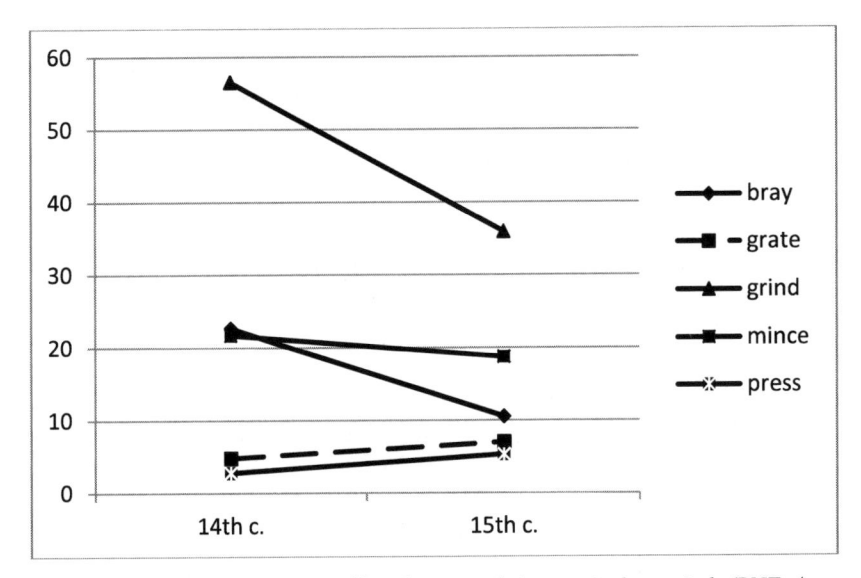

Fig. 10: Distribution of the major[49] 'reducing verbs' at particular periods (RNFs / 10,000 words)

---

49 By 'major' we mean those verbs whose relative normalized frequency exceeded 5 (at least in one of the analysed periods).

The most general verbs in this group were *grind* and *bray*. They were used with a wide variety of foodstuffs. The only tool for both actions was a mortar. Grinding and braying were conducted not only in order to pulverize a particular foodstuff, but also to mix ingredients (e.g., (85)–(86)). Additionally, grinding might have been applied in order to colour a dish (e.g., (87)). Neither grinding nor braying were followed by any other cutting procedures, which suggests that the result of both actions was so small that no further reduction could be applied (unlike for the other reducing verbs).

(85) Take persel, mynt, garlek, a litul serpell and sawge; a litul canel, gynger, piper, wyne, brede, vyneger & salt; **grynde** it smal with safroun,

(FC_144)

(86) Take the rowe of a female pike, or any rowe, and bray hit in a morter; thenne take xx or xxx almoynes and bray theym and put theym to the rowe and **bray** theym togeder verry small.

(GR_SA_7)

(87) (…) & **grynd** egges and safroun or sandres togedere þat it be colourd

(DS_34)

Both verbs tend to decrease in frequency (see Fig. 10). This might have been caused by the tendency towards the replacement of non-specific vocabulary with words carrying a narrow meaning. *Press* for instance, which was of a specific meaning (referred to liquid or liquid-like products), shows a considerable increase in frequency.

The corpus shows that a considerable number of reducing verbs became available in the Middle English period (via borrowing from French). If we compare the semantic field from the Old English period with that of the Middle English period, the number of verbs will be much greater.

However, a great deal of the verbs belonging to this group were peripheral, i.e., they occurred with extremely rare frequency (*beat$_1$, bruise, crumb, powder$_1$, quest, stamp*).[50] The other verbs, i.e., *grate* and *mince* correlated, to a certain extent, in their meaning. In the 14th c. the former referred to bread and cheese, in the 15th c. its reference became limited to bread only. The latter had a wider range of referents, bread being one of the dominant ones in the 14th c. but not a century later (see Fig. 9 in section 3.3.1.7). Thus, it is believed that *mince* lost its reference to bread in favour of the verb *grate*, or due to the fact that *grate* narrowed its meaning

---

50   This might be accounted for by the fact that most of them were newly introduced to English, thus, they had not been fully assimilated into the language.

and in the 15th c. bread became its sole referent. At the same time the normalized frequency of *grate* rose slightly, and that of *mince* diminished. Additionally, it is believed that the size of the foodstuff resulting from both actions might have differed. Grating bread resulted in bread crumbs, whilst mincing most probably resulted in coarser pieces, for instance the recipe under (88) calls for both minced ginger and powdered ginger – which proves that mincing resulted in a different form of the foodstuff than powder. Also, minced ingredients could have been further ground or brayed (see examples (76) and (77) in the sections above). On the other hand, the fact that not a single recipe specifies the way of mincing suggests that the verb is rather a reducing than a cutting verb.[51]

(88) cast on almondys fryed & cuttyd, **ginger mynsyd**, & **poudyr of ginger**.

(OP_73)

Finally, phrases such as 'do powder', 'do in a morter' or 'pull to powder' should be mentioned, since they also referred to the reduction of foodstuffs into powder. They were rather infrequent, with only 9 records [RNF: 3.1] in the 14th c.

3.4 Removing verbs

3.4.1 The corpus

The group of 'removing verbs' comprises 21 verbs: *blanch, bone, break₃, chop off, cut₂, do₁ (away, off, out), flay, ⁺hild, hull, pare, peel/pill/pull, pick (away/off/ out), scale, scrape, shave, shell, skin, smite off, strip, take₂ (away/off/out)* and *whiten* (see Table 8). All of them refer to the action of removing some part of the foodstuff, such as skin, kernel, bone, hull, hair, etc. from its main part. Due to a certain degree of synonymity, in what follows, some verbs shall be discussed together. Moreover, a number of the verbs seem to have been peripheral due to a small number of occurrences, thus, they shall be discussed together in one section. Hence, verbs whose relative normalized frequency is equal or lower than 1, have been grouped in the section 'peripheral verbs', unless they are synonymous with one of the non-peripheral verbs, then they shall be discussed in the same section as their synonym.

---

51 The fact that *mince* has been classified as a 'reducing verb' rather than 'cutting' can also be supported by the fact that Marttila (2009) did not include it in his study, from which verbs referring to pulverizing and squeezing have been excluded.

Table 8: *The number of occurrences of the 'removing verbs' in the analyzed material. Relative normalized frequencies have been given in brackets [RNFs / 10,000 words.]*

	14th c.	15th c.
blanche	42 [14.5]	138 [13.9]
bone	0	1 [0.1]
break₃	6 [2]	21 [2.1]
chop off	0	4 [0.4]
cut₂	0	78 [7.9]
do₁ (away, off, out)	9 [3.1]	52 [5.2]
flay	5 [1.7]	30 [3]
†hild	3 [1]	0
hull	2 [0.7]	1 [0.1]
pare	15 [5.2]	69 [7]
peel, pill, pull	7 [2.4]	52 [5.2]
pick (away, off, out)	8 [2.8]	56 [5.6]
scale	0	16 [1.6]
scrape	1 [0.3]	4 [0.4]
shave	1 [0.3]	10 [1]
shell	1 [0.3]	7 [0.7]
skin	0	2 [0.2]
smite₂ off	0	2 [0.2]
strip	0	9 [0.9]
take₂ (away, off, out)	8 [2.8]	41 [4.1]
whiten	6 [2]	0

3.4.1.1 *blanch* and *whiten*

The verb *blanch* derived from Fr. *blanchir* 'to whiten' and referred mostly to almonds. According to the *OED*, it denoted 'to whiten almonds, or the like, by taking off the skin; hence, to scald by a short rapid boil in order to remove the skin, or for any other purpose' (s.v. *blanch*, v.[1] 2a). It was introduced into English in the 14th c. Additionally, the *OED* records the adjective *blanched* from the early 15th c. with the sense 'whitened (by loss of colour)', and with reference to almonds (as found in the analyzed material): 'whitened by removal of the skin; peeled' found from the 2nd half of the 15th c. (*OED*: s.v. *blanched*, adj.)

In the analyzed corpus the verb *blanch* was found 42 times [RNF: 14.5] in the 14th c. and 138 [RNF: 13.9] in the 15th c. In the 14th c. the majority of records (73%) were in the adjectival form (i.e., the past participle *blanched*, meaning 'peeled'); additionally, 22% of records were used as an adjective (without the *–ed* ending) denoting 'white' (see (89)–(90)), and 5% of the forms were used as an active transitive verb. In the 15th c. 39.2% of records were in the form of the past participle (= 'peeled'), 30.4% were non-*ed* adjectives (= 'white') and 30.4% were used as active transitive verbs. Fig. 11 shows the ratio of the occurrences of particular forms in the respective centuries. Although, following the *OED*, *blanch* was used earlier in its verbal rather than adjectival form (the former was used already in the 14th c., the latter only in the 15th c., and what is more with reference to almonds it started to be used only in the 2nd half of the 15th c.)[52], the corpus shows an opposite tendency. In the 14th c. the adjectival use was the most frequent, with 73% of the *–ed* forms (= 'peeled') and 22% of the non-*ed* forms (= 'white'). The 15th c. corpus shows a more balanced division, with only a slight advantage of the *–ed* forms.

All of the 14th century records referred to almonds. In the later century meat could have been blanched as well; however, this was sporadic, see (91).

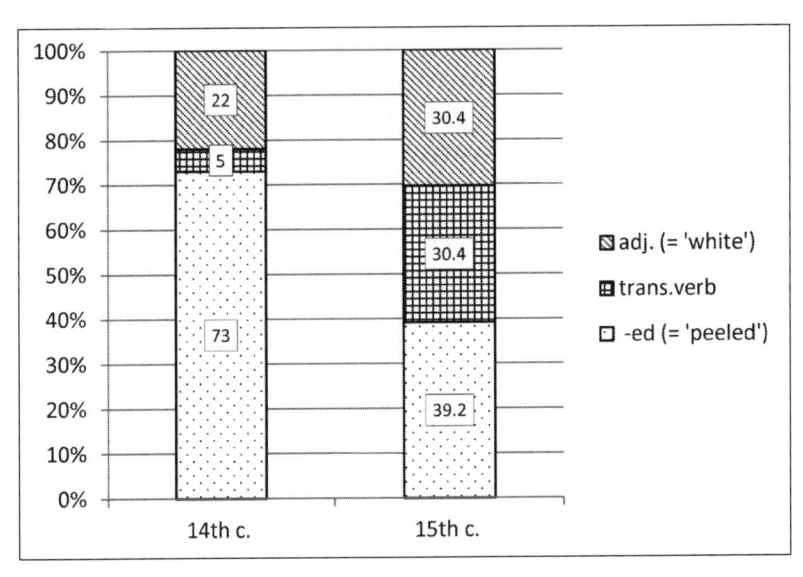

Fig. 11: The ratio of the occurrence (%) of particular forms of blanch in the analyzed centuries

---

52   See: *OED*: s.v. *blanch*, v.[1] 2a and *blanched*, adj. 1 & 2.

(89) For to make **Blawnche** Perrye. Take þe Whyte of the lekys, an seþe hem in a potte, an presse hem vp, (…)

(PD_45)

(90) **Blanch** Bruett. Blanch almundys in colde water; grynd tham small. Draw tham with whyte wyne; do to tham ffyges small mynsyd, & do in pouder gynger, suger, & salt.

(GR_Sl7_14)

(91) take Capoun, Conyngys or Pertriches; smyte þe Capoun, or kede, or Chykonys, Conyngys: þe Pertriche shal ben hol: þan **blaunche** þe Fleyssh, an caste on þe mylke;

(PD_67)

The corpus contains also a Germanic synonym of *blanch*, i.e., *whiten*, which was formed from the adjective *white* and the verbal suffix *–en*. The *OED* (s.v. *whiten*, v.) defines it as denoting (i) 'to make or render white; to impart a white colour or appearance to'. Additionally, the form *white*, denoting 'to whiten, to blanch', first occurred in the 16th c. (*OED*: s.v. *white*, v.[1] 2c). In the analyzed material, the verb *white(n)* was found 6 times [RNF: 2] in the 14th c. No record was found in the 15th c. Semantically, the verb might have referred to both peeling/blanching and colouring/whitening, even within the same recipe, see for instance (92). The dish in (92) is based on layers of different colours, thus 'whitened' almonds boiled with saffron are to be coloured, and thus the verb refers rather to taking off the skin than dyeing the almonds white. It should be noted that all the occurrences of the verb were found only in one of the analyzed collections, i.e., *Diuersa cibaria* (DC), which may suggest some dialectal restrictions of the use of the verb.

(92) (…) & soþþen nim þe alemaundes **ihwyted** [= 'peeled'] & saffron & make boillen togederes in water. & soþþen fryen in oylee oþur in grecee, & vnder þe metee þat is **ihwyted** [= 'white'] schulen beon iset alemauns icoloured, & abouen þe mete icoloured schulen beon iset alemauns **iwyted** [= 'white'] & rys & penides.

(DC_33)

3.4.1.2 *break₃*

Break is one of the verbs with a particularly broad meaning. Hence, it has been divided into four sections, depending on its reference:

- *break₁* – dividing verb (discussed in section 3.2.1.1),
- *break₂* – reducing verb (discussed in section 3.3.1.3),

- *break₃* – removing verb (the present section),
- *break₄* – penetrating verb (discussed in section 3.5.1.1).

Break₃ was used as a removing verb six times in the 14th and 21 times in the 15th c. [i.e., RNF: 2 and 2.1 in the respective centuries]. It referred to removing shells (of eggs and nuts), but also to removing some parts of meat (bones, beaks, legs, etc.).

3.4.1.3 *cut₂ (away/off/out)*

Cut is one of the major verbs belonging to the group of dividing verbs (see section 3.2.1.4). However, 78 of its 15th c. occurrences [RNF: 7.9] were classified as 'removing'. They refer to the removal of certain parts of meat (wings, legs, head, etc.) and fish (fin, etc.). Usually the verb was followed by the preposition *away, off* or *out*, but not always (e.g., (93)–(94)). None of the 14th c. records of *cut* qualifies it into the category of 'removing verbs'.

> (93) (…) & breke awey the boon fro the kne to the fote, and lete the skyn be stille, and **cutt** the wyng att the Joynte next the body,
> (Aus_Douce_6)

> (94) & lett the skyn be still. & **cut awey** the whyngys by the joynte nexte the body,
> (OP_145)

3.4.1.4 *flay, †hild* and *skin*

All these verbs are of Germanic origin (*flay* < OE *fléan*, *hild* < OE *hyldan*, *skin* developed from the noun, which in turn was borrowed from ON). They denoted 'to strip or pull off the skin; to skin', 'to peel off (the skin)'. *Hild* became obsolete in the 17th c. The other two verbs have remained in use until the Present Day English.

In the analyzed corpus *flay* occurred only 5 times [RNF: 1.7] in the 14th c. and 30 times [RNF: 3] in the 15th c. The action referred to taking off the skin (and sometimes the feathers) of various fish and sometimes meat, see (95).

> (95) Take a Pecok, breke his necke, and kutte his throte, And **fle** him, þe skyn and the ffethurs togidre,
> (BK_55)

Hild was found only 5 times in the 14th c.; only three of the records [RNF: 1.4] were synonymous with *flay* – compare (96)–(97). No occurrences of the verb were noted in the 15th c., which may suggest an earlier obsolescence than suggested in

109

the *OED*[53]. The three records referred to meat and fish. The other two records, in which the verb refers to sauce and broth respectively, seem to have a different denotation, such as 'to pour', see (98).

(96) Take eles & **fle** hem & cut hem on thynne gobetes, & frye hem in oyle dolif, (…)

(UC_1)

(97) Take sooles and **hylde** hem; seeþ hem in water. Smyte hem on pecys (…)

(FC_122)

(98) (…) & ley it in the disches with yolkes and take the sauche [= sauce] and **hilde** hit into the disches & do aboue clowes & serue it forth.

(UC_20)

Even though, following the *OED* (s.v. *skin*, v. I.2.a), *skin* was used only from the middle of the 16th c., we have found two occurrences [RNF: 0.2] of the verb in the 15th c. (e.g., (99)). The verb was used with the sense 'to remove the skin from (an animal or occas. a person); to peel or pare off the skin of (a vegetable or piece of fruit), decorticate', and was formed by conversion from the noun *skin*. The early occurrence may serve as evidence that the conversion process started earlier than stated in the dictionary.

(99) Take a pigge, & make hym clene, and **Skynne** hym, & Fylle it ful of suche mete…

(LV_38)

3.4.1.5 *pare*

The verb *pare* derives from AN and OF *parer* 'to adorn, beautify; to prepare, arrange' and 'to peel, to trim'. It was borrowed into English in the 14th c. with the latter sense. The analyzed corpus contains 15 records [RNF: 5.2] of *pare* found in the 14th c. and 69 [RNF: 7] a century later. The verb referred mostly to fruits (e.g., (100)), but also to meat (101), ginger (102) and cheese (103). The action of paring was often followed by various cutting procedures, e.g., grinding (101), leaching (100), hewing (102), carving, braying, etc.

(100) And then take pere Wardones, and **pare** hem, And seth hem, And leche hem in faire gobettes, and pike out the core,

(BK_97)

(101) Take Freyssch Brawn & seethe yt y-now, & **pare** it & grynde it in a mortere,

(LV_1)

---

53   According to the *OED*, *hild* became obsolete in the 17th c.

(102) soþþen nim gynger & **par** yt wel & heuw hit.

(DC_56)

(103) Take nessh chese, and **pare** it clene, and grinde hit in a morter small,

(BK_29)

3.4.1.6 *peel, pill* and *pull*

Peel is a variant of *pill*, which, in turn, derived from an unattested OE **pilian*, **pylian*, from classical Latin *pilāre* 'to deprive of hair or feathers', later also 'to scalp, pluck wool'. The verb might have been influenced by French *peler* 'to make bald; to remove hair; to remove the skin; peel; bark' (*OED*: s.v. *pill*, v.[1] and *peel*, v.[1]). *Pull* is a Germanic verb of uncertain etymology, related to Low German *pūlen* 'shell, strip, pluck', MDu *polen* 'strip' and MLG *pūle*, and Du *peul* 'husk, shell' (*ODEE*: s.v. *pull*). According to the *OED* (s.v. *pull*, v.), in the Old English period the prefixed form *apullian* 'to pull or tear off (hair)' was also attested. The verb was used with the sense 'to pluck the feathers from (a bird); [†]to strip the wool or fur from (a sheep or animal skin), to fleece' (*OED*).

In the 14th c. 7 occurrences [RNF: 2.4] of these verbs were found (3 of the form *pill* and 4 of *pull*). The forms were used synonymously, they referred to peeling meat and vegetables. Occasionally, the preposition 'off' followed the verb. Only one record specifies what was removed, see (104).

(104) Take rawe pork and **pull** of the skyn, and pyke out þe synewes,

(FC_66)

In the 15th c. not only were more records found but we can also see a greater diversity of the forms. Altogether, the corpus contains 49 occurrences of the verbs [RNF: 4.9] (i.e., 36 of *pull*, 3 of *peel* and 10 of *pill*). However, they were no longer synonymous. Thus, we can distinguish the following senses:

(i) 'to remove the skin, feathers, hair, etc.':
    pull: 13 records
    peel: 1 record
    pill: 10 records

(ii) 'to remove blood':
    pull: 23 records

(iii) 'to remove shell, hull, etc.':
    peel: 2 records

Sometimes the verb was followed by the preposition 'away' or 'off'. The recipes prove that pulling could have affected meat/fish but also a live animal, see (105)–(106).

(105) (…) an porke þer-ynne, an **pulle** of þe swerde [= rind] an pyke owt þe bonys, an þan hewe it,

(PD_7)

(106) Take a rede coke of v yere age; **pull** [= 'remove feathers'] hym all quykke & after þat lett hym lyfe a while, & þan kylle hym.

(GR_CUL_124)

3.4.1.7 *pick (away/off/out)*

This verb was used throughout the corpus 29 and 99 times in the respective centuries. However, it was found with a number of senses:

(i) 'to remove some unwanted parts of foodstuffs, such as hair, skin, bones, stone, etc.'; the sense corresponds to that found in the *OED* (s.v. *pick*, v.[1] I.3.a) – used from the end of the 14th c.;
(ii) 'to pick up, take from; to put somewhere', which corresponds to the *OED* (II.12.a) – used from the 14th c.;
(iii) 'to choose out, select carefully' – from the end of the 14th c. (*OED*: III.15.a);
(iv) 'to make an incision', which corresponds to the *OED*'s sense (I.2.a) 'to probe or penetrate with a pointed instrument so as to remove extraneous matter; to probe or penetrate with finger, beak, etc., in a similar manner'. Following Marttilla's (2009) division of verbs, this sense would belong to the group of penetrating verbs;[54]
(v) 'to cut, make smaller' – which does not have any corresponding sense in the *OED*.[55]

In the present section only sense (i) will be discussed. The ratio of the occurrence of particular senses, as found in the analyzed corpus, has been shown in Fig. 12.

Pick usually referred to the removal of skin, bones, stones, cores, hair, etc. This sense was definitely the dominant one in the 15th c. (= 54.4%). In the 14th c.

---

54 This sense has been found only once in the 15th c. material (see example below), thus it will not be discussed in the section on 'penetrating verbs'.
(…) an whan þe beef hath y-boylid, take it vp an pyke it, an lete it blede in-to a vessel,
(PD_24)
55 This sense was reflected in the analyzed corpus only three times in the 15th c. Thus, it will not be discussed in the present study.

the verb (with the removing sense) was always followed by the preposition 'out'. In the 15th c. the majority of records were accompanied by 'out, away' or 'off', e.g., (107). However, plain forms also occur with sense (i), e.g., (108)–(109). In the former example, *pick* is closer in meaning to 'to detach', whilst in the latter 'to peel'.

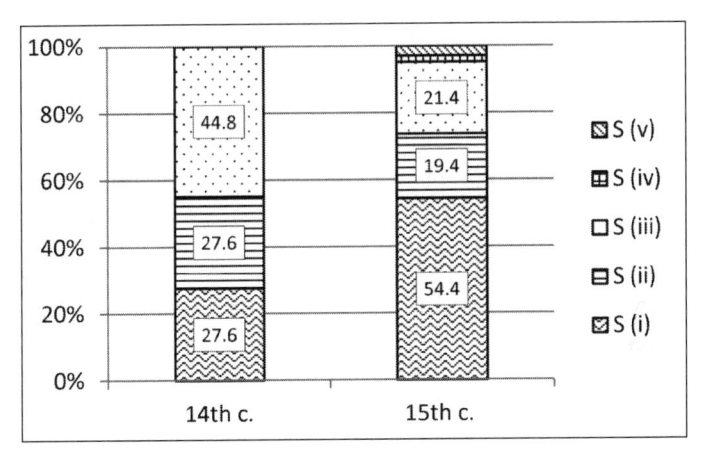

Fig. 12: *The ratio of the occurrence (%) of particular senses of* pick *in the respective centuries [S = sense]*

(107) Take otemele, an grynd it smal, an seethe it wyl, an porke þer-ynne, an pulle of þe swerde an **pyke owt** þe bonys,

(PD_7)

(108) Take porke sodyn; **pyke** hit clene from the bonys, grynd hit small.

(OP_119)

(109) then take hole oynones, **pike** hem, And cast hem al hole there-to;

(BK_13)

3.4.1.8 *scrape* and *shave*

Although, according to the *OED*, *scrape*[56] was present in English from the 14th c., only five occurrences of the verb were found in the analyzed material (one in

---

56 Probably representing OE *scrapian* (*OED*).

113

the 14th and four in the 15th c.). They referred to the peeling of roots of vegetables (in the 14th c.) and fish (in the 15th c.), see (110)–(111).

> (110) Take rote of persel, of Pasternak, of rafens, **scrape** hem waische hem clene,
>
> (FC_103)
>
> (111) Recipe þe pokes of þe pike & wesch it clene, & **scrape** it, þe pike, & wesh it clene,
>
> (Ht_Hrl_19)

Shave, from OE *sceafan*, was recorded much earlier than *scrape* (i.e., from the 8th c.). Originally the verb denoted 'to scrape, to scrape away the surface of, to cut down or pare away with a sharp tool, thereby removing very thin portions of the surface'. From the 14th c. the following senses were also found: 'to remove by scraping or paring; to cut off in thin slices or shavings', and 'to cut off (hair) close to the skin with or as with a razor' (*OED*).

Shave was found only once [RNF: 0.3] in the 14th c. and 10 times [RNF: 1] in the 15th c. It referred to removing hair of fish (112) or of certain parts of meats (113). It might have been followed by the preposition 'away' (112).

> (112) Take and scalde a congur; (…) **shave away** þe herys fro the bake and off the bely unto þe tayle,
>
> (Gr_CUL_163)
>
> (113) Take the hert of a swan, the geser, and the tharmes; slete hem, **shave** hem, seth hem, & the fetys & the whyngys.
>
> (OP_116)

3.4.1.9 do_1 / $take_2$ (away/off/out)

The verbs *do* and *take* were extremely frequent in the analyzed corpus, but with the general sense (see sections 5.3 and 5.6, respectively). Both could also be classified as 'removing verbs', and, in such a case, they were followed by one of the prepositions *away*, *off* or *out*, and were used with reference to the removal of any part of fruit, vegetable, meat or fish. Do_1 as a removing verb was found 9 [RNF: 3.1] times in the 14th c. and 52 times [RNF: 5.2] in the 15th c. $Take_2$ was used 8 times [RNF: 2.8] in the 14th and 41 [RNF: 4.1] in the 15th c.

It is worth noting that the use of a general verb followed by a particle which modified its meaning into a more specific one became more popular in the 15th c.

3.4.1.10 Peripheral verbs

Additionally, the corpus contains a number of verbs which were peripheral due to a very small number of their occurrences. These shall be discussed together in this section rather than in separate sections.

(a) bone

The verb, formed from the noun *bone*, was found only once in the 15th c. It referred to detaching/removing the bone from meat. The single record of the verb may be explained by the fact that it was only just entering English – according to the *OED*, *bone* started to be used at the end of the 15th c.

(b) chop off

Among the 15th c. occurrences of *chop*, which was one of the major dividing verbs[57], four records definitely qualify the verb as 'removing' [RNF: 0.4]. They were all followed by the preposition *off* and referred to the removal of certain parts of fish or meat, such as legs, head or hair, e.g., (114).

(114) Draw þe plays; **chop of** þe hedes & þe fynnes.

(GR_Rwl_85)

(c) hull, shell and scale

Hull was derived from the noun *hull* 'the shell, pod, or husk of peas and beans; the outer covering or rind of any fruit or seed' (*OED*: s.v. *hull*, n.¹). The verb was used from the end of the 14th c. with the sense 'to remove the hull, shell or husk of; to strip of the outer covering'. The analyzed material contained only 2 occurrences of the verb in the 14th c. and 1 in the 15th c. [RNF: 0.7 and 0.1, respectively]. Phrases with the noun (e.g., 'till the hulls go off', 'to do off the hulls') occurred 8 and 12 times in the respective centuries, i.e., 2.8 and 1.2 times per 10,000 words. Both the verb and the noun referred to grains (wheat) and pulses (peas and beans).

Shell was derived from the noun *shell* (OE *sciell, scill*). Following the *OED*, the verb with the senses (i) 'to remove (a seed) from its shell, husk, or pod' and (ii) 'to remove the shell, husk, etc. of' was first recorded in the 2nd half of the 16th and the end of the 17th c., respectively. Nevertheless, we have found one record [RNF: 0.3] of the verb at the end of the 14th c. (see (115)), and 7 records [RNF: 0.7] in the 15th c. (e.g., (116)). All the occurrences of the verb referred to oysters.

(115) **Schyl** oysters and seeþ hem in wyne and in hare owne broth;

(FC_124)

---

57 See section 3.2.1.3.

(116) Take oystres and **shell** hem and put hem in a vessel,

(BK_148)

Similarly, the verb *scale*, formed from the noun *scale* (from French *escale*), was found with the sense 'to remove scales'. All of its 16 records [RNF: 1.6] referred to fish. It was found only in the 15th c., which agrees with the *OED* (s.v. *scale*, v.²).

(d) smite off

In the 15th c. the verb *smite* (categorized as a 'dividing verb', see section 3.2.1.15) started to be used with the preposition *off*, which changed its meaning into 'to cut off', and in turn it broadened the reference of *smite* to 'removing verbs'. However, only two occurrences were found [i.e., RNF: 0.2], which may be accounted for by the fact that the formation was only just entering the language.

(e) strip

Strip, from OE **striepan, *strepan, *strypan*, belongs to the category of cutting ('removing') verbs with the following senses: (i) 'to remove (an adhering covering of skin, bark, lead, paper, etc.); to pull off (leaves, fruit) from a tree, etc.', and (ii) 'to skin (an animal)' – the latter being obsolete from the 18th c. We have found only 9 occurrences [RNF: 0.9] of the verb in the 15th c. Sometimes it was accompanied by the particle 'away' or 'off'. It referred to removing the skin, bones or buds (from stalks).

3.4.2 Discussion

The group of the 'removing verbs' comprises 21 verbs. However, only few of the types had a significant number of tokens, a great number of the verbs had their relative normalized frequency below 1 (per 10,000 words), see Table 9. This can be accounted for by the fact that removing bones or hair, or peeling fruit and vegetables, were such basic activities that they did not have to be indicated in the recipes.

Unlike in the other verbal groups, the majority of the 'removing verbs', except *blanch, pare* and *scale*, are of Germanic origin. All of them were extremely specific in meaning – *blanch* referred to removing the skin of almonds (except one 15th c. reference to meat), *scale* to removing the scales of fish. *Pare*, in most of its occurrences referred to fruit.

The Germanic origin of the majority of verbs belonging to this group may be justified in a similar way as the idea concerning meat vocabulary, introduced by John Wallis and popularized in Scott's *Ivanhoe* (Jespersen 1912, Knowles 1997)[58].

---

58   Wallis suggested that names of animals were referred to with Germanic terms since they were handled by the servants, whilst the terms for meat were of French origin,

Thus, the most basic cutting activities, which were known to the Englishmen were referred to with native terms, whilst the more sophisticated procedures introduced by the French cooks, and consequently the vocabulary used for these activities was named with the borrowed lexemes.

Table 9: Number of occurrences of the 'removing verbs' found in the analyzed material

	verb	14th c.	15th c.		verb	14th c.	15th c.
9a. Absolute frequencies:	blanch	42	138	9b. Normalized frequencies:	blanch	14.5	13.9
	bone	0	1		bone	0	0.1
	break₃	6	21		break₃	2	2.1
	chop off	0	4		chop off	0	0.4
	cut₂	0	78		cut₂	0	7.9
	do₁ (away/ off/ out)	9	52		do₁ (away/ off/ out)	3.1	5.2
	flay	5	30		flay	1.7	3
	ᵗhild	3	0		ᵗhild	1	0
	hull	2	1		hull	0.7	0.1
	pare	15	69		pare	5.2	7
	peel/pill/pull	7	49		peel/pill/pull	2.4	4.9
	pick (away/ off/ out)	8	56		pick (away/ off/ out)	2.8	5.6
	scale	0	16		scale	0	1.6
	scrape	1	4		scrape	0.3	0.4
	shave	1	10		shave	0.3	1
	shell	1	7		shell	0.3	0.7
	skin	0	2		skin	0	0.2
	smite off	0	2		smite off	0	0.2
	strip	0	9		strip	0	0.9
	take₂ (away/ off/ out)	8	41		take₂ (away/ off/ out)	2.8	4.1
	whiten	6	0		whiten	2	0

since it was eaten by the French masters. The idea that the origin of vocabulary reflects the master – servant relation, which leads to the superstratal position of French, has been questioned by Lutz (2013: 575), who on the example of food vocabulary shows that similar borrowings from French can be found in Middle English and Middle High German, despite the fact that in the latter case we cannot talk of "an unequal stratal relation" between the two languages involved.

Another interesting fact concerning the 'removing verbs' is that many of the verbs were general verbs followed by one of the prepositions which added the meaning of removal to the general verb, e.g., *take away, pick out, cut away, pull out*, etc. Hardly any of the Germanic 'removing verbs' are specific in meaning, and those which are, are peripheral in terms of their frequency of occurrence. Additionally, many of the verbs were formed in the process of conversion (similarly to 'dividing verbs', see section 3.2.2), e.g., *hull, scale, shell, skin*.

Additionally, a number of phrases referring to the removal of certain parts of foodstuffs were used. These were some general verbs followed by a specifying phrase (e.g., *make them clean* = 'remove hair', *let blood at the navel* = 'remove blood', etc.). The corpus contained 26 [RNF: 9] such phrases in the 14th c. and 99 [RNF: 10] in the 15th c. They referred to removing bones, skin, stones, etc.

3.5 Penetrating verbs

3.5.1 The corpus

The group of penetrating verbs was the poorest in terms of the verbal types belonging to it. Only five verbs were categorized as penetrating: *break$_4$, cut$_3$, draw$_4$, open* and *slit$_2$*. They refer to the action of making an incision or cutting foodstuff without dividing it into smaller parts. An instrument such as a knife was not necessary – the action might have been done with one's hands.

3.5.1.1 *break$_4$*

Break had such a broad meaning that it was categorized into all the four subgroups of cutting verbs (see sections: 3.2.1.1 for *break* as a 'dividing verb', 3.3.1.3 as 'reducing' and 3.4.1.2 as 'removing'). A number of its occurrences qualify it also as a 'penetrating verb'. In the 14th c. we have found only 3 records [RNF: 1] of *break$_4$*, but in the following century this sense became the dominant one, with 46 records [RNF: 4.6], which makes up 20% and 49.5% of all the occurrences of *break* in the respective centuries (see also Fig. 2 in section 3.2.1.1).

In the 14th *break$_4$* was used with reference to various grains (e.g., wheat, rice). It denoted breaking of the structure of the grain, without the use of any instrument, but rather due to various cooking procedures (e.g., (117)). In the 15th c. this sense was still used, with 17.4% of all the records. This sense was used next to the synonymous *burst*, which was rather infrequent. *Burst* was found only 9 times [RNF: 3.1] in the 14th and 4 times [RNF: 0.4] in the 15th c. This suggests that it might have been replaced by the more general *break*, which gained in frequency in the 15th c. Additionally, $break_4$ referred to making an incision in fish or meat (either with a knife or with one's hands), in order to remove blood, to kill or to reshape it. This use of $break_4$ constituted 69.6% of all its records, e.g., (118); and 13% of its records referred to breaking vessels or pastry coffins.

>(117) wasch clene þe rys in leuk water & turne & seth hem til þay **breke** & lat it kele,
>
>(UC_28)

>(118) Sle hym in the mouth as a curlew. Scall hym; draw hym as a henne. **Breke** his leggys at the kne & take awey the bone from the kne to the fote, as an heyron,
>
>(OP_149)

3.5.1.2 cut_3

Similarly to *break*, the verb *cut* was also used with a range of senses, which allow to categorize it in a number of sub-groups of cutting verbs (see sections 3.2.1.4 for the 'dividing' sense, and 3.4.1.3 for the 'removing' sense). The penetrating sense of *cut* was found only in the 15th c., with 18 records [RNF: 1.8], which constitutes 5.5% of all the records of *cut*. Cut_3 referred to incising meat or fish, either in order to remove the blood (119) or to reshape it (120). Fig. 3 in section 3.2.1.4 shows the ratio of occurrence of the particular senses of *cut*.

>(119) Take a crane, and **cutt** hym in the rofe of the mouth, and lete him blede to deth;
>
>(Aus_Douce_4)

>(120) (…) and if þou wilt haue him rounde, **kut** him in þe bake in two or þre places, but no3t þorgh,
>
>(BK_155)

3.5.1.3 $draw_4$

The verb *draw* will be discussed in detail in section 5.3.2, since its major culinary reference categorizes it as a 'verb of preparation'. However, one of its senses puts it also in the group of 'penetrating verbs', thus it has to be mentioned here as well. $Draw_4$ was found only twice [RNF: 1.7] in the 14th c. and 96 times [RNF: 9.7] in the 15th c. It was used with reference to making an incision in meat (or rather in an animal) or a fish.

3.5.1.4 *open*

According to the *OED* (s.v. *open*, v. 5b), this verb was found with the 'penetrating' sense, i.e., 'to make or produce (an opening or open space of some kind) by cutting, breaking in, or breaking up', from the Old English period. Thus, it is surprising that the analyzed corpus contained only 2 occurrences [RNF: 0.7] of the verb in the 14th c. and 7 [RNF: 0.7] in the 15th century. Some of its records indicate that it was used in the same context as the other penetrating verbs, see for instance (121)–(122) or (123)–(124) in the next section.

(121) Nym caponys & schald hem. Nym a penne & **opyn** þe sckyn at þe heuyd & blowe hem tyl þe sckyn ryse from þe flesche, & do of þe skyn al hole.

(DS_28)

(122) Scall chikens; **breke** the skyne at the necke byhynd & blow hym that the skyn aryse fro the flesch.

(OP_160)

3.5.1.5 $slit_2$

The verb *slit* has already been presented in section 3.2.1.12, since, apart from belonging to the 'penetrating verbs', it has been categorized as a 'dividing verb'. In the 14th c. *slit* was extremely rare, with only 4 occurrences, only one of which referred to 'penetrating' cuts. In the 15th c. the sense 'to cut open' became the dominant one, with 18 occurrences [RNF: 1.8] (out of 21).

It is suggested that the verb was synonymous with the other penetrating verbs, see for instance (123)–(124). The examples are extracts from two very similar recipes (for 'lamprey in galantine' and 'fresh lamprey'), which might even have been two versions of the same recipe reconstructed in two different culinary collections.

(123) Take laumpreys (…) **Slyt** hem a litel at þe nauel, & rest a litel at the nauel. Take out the guttes at the ende. Kepe wele the blode. Put the laumprey on a spyt; roost hym (…)

(FC_130)

(124) Tak & **open** hym [lamprey] ate nauele & lete hym a litel blod, & gadere þat blod in a vessel & do awey þe galle & scorche hym & wasch hym wel (…)

(UC_24)

3.5.2 Discussion

The group of penetrating verbs is rather poor, both in terms of types and tokens (see Table 10). All the verbs are of Germanic origin, except *cut*, which is of dubious etymology. None of the French borrowings belongs to this group of verbs. It is suggested that the verbs, with the exception of *break₄*, were synonymous. This can be accounted for by the fact that they occur in similar contexts, in different versions of the same recipes, as if they were used interchangeably. *Break₄* seems to have been broader in meaning, and it might have referred to penetration with one's hands rather than with a bladed instrument. Although no cutting instrument was indicated in the recipes, the context suggests that a knife or a similar tool might have been used for cutting, opening and slitting.

Moreover, it should be noted that all the 'penetrating verbs', with the exception of *open*, are very general in meaning, having a number of other culinary senses, and their reference to this group is rather peripheral comparing to their other senses.

Table 10: The number of the 'penetrating verbs' found in the analyzed material. [AF = absolute frequencies; RNF = relative normalized frequencies]

	verb	14th c.	15th c.		verb	14th c.	15th c.
10a. AF	break₄	3	46	10b. RNF	break₄	1	4.6
	cut₃	0	18		cut₃	0	1.8
	draw₄	2	1.7		draw₄	96	9.7
	open	2	7		open	0.7	0.7
	slit₂	1	18		slit₂	0.3	1.8

3.6 Conclusions

The verbs of cutting found in the analyzed material have been divided into four groups:

- dividing verbs – referring to cutting into smaller, but distinguishable, parts;
- reducing verbs – referring to pulverizing, squeezing, etc.;
- removing verbs – referring to removing the unwanted parts of foodstuffs;
- penetrating verbs – referring to cutting or opening a particular foodstuff, without the removal of any of its parts.

The group of dividing verbs was the most numerous in terms of types, with 23 types (i.e., 21 in each of the analyzed centuries). However, a number of verbs were rather infrequent in terms of tokens. Similarly, the removing verbs, with 21 types (14 in the 14th and 19 in the 15th c.), were mostly represented by tokens whose relative normalized frequency was below 1 per 10,000 words. On the other hand, the reducing verbs, with only 10 types (9 in each century), were relatively rich in terms of tokens (see Fig. 1 at the beginning of the chapter).

The dividing verbs can be divided into those that are general and specific (in meaning). The former being dominated by verbs of Germanic origin, the latter by verbs borrowed from French. It seems that the general verbs were more frequent than the specific ones, partly due to the fact that they could have been used to express both meanings – the general and the specific one – the latter with the use of specifying nominal phrases, e.g., 'to cut to dice', etc. The dominant role within the semantic field of dividing verbs was taken over by the verb *cut*, which was introduced in the late 13th c. The number of its records clearly shows that it outnumbered all the other verbs present in English from the Old English period.

The general dividing verb could have been categorized into the other groups of cutting verbs: either with the use of a preposition following the verb, as in the case of removing verbs, e.g., *chop / do / pick / take + away / off /out*; or as a bare verb, e.g., *break*. Sometimes, as in the case of *cut*, the verb might have been followed by a particle to change its category but it did not have to, e.g., *cut* (= 'dividing verb' or 'removing verb') vs. *cut off/away* (= 'removing verb').

In the group of the reducing verbs (containing altogether 10 verb types) three verbs were especially dominant, i.e., *bray, grind* and *mince*. All of them might have involved mixing and were the final cutting procedures (no further cutting action could have been applied)[59]. In the 14th c. the verbs *grate* and *mince* shared

---

59 Only single records (in both centuries) indicate that mincing might have been followed by braying.

their meaning to a certain extent (with reference to bread); however, in the 15th c. *grate* narrowed its meaning to 'pulverizing bread' only, while at the same time *mince* lost this particular reference.

The two groups of verbs discussed above are very close in meaning – they differ only in terms of the size of the cut foodstuffs. Looking at the sequence of particular cutting procedures, it turns out that some cutting activities can be followed by others and some cannot. Thus, a certain hierarchy of the most prominent cutting verbs can be formed depending on the received size of the foodstuffs:

GROSS >	**MEDIUM** >	**MINUTE**
carving	hewing	braying
chopping	leaching	grating
cutting	mincing	grinding
hacking		
smiting		

The third group, i.e., the removing verbs, comprises verbs which referred to the removal of certain parts of foodstuffs, such as *bone, peel, shell, skin*, etc. This group was rich in types, but insignificant in terms of tokens. The dominant role was played by verbs of Germanic origin. What is more, the most prominent verbs included in this group belong at the same time to the category of the general dividing verbs. As 'removing verbs', they were usually followed by a particle such as *away, out* or *off*. This tendency was especially popular in the 15th c., when the frequency of the occurrence of these verbs was much higher than in the previous century.

The last group of cutting verbs, i.e., the penetrating verbs, were also dominated by Germanic verbs. This group comprises only 4 verbs. All the verbs referred to incising a foodstuff either in order to remove blood or to change the shape of that foodstuff (mostly meat or fish).

A number of verbs found in the corpus were derived from nouns in the process of conversion; these were mostly 'dividing verbs' (e.g., *dice, leach, quarter*), and 'removing verbs' (e.g., *skin, bone, shell*).

Finally, the culinary material shows many cases of an earlier use of verbs than indicated in the *OED*. These verbs are usually peripheral in terms of their frequency; however, this could be accounted for by the fact that they were new in English and had not been adapted into the language yet. A great deal of these verbs are the verbs formed by conversion, e.g., *gobbon, shell, skin*.

Chapter Four: Verbs of cooking

4.1 Introduction

The semantic field of cooking verbs in its contemporary state has been analysed by Lehrer (1969) and in a more general work on verbs by Levin (1993). The former (1969: 49) enumerates the following cooking verbs: *bake, barbecue, boil, braise, broil, brown, burn, charcoal, cook, deep-fry, flamber, French-fry, fry, grill, oven-fry, oven-poach, pan-broil, pan-fry, parboil, parch, plank, poach, pot-roast, reduce, rissole, roast, saute, scallop, sear, shirr, simmer, steam, steam-bake, stew* and *toast*. The latter (1993: 243) adds *blanch, charboil, charcoal-broil, coddle, crisp, hardboil, heat, microwave, overcook, percolate, perk, scald, softboil* and *stir-fry*. As far as the present author is concerned, no diachronic study of the cooking verbs has been conducted so far, with the exception of her own articles based on a small sample of recipes (Bator 2013a, 2013c).

The verbs found in the analyzed material describe different cooking methods, from the basic ones, such as *boil, fry, roast* or *bake*, to the more specific ones such as *broil, toast* or *stew*. Verbs such as *burn, scorch* and **ouerstep*, which describe the degree of cooking, have also been included in the present study.

Cooking verbs are not as numerous in terms of types as the other investigated groups, i.e., verbs of cutting or verbs of preparing, but this group is the most numerous in terms of tokens. They have been subdivided, with reference to the medium in which the action takes place, into:

(i) verbs of cooking in liquid, e.g., *boil, parboil, scald, seethe*, etc.;
(ii) verbs of cooking with fat, e.g., *bake, fry*, etc.;
(iii) verbs of cooking in any or no medium, e.g., *burn, heat, toast*, etc.

The last group of verbs refers rather to the degree of cooking than to the medium in which the action is conducted. The ratio of types and tokens of verbs belonging to particular groups is presented in Fig. 1 below. The tokens have been normalized to 1,000 words. Where the type bar is higher than the token bar, the subgroup contains the number of lexemes with single or few occurrences, and consequently, where the type bar is lower than the token bar, the subgroup contains the number of lexemes which were very frequently represented in the analyzed corpus.

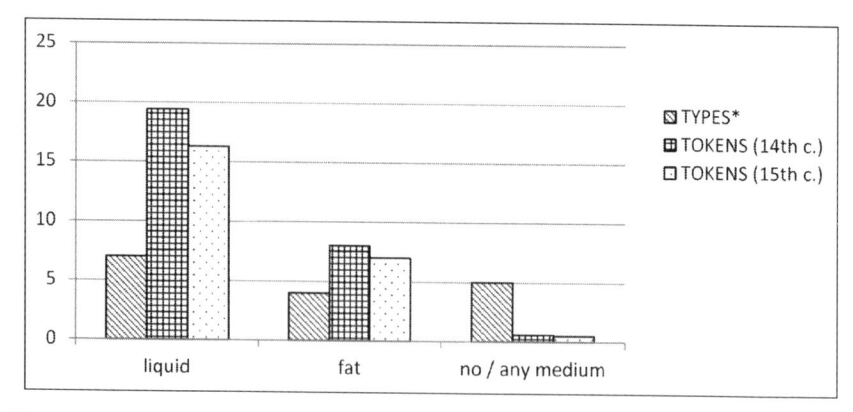

Fig. 1: Types and tokens (RNFs / 1,000 words) of particular verbal groups
(* The number of types is the same for both centuries)

4.2 Verbs of cooking in liquid

4.2.1 The corpus

This group of verbs is not very numerous as it contains only 7 verbs: *boil, parboil, seethe, scald, *ouerstep, stew* and *well*. However, most of them have numerous records. Such a frequency of occurrence of the verbs (for the exact numbers see Table 1 below) indicates that the action of cooking in liquid must have been one of the most basic cooking procedures. This can also be accounted for by the fact that very often the process of cooking is not indicated at all, but can be deduced from the recipe, e.g., in (1) there is no mention of any cooking procedure but the cook is told to 'take the fish from the fire'; moreover, he is instructed what to do with 'the broth' (which results from cooking meat, fish or vegetables in water). It should also be mentioned here that the verb *cook*, which has been suggested by Lehrer (1969) to be the most general of the cooking verbs, has been found in the corpus not even once, even though according to the *OED*, it has been present in English since the 14th c. It is suggested that it might have been too general to use in the culinary instructions.

> (1) Take fayre Freysshe Storgeoun, an choppe it in fayre water; þanne **take it fro þe fyre**, an strayne þe **brothe** þorw a straynoure in-to a potte, an pyke clene þe Fysshe, (...)
>
> (PD_38)

Table 1: *The number of occurrences of the 'verbs of cooking in liquid' in the analyzed material. Relative normalized frequencies have been given in brackets [RNFs / 10.000 words]*

verb:	14th c.	15th c.
boil	200 [68.9]	892 [89.9]
*ouerstep	1 [0.3]	0 [0]
parboil	38 [13]	94 [9.5]
scald	24 [8.3]	107 [10.8]
seethe	288 [99.2]	494 [48.8]
stew	11 [3.8]	34 [3.4]
well	2 [0.7]	3 [0.3]

4.2.1.1 boil

The verb *boil* derives from Old French *boillir* (from Latin *bullīre*) 'to form bubbles, to boil'. According to the *OED*, its first attestations in English come from the 13th c. It was used with the following senses:

(i) 'to reach the boiling point, to turn from the liquid into the gaseous state' (intrans.; 1225-);
(ii) 'to move with an agitation like that of boiling water; to bubble, to seethe' (trans.; 1300-);
(iii) 'to cause (a liquid) to bubble with heat; to bring to the boiling point: esp. said of food, wholly or partly liquid, in the process of cooking; also of the containing vessel' (trans.; 1475-);

The verb *boil* was found 200 times [RNF: 68.9] in the 14th c. and 892 [RNF: 89.9] in the 15th-c. material. The majority of its 14th-c. occurrences, i.e., 60.5%, are transitive, e.g., (2), comparing to only 24% of intransitive records[60], e.g., (3)–(4). In the 15th c. the ratio of transitive and intransitive uses of *boil* changed: to the

---

60 In the intransitive context *boil* was used either in ergative structures or as an imperative followed by a zero object. In the former case, the referent, instead of functioning as the object of the verb, was transferred to the position of the subject. For more on ergative structures, see for instance Radford (2005). In the latter case, the referent was contextually defined, being mentioned earlier in the recipe and deleted from the object position. For more on the deletion of object used in the recipes (which, depending on the source is referred to as ellipsis, null-object, zero-anaphor, etc.), see for instance

advantage of the intransitive forms (42%), e.g., (5)–(6), over the transitive ones (37%), e.g., (7)–(8). Fig. 2 below shows the ratio of particular forms in the two centuries. A great deal of the intransitive records consisted of phrases such as 'let boil', 'make boil', 'do boil', etc. as in (9).

(2) (…) do þerto powdour of galingale, powdour douce and salt and **boyle** the sawse,

(FC_32)

(3) tak triyd gyngeuer & safroun & grynd hem in a morter & temper hem vp wyþ almandys & do hem to þe fire; & wan it **boylyþ** wel do þerto 3olkys of egges sodyn (…)

(DS_79)

(4) (…) & þe ferst mylk cast þerto & **boyle** wel, & serue yt forth.

(DS_89)

(5) Take almaunde Mylke, & Sugre, an powdere Gyngere, & of Galyngale, & of Canelle, and Rede Wyne, & **boyle** yfere: (…)

(PD_111)

(6) (…) And drawe hem þorgh a streynour; And whan the potte **boyleth**, cast þe licour to,

(BK_122)

(7) Take half figges and half reysons, and **boile** hem in wyn, and (…)

(BK_126)

(8) Do þerto wyne & hole spyces & pouder of peper & canel. **Boyl** hit vp with a pertye of swete brothe.

(GK_20)

(9) Also mencyd Datys, Clowes, Maces, Pouder Pepir, Canel, Safroun, & a gode dele Salt, & let **boyle** a whyle;

(PD_48)

Massam and Roberge (1989), Massam (1992), Culy (1996), Görlach (1992, 2004) or Carroll (1999). Also, see section 1.3 of the present book.

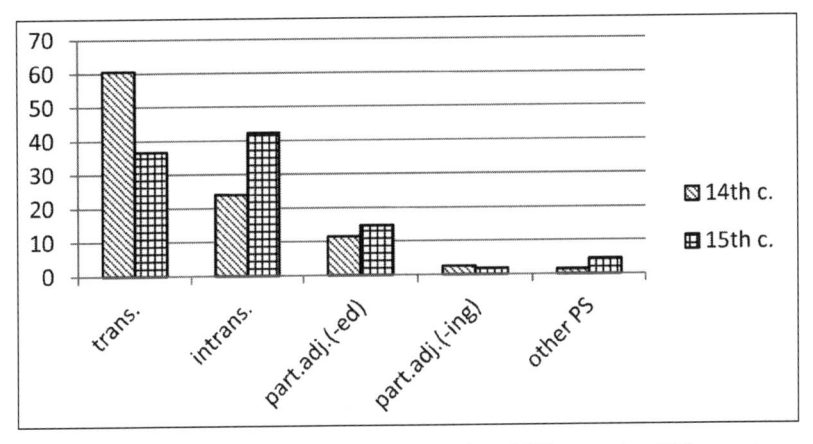

Fig. 2: *The percentage of forms of* boil *in the 14ᵗʰ and 15ᵗʰ centuries. [PS = parts of speech]*

56% and 53% of the uses of *boil*, in the 14th and 15th c. respectively, referred to the final operation applied to an almost completed dish or to a mixture of ingredients which had been already processed (in isolation), rather than to separate ingredients in the initial stage of a meal's preparation (see (10)–(12)). Boiling of individual foodstuffs was rather infrequent, and was mostly applied to meat and fish (11% and 21% in the respective centuries), as well as to vegetables and fruit (10% and 9% in the respective centuries). Herbs and spices were also boiled separately from other foodstuffs (7% and 6% in the respective centuries); however, these were usually various mixtures, thus they are somewhere between the two categories, e.g., in (13) a selection of various herbs are boiled before they are mixed with other ingredients and further processed. It was seething which applied to the individual ingredients much more frequently than boiling (see section 4.2.1.4).

(10) Nym hennyn & porke & seþ hem togedere. Nym þe lyre of þe hennyn & þe porke and hake small, & grynd hit al to dust, and wyte bred þerewyþ; (...) & **boyle** it, & disch it,

(DS_5)

(11) Take þe lyuer of capouns and roost it wel. Take anyse and greynes de parys, gynger, canel, & a lytull crust of brede, and grinde it small, (...) **Boyle** it and serue it forth.

(FC_141)

(12) Take kowe mylke, & do þer-to Eyroun y-swonge; (...) Porke y-sothe, (...) pouder Gyngere, Galyngale, or Pepir; (...) Safroun, & caste all þese to-gederys, & **boyle** it.

(LV_8)

(13) Take Borage, Vyolet, Malwys, Percely, Yong Wortys, Bete, Auence, Longebeff, with Orage an oþer, pyke hem clene, and caste hem on a vessel, and **boyle** hem a goode whyle;

(PD_3)

4.2.1.2 parboil

Parboil comes from Anglo-Norman *parboillir, perboillir* 'to cook partially by boiling, to cook thoroughly by boiling' and Old/Middle French *parboilir* 'to cook thoroughly by boiling' (*OED*: s.v. *parboil*, v.). It has been present in English since the 14th c. when it was recorded with the sense 'to cook partially by boiling' (trans.). The other (Anglo-Norman) meaning appeared in the written records of the 17th c., but became obsolete shortly afterwards.

In the analyzed recipes, *parboil* occurred 38 times [RNF: 13] in the 14th and 94 times [RNF: 9.5] in the 15th c. The verb was used transitively, with the exception of one 14th-century occurrence, in which the object seems to have been ellipted[61], see (14), and two intransitive records in the 15th c., see (15).

(14) Nym þe thermes with all þe tallow; wasche ham clene & **perboyll** & sithen hak ham small.

(GR_AshmB_25)

(15) ... And let hong yn to þe boyling potte, and **parboile**; and take hit vppe, and lette hit kele,

(BK_84)

Additionally, a number of passive forms were recorded: 7 in the 14th c. and 12 in the 15th c. (plus one active participial adjective, see (16)).

(16) (...) and take faire parcelly, and parboyle hit in a potte, & **parboylingge** broþe;

(BK_84)

The action of parboiling was usually conducted in order to prepare the particular foodstuffs for further cutting (19 times in the 14th and 26 in the 15th c.), or for further cooking – mostly roasting, but also seething and frying – (8 and 24 times

---

61 The object ellipsis was often used with the verb *boil* (see section 4.2.1.1).

for the two centuries, respectively). Less frequently were the foodstuffs cut before parboiling (3 and 18 times in the respective periods) and only once were they scalded (see (17)[62]). This suggests that parboiling must have been a preliminary cooking procedure applied to food.

(17) Cormoraunz schul be scalded & **perboyled** & larded & rosted.

(UC_15)

When it comes to the foodstuffs being parboiled, there are almost twice as many references of *parboil* to meat and fish than to fruit and vegetables. This may be accounted for by the greater number of meat/fish dishes in the corpus but also by the fact that meat requires longer processing in order to become soft and ready for consumption than vegetables and fruit and parboiling was to prepare meat and fish (i.e., hard products) for further procedures (cooking or cutting).

4.2.1.3 *scald*

Following the *OED*, *scald*, from Old Northern French *escalder*, *escauder*, deriving from late Latin *excaldāre* 'to wash in hot water', was first used with reference to burning or washing with hot liquid or steam. Only later, i.e., in the 15th c., did the culinary senses 'to heat liquid to a point just short of boiling point' and 'to subject to the action of hot water; to pour hot liquid over' appear.

In the 14th c. *scald* was found only 24 times [RNF: 8.3], mostly with reference to meat and fish (10 times each); but also fruit (plums), figs and raisins (3 times) and to water (once). The action was the most preliminary procedure applied to the foodstuffs and was followed by some kind of cutting and cooking. Figs, raisins and plums were scalded in wine, otherwise the medium was not specified (we may assume that if not specified the medium was water).

In the 15th c. material, the verb *scald* was found 107 times [RNF: 10.8]. Fig. 3 shows the ratio of various foodstuffs which were scalded at that time. The aim of scalding (and at the same time, the meaning of the verb) seems to have varied depending on the ingredients. Thus, milk and bread were scalded in order to kill all the dangerous bacteria and to avoid lumps. Scalding fruit (plums and figs) was to change their taste – since they were scalded in wine or ale in order to become soaked with the liquid. Scalding meat and fish usually took place in water and was followed by washing or cleaning (e.g., removing the entrails) and only later

---

62 The particular instructions in medieval recipes were enumerated in a chronological sequence.

by cutting and cooking, e.g., (18). A number of examples suggest that the aim of scalding meat and fish was to prepare it for the removal of feathers, hair (see (19)) or scales (see (20)). In the latter case, sometimes the recipe did not contain the instructions to remove scales, as if this action was included in the process of scalding, or as if the authors of the recipes misinterpreted the meanings of the verbs *scald* and *scale*[63], since they are used interchangeably in the same recipes found in different manuscripts, e.g., (21a–b).

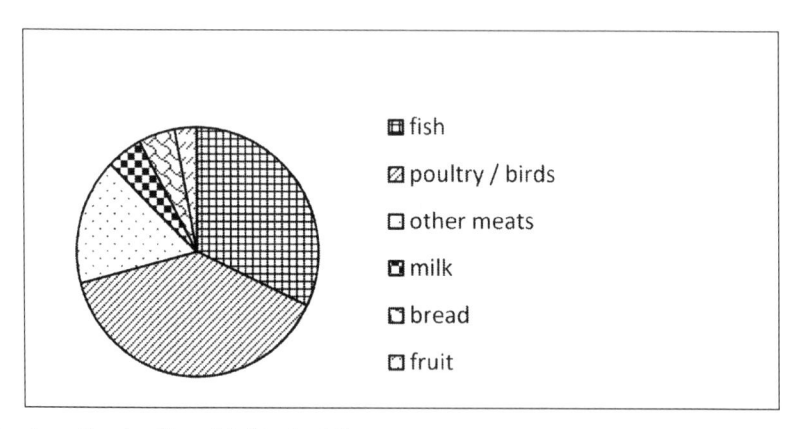

Fig. 3:   Foodstuffs scalded in the 15th c

(18) Take þe hennys, & **skalde** hem, & ope hem, & wasshe hem clene, & smyte hem to gobettys, & seethe hem with fayre porke;
(PD_65)

(19) Take to ii gangge of calve fete, half a gange of rodor fete, and seth hem or **scalde** hem and pyke away the hayr.
(GR_Hunt_3)

(20) (…) & **skald** hym [tench] in hot water, & rub it with a cloth till he be clene;
(Ht_Hrl_59)

(21) (a) MS Douce 55:
Scale a mulet and draw hym in the bely and seth hym in water and salt (…)
(b) MS Add. 5467:
Tak a milet and **scald** hym and then make sauce of water and salt (…)
(MAe_148)

---

63   For the discussion on *scale*, see section 3.4.1.10.c.

To conclude, it is suggested that the verb *scald* was used with the sense 'to pour hot liquid over something in order to (a) remove the unwanted parts, such as skin, hair, feathers, etc.; (b) soak with the liquid (and thus, change the taste); or (c) to kill bacteria and avoid the formation of lumps'.

4.2.1.4 *seethe*

Seethe is a Common Germanic verb (OE *séoðan*), which initially was used with the transitive sense 'to boil; to make or keep boiling hot; to subject to the action of boiling liquid, esp. to cook (food) by boiling or stewing; also to make an infusion or decoction of (a substance) by boiling or stewing' (*OED*: s.v. *seethe*, v.). At the end of the 14th c. the intransitive and passive sense 'to be boiled; to be subjected to boiling or stewing; to become boiling hot. Said of a liquid, or a substance boiled in liquid; also of the pot or other receptacle' was found. The reference to cooking, however, became obsolete or archaic in the 19th c. (*OED*). Carroll (1999: 32) categorized the verb as belonging to 'the technical language of cookery', due to the fact that it "is used in a more specific sense in recipes than elsewhere".

The verb was found 288 times [RNF: 99.2] in the 14th c. and 494 times [RNF: 48.8] in the 15th c. In the 14th c. over half of the forms were transitive (see (22)–(23)), comparing to 16% of the intransitive records; passive uses were also frequent (26.5%), see examples (24)–(25). The later recipes included 54% of the transitive records (comparing to only 12% of the intransitive ones) and 33% of passive uses of *seethe*. For the ratio of forms of *seethe* in both periods, see Fig. 4 below.

Similarly to *boil*, *seethe* might have occurred with no object. Following Görlach (2004: 125), the deletion of objects is one of the typical linguistic features of the cooking recipe. Although in the Middle English period object ellipsis was rather uncommon, i.e., Görlach (1992: 749, 2004: 130) found it with less than 10% of cases of the analyzed transitive verbs and Culy (1996: 98) assigns it to slightly more than 4% of verbs, this feature accounts for the 12% and 16% of intransitive records of *seethe* found in the analyzed material.

(22) Take sooles and hylde hem; **seeþ** hem in water.

(FC_122)

(23) For to make a potage fene boiles, tak wite benes & **seþ** hem in water, & bray þe benys in a morter al to no3t; & lat þem seþe in almande mylk & do þerein wyn & hony. & **seþ** reysouns in wyn (…)

(DS_81)

(24) (…) & wane þe chese and þe eggys ben wel **sodyn**, tak hem (…)

(DS_38)

(25) Do þerto oynouns **ysode** and ymynced, (...)

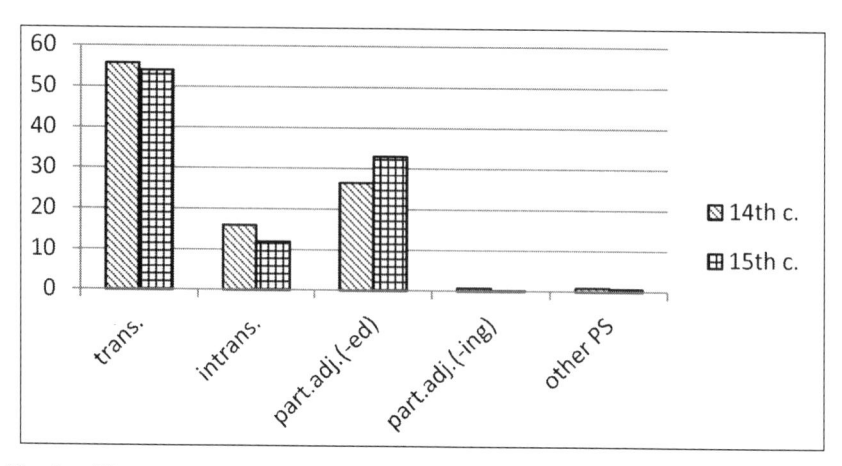

(FC_189)

Fig. 4: The percentage of forms of seethe *in the 14th and 15th centuries. [PS = parts of speech]*

Both in the 14th and 15th centuries the majority of records of *seethe* indicate that the action was conducted on individual ingredients rather than a mixture of various foodstuffs, which suggests that seething was an essential and preliminary culinary activity. It was hardly ever preceded by other procedures, except cutting of larger foodstuffs, such as meat, see (26)–(27). Occasionally, seething might have been preceded by parboiling or scalding, see (28)–(30). Most of the foodstuffs seethed were meat and fish (41% and 58% for the two centuries, respectively). For a detailed ratio of ingredients which might have been affected by seething in the two analyzed centuries, see Fig. 5 and 6, respectively. Usually, after seething, foods were further processed, e.g., cooked (roasting, frying, boiling), cut (hewed, brayed, ground, minced), or cleaned (of hair, bone, skin, shell, stone), etc.

(26) Take veel oþer motoun and <u>smyte it to gobettes</u>. See**þ** it in gode broth;

(FC_18)

(27) Take harys, & Fle hem, & make hem clene, an <u>hacke hem in gobettys</u>, & **sethe** hem in Water (...)

(PD_63)

(28) Take the lire of the boor oþer of the roo, <u>perboile it</u>. Smythe it on smale peces; see**þ** it wel half in water and half in wyne.

(FC_16)

(29) Take the congur and <u>scald hym</u>, and smyte hym in pecys, & **seeþ** hym.

(FC_107)

(30) Take þe hennys, & <u>skalde hem</u>, & ope hem, & wasshe hem clene, & smyte hem to gobettys, & **seethe** hem (…)

(PD_65)

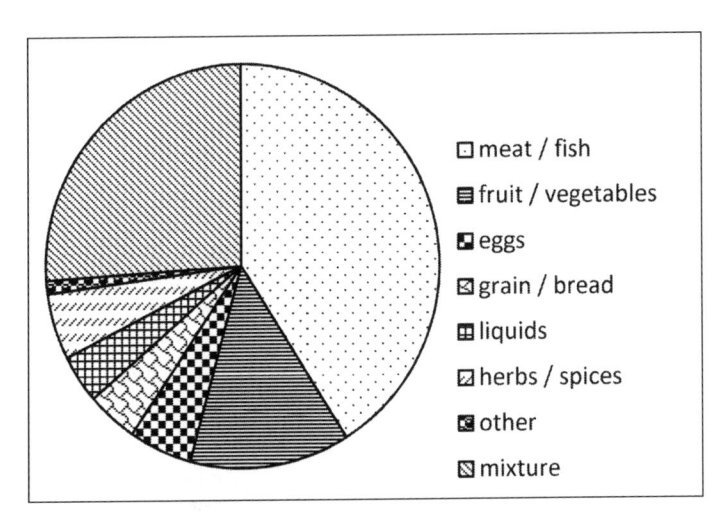

Fig. 5: The ratio of ingredients seethed in the 14th c

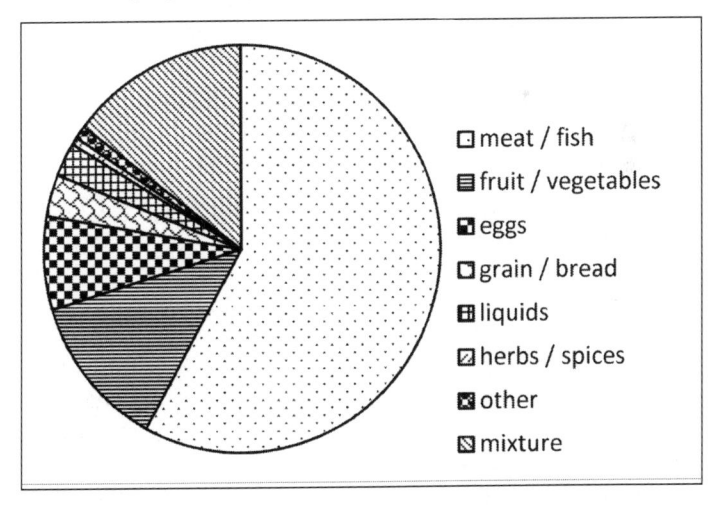

Fig. 6: The ratio of ingredients seethed in the 15th c

135

4.2.1.5 *ouerstep*

The form *ouerstepid*, found once in the 14th c. material, has been translated by Hieatt and Butler (1988) as 'overcooked'. The *OED* does not enumerate such a verb. However, it might be related to the verb *steep* (*OED*: s.v. *steep*, v.[1]). Its etymology is uncertain; it might be derived from the Old English forms **stiepan, *stepan*, which would be related to Scandinavian languages. The verb was used with the following senses:

(i) 'to soak in water or other liquid; chiefly to do so for the purpose of softening, altering in properties, cleansing, or the like, or for that of extracting some constituent' (1400-);
(ii) 'to undergo the process of soaking in liquor' (1412-);

*Ouerstepid was found only once in the analyzed corpus, thus it is rather irrelevant for the analysis of the semantic field of culinary verbs.

4.2.1.6 *stew*

Following the *OED*, *stew*, from Old French *estuver*, was present in English from 1400; its reference to cooking, i.e., (trans.) 'to boil slowly in a close vessel; to cook (meat, fruit, etc.) in a liquid kept at the simmering-point', appeared in the 15th c. (*OED*: s.v. *stew*, v.[2]). The analyzed material shows its early records with reference to cooking already at the end of the 14th c. Moreover, it seems to have been more frequent at that time than in the 15th c., i.e., its RNFs equal 3.8 and 3.4 for the two periods, respectively. It should be noted that in the 15th c. half of the occurrences of *stew* were found in the titles of the recipes (comparing to only 9% of such uses in the 14th c.). What is also interesting is that stewing was conducted not only in liquids but also in grease, especially in the 14th c. (see (31)).

> (31) cast þerinne raysouns of coraunce, sugur, powdour ginger, erbes **ystewed in grees**, oynouns and salt.
>
> (FC_19)

4.2.1.7 *wall* / *well*

The form refers to two verbs: *well* and *wall*. The former (from Old English *wiellan*) derives from the stem of *weallan* 'to boil'. Originally, *well* was used only in transitive contexts, meaning 'to boil (a liquid, ingredients, etc.)'. The intransitive uses started to appear only at the end of the 14th c. (*OED*: s.v. *well*, v.[1]). The latter corresponds to the Old English *weallan*, which occurred only intransitively in the

Old English period and denoted '(of a liquid): to boil', 'to bubble up; to boil up' (*OED*: s.v. *wall*, v[1]).

The analyzed material revealed only 5 occurrences of the verb (2 in the 14th c. [RNF: 0.7] and 3 in the 15th c. [RNF: 0.3]). These few occurrences indicate that it might have referred either to the action of cooking without any indication of the degree, see for instance (32), or to the action of boiling up, see for instance (33).

(32) þan tak water & **well** it in a frying panne;

(Ht_Hrt_64)

(33) (…) & set it oure by fyre & styr it were, & when it is in poynt to **welle** set it of & let it be standing & serof.

(Ht_Hrl_66)

4.2.2 Discussion

The group of the 'verbs of cooking in liquid' has been definitely dominated by verbs of French origin. The only native verbs were *seethe, *ouerstep* and *well*, with the last two being far too infrequent to influence the semantic field. *Seethe* diminished in the number of records in the 15th c. by half, most probably due to the growing popularity of the French *boil*, which originally was used as a synonym of the native word and later took over its meaning – pushing the latter to the metaphorical use. Table 2, as well as Fig. 7 show the number and ratio of occurrence of the 'verbs of cooking in liquid'.

Table 2: The number of occurrences of the 'verbs of cooking in liquid' found in the analyzed material

2a. Absolute frequencies:

	boil	parboil	scald	seethe	overstep	stew	well
14th c.	200	38	24	288	1	11	2
15th c.	892	94	107	494	0	34	3
Total:	1092	132	131	782	1	45	5

2b. Normalized frequencies (to 10,000 words):

	boil	parboil	scald	seethe	overstep	stew	well
14th c.	68.9	13	8.3	99.2	0.3	3.8	0.7
15th c.	89.9	9.5	10.8	48.8	0	3.4	0.3

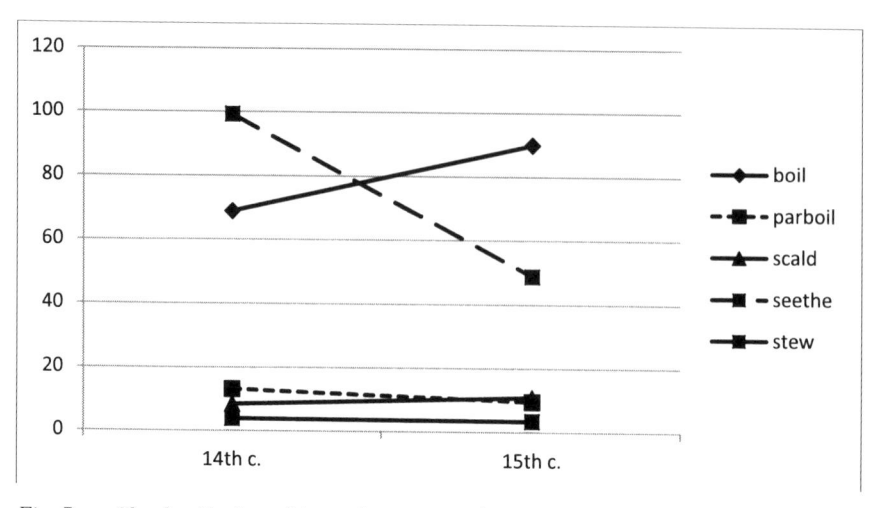

Fig. 7: The distribution of the verbs at particular periods (RNFs / 10,000 words)

Scald and *parboil* referred to preparatory cooking actions and were not very popular in the analyzed material. Moreover, *scald* as well as *stew* were only just entering the English language, which also explains their low frequency.

In the 14th c. material *seethe* was definitely the dominant verb (see Fig. 7 above). In the next century the number of its records diminished by half. In the case of *boil* the tendency is quite the opposite: the number of its records is almost one third bigger in the 15th c. than a century earlier. The increase in the number of uses of *boil* in the 15th c. may be justified by a number of causes:

(a) Vocabulary of French origin was more prestigious than native items;[64]
(b) *Boil* could have been used as both a transitive and an intransitive verb. The use of verbs without the object, which is a typical feature of the culinary recipe, becomes more and more common. Following Culy (1996: 97), "[t]he use of zeros in recipes has increased dramatically over time. (…) 23.6% zeros in the historical survey vs. 40.6% in the contemporary survey". Thus, the greater popularity of the verb *boil*, which as a rule may be used without the object.
(c) Some changes in the denotation of the two verbs have taken place: in the 14th c. *seethe* and *boil* were used synonymously with (i) a general meaning

---

64 Although, Lutz (2013) claims it was rather the "stratal relation" between English and French than simply prestige which contributed to the high degree of borrowing.

(= 'to cook' – without specifying the vigour of cooking or below the boiling point), see (34)–(35) and with (ii) a specific meaning (= 'to cook in the temperature of 100° C; to bubble', categorized by Lehrer (1969) as 'full boil'), see (36)–(39). Sometimes the 14th c. recipes for dishes whose name suggests boiling, were seethed (e.g., (40)) (with no mention of the verb *boil* throughout the entire recipe), which suggests the synonymous and interchangeable use of the two verbs.

Additionally, Lutz (2013: 576–7) suggests that "in medieval England the replacement of inherited words with French loans was often due to the fact that, for an extended period of time, servants needed to know them in the language of their masters (…). Thus, eventually, the inherited terms went out of use or were restricted to a fraction of their original meaning range whereas the loans, though apparently unnecessary, could become part of the very basic vocabulary".

(34) (…) take garlic & grapes, and stoppe the chikenus ful, and **seeþ** hem in gode broth, so þat þey may esely be boyled þerinne.
(FC_36)

(35) (…) and **boile** it with esy fyre
(FC_68)

(36) Or hit bygene to **boyle**, do in þi spicery;
(FC_205)

(37) (…) & let yt na3t **boyle** non ofter þan onys.
(DS_37)

(38) (…) and lat it not **seeþ** after þat it is cast togyder, & serue it forth.
(FC_66)

(39) (…) & when it is in poynt to **seth** cast þe bred þerin (…)
(Ht_Hrl_69)

(40) "For to **boile** fesauntes, pertruches, capouns, and curlews"
Take gode broth and do þerto the fowle, and do þerto hool peper and flour of canel, a gode quantite, and lat hem **seeþ** þerwith; and messe it forth, and cast þeron powdour dowce.
(FC_37)

Already in the 14th c. some difference in the usage of the two verbs can be observed. If both verbs were used in the same clause, they represented two different senses. In such cases, *seethe* is used with the general meaning, referring to cooking without boiling up (i.e., without bubbling), whilst *boil* – with the specific meaning referring to boiling up (see (41)–(43)). This puts seething in the position of a preparatory action for boiling.

(41) (...) & seþe hem wel togidere til it **boile**.

(GK_8)

(42) (...) & do þer-to a porcyon of flower of Rys, & do þer-to þen pouder Gyngere, Galyngale, Canel, Sugre, Clowys, Maces, & **boyle** it onys & seþe it;

(PD_62)

(43) (...) & than **seth** þam in clene water til þai begyn to **boyle**.

(Ht_Hrl_5)

The difference in denotation led to the creation of some hierarchy of the cooking procedures. Sometimes the recipes specify the state of the liquid in which food is cooked. The hierarchy, based on the degree of cooking, is presented in Fig. 8 below. The cooking associations can take place only in one direction, hence, food can be seethed in boiling water, or it can be parboiled in seething or boiling water, but no record of boiling in seething water or seething in parboiling water was found, see examples (44)–(46).

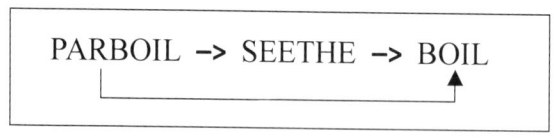

```
┌─────────────────────────────────┐
│   PARBOIL  ->  SEETHE  ->  BOIL │
│           ▲                   │ │
│           └───────────────────┘ │
└─────────────────────────────────┘
```

Fig. 8:   *The hierarchy of the cooking verbs*

(44) Take spynoches; **perboile** hem in **seþyng water**.

(FC_188)

(45) (...) & **parboyle** it in a potte with **boyling broþe**;

(LV_50)

(46) (...) & do it to **seeþ** in **boillyng water**.

(FC_182)

The two verbs *seethe* and *boil* seem to have differed also in terms of the foods they affected. *Boil* referred in the majority of cases to almost completed dishes, and it affected mixtures of already processed foodstuffs, while *seethe* was used rather with individual ingredients, and the action was to prepare particular foodstuffs for further processing (see (47)). This may also serve as evidence for the hierarchy of verbs mentioned above. It should be mentioned that with time the verbs started to collocate with specific products, e.g., *seethe* seems to have been the only appropriate verb to apply to eggs; but on the other hand, in the 15th c. it was no longer used with herbs and spices (see Fig. 9–12 below).

(47) Nym þe þarmys of a pygge & wasch hem clene in water & salt, & seþ hem wel; & þan hak hem smale, & grynd pepyr and safroun, bred & ale, & **boyle** togedere.

(DS_16)

Summing up, *seethe* moved closer in meaning to *parboil* than to *boil*, and it was used either to describe the action which was to prepare food for further procedures or to describe the preliminary process to boiling.

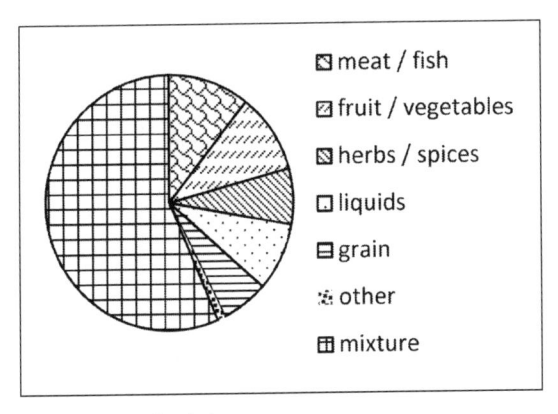

Fig. 9:   *Foodstuffs boiled in the 14th c*

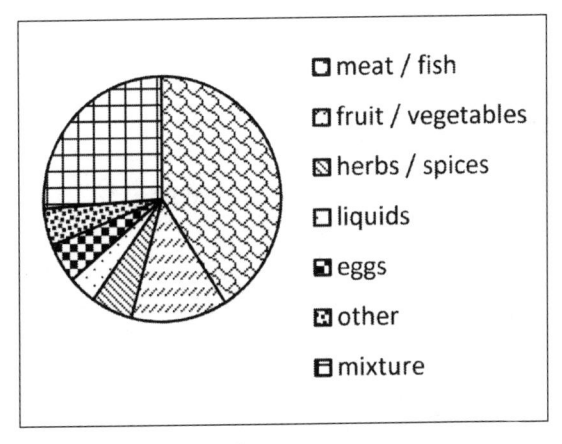

Fig. 10:   *Foodstuffs seethed in the 14th c*

141

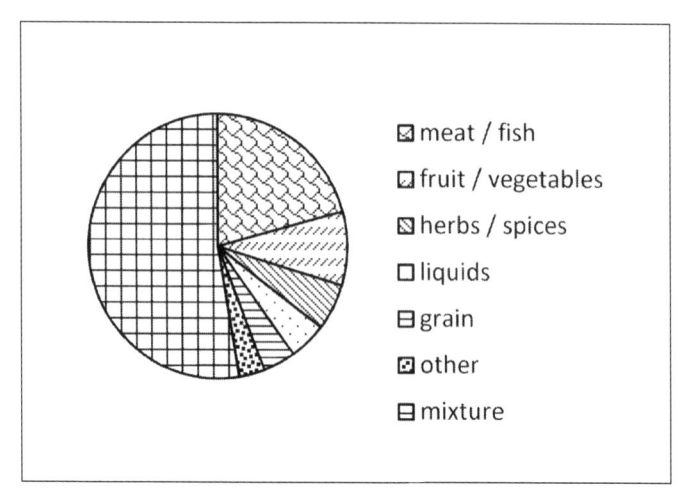

Fig. 11: Foodstuffs boiled in the 15th c

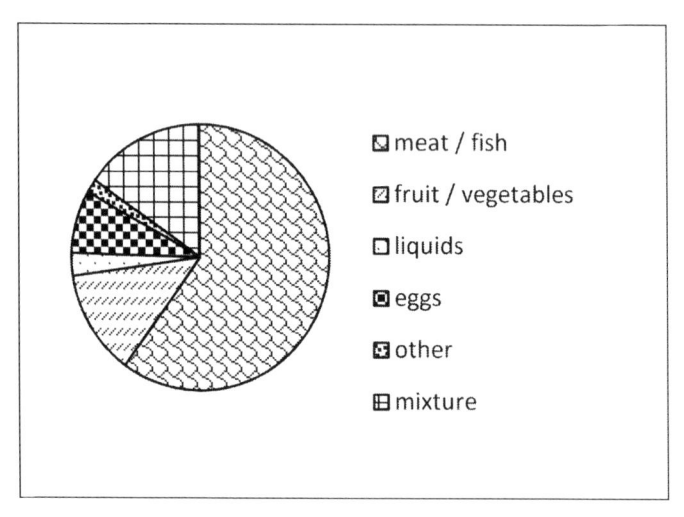

Fig. 12: Foodstuffs seethed in the 15th c

4.3 Verbs of cooking with fat[65]

4.3.1 The corpus

Only four verbs of cooking with the incorporation of some fat were found, i.e., *bake, broil, fry* and *roast*. Sporadically, some of the verbs which referred to 'cooking in liquid' were used with some kind of fat, e.g., (48)–(50).

(48) Leshe it in dishes, þanne take oynouns and mince hem smale and **seeþ** hem in oile til þey be al broun, (...)

(FC_76)

(49) (...) & nym þe lyre of þe hennyn or of capouns & grynd hem small; kest þere to wite grese & **boyle** it.

(DS_14)

(50) tak an hundred onions oþer an half, & tak oyle de olyf & **boyle** togedere in a pot;

(DS_88)

We have classified to the present group not only those verbs which describe the action of cooking with the addition of fat, such as oil or butter, e.g., *fry*, but also verbs, such as *roast*, which themselves do not necessarily involve the addition of any extra fat, but refer to cooking foodstuffs which contain fat and thus, even though not added on purpose, it is necessary and it does take part in the process of the food preparation. Table 3 below shows the list of the verbs classified into this group and the frequencies of their occurrence (both absolute and normalized).

Table 3: *The number of occurrences of the 'verbs of cooking in fat' in the analyzed material. [RNFs / 10.000 words]*

verb	14th c.	15th c.
bake	37 [12.7]	147 [14.8]
broil	2 [0.7]	15 [1.5]
fry	93 [32]	212 [21.4]
roast	102 [35.1]	328 [33]

---

65 In this section those verbs which refer to the action of cooking with the addition of some kind of fat will be discussed, but also those which apply to food containing its own fat.

4.3.1.1 *bake*

Bake is a Common Germanic verb (OE *bacan*), which, following the *OED*, denotes 'to cook by dry heat acting by conduction, and not by radiation, hence either in a closed place (oven, ashes, etc.), or on a heated surface (bakestone, griddle, live coals)'. Originally it was used with reference to bread, then potatoes, apples and meat (*OED*: s.v. *bake*, v.).

This verb appeared 37 times [RNF: 12.7] in the 14th c., mostly transitively (68%). 81% of its records referred to flour products, such as tarts, crusts and coffins, filled with meat stuffing. The other occurrences referred to meat and fish. In the 15th c. 147 records [RNF: 14.7] were found, most of which were used intransitively, i.e., 47% (comparing to only 8% in the earlier period). Additionally, 34% of the later occurrences were transitive and 18.5% were used as the passive participles. Semantically, 89% of the 15th c. records referred to flour products filled with meat or fish stuffing, the rest applied to meat and fish, the yolks of eggs and to quinces. However, a great number of the references to meat and fish were found in titles, e.g., "Baked chickens" (OP_126), whilst, when found within the recipes, *baking* was mostly applied to meat or fish closed in a crust rather than to the individual products.

Baking might have been conducted in an oven or in an open fire. The former was rather rare in the 14th c. material. The latter in the 14th c. involved using a trap, i.e., 'a kind of dish or pan' (*OED*: s.v. *trap*, n.[6]), and in the 15th c. a pan, which actually involved using two identical pans. The pans had to be preheated, one of them greased; first a batter was baked to form some kind of a coating, which in turn was filled with various fillings, and then the process of baking continued. The process has been described in (51). In the 15th c. baking in an open oven was also possible but rare, and in such cases the cook was to decide whether to close it or not.

> (51) Take ij lytel erþen pannys, & sette on þe colys tyl þey ben hote; make a dyssche-fulle of þikke bature of Floure & Watere; take & grece a lytel þat oþer panne, & do þe bater þer-on; & lat renne al a-bowte þe panne, so þat þe pan be al y-helyd; take & sette þe panne a-3en ouer þe fyre of cloys; do þat oþer panne a-boue þat oþer panne, tyl it be y-baken y-now; whan it is y-bake, þat it wol a-ryse fro þe eggys of þe panne, take kydes Fleyssche & 3ong porke, & hew it; take Percely, ysope, & Sauerey (...); & do it in a panne, & þe cofynne, do it to þe cloys; hele it with þat oþer panne, & do cloys a-bouyn, & lat baken wyl;

(BM_30)

Fat (grease, butter or oil) was indicated sporadically. However, some fat must have been used in order not to burn the pastry.

Apart from the verb, the compound *bakemeat*[66] was found 21 times [RNF: 2] in the 15th c.

4.3.1.2 *broil*

The verb *broil* is of uncertain etymology. Following the *OED*, it might be related to the French *bruler*, which according to the *AND*, denoted 'to burn, scorch, broil' (*AND*: s.v. *bruler*). It was found only twice [RNF: 0.7] in the 14th c. and 15 times [RNF: 1.5] in the 15th c. It referred to meat or fish, in which case it denoted 'to grill'. Additionally, one 15th-c. record referred to 'broiling bread', which suggests a meaning synonymous with 'to toast'. The action always took place on a griddle, except for broiling bread, which took place on coals, see (52).

(52) Take brede, and **broil** it vpon þe colous, and make it broune, (...)
(Aus_Ashm_7)

4.3.1.3 *fry*

Fry was derived from French *frire* (from Latin *frigere*) 'to roast, fry'. It was present in English from the end of the 13th c. with the meaning 'to cook (food) with fat in a shallow pan over the fire'.

The analyzed corpus revealed 93 records [RNF: 32] of the verb in the 14th and 212 [RNF: 21.4] in the 15th c. This includes 60 transitive, 2 intransitive and 31 passive uses in the 14th c. and 164 transitive, 14 intransitive, 32 participles (30 passive + 2 active), and 2 gerunds in the 15th c. Apart from the 212 records of the verb in the later period, we have found 17 occurrences of the compound *frying pan*, which was not found in the 14th c., and 5 records of the noun *fries*, which stood for pieces of a particular shape (lozenge or strips) made of meat or pastry and fried in some fat.

The majority of the 14th -c. occurrences (78%) refer to individual foodstuffs, mostly fish, fruit or nuts (almonds, raisins, pines, nuts, dates), and onions. But also (sporadically) such products as bread, the yolk of eggs, vegetables other than onions (e.g., spinach or beans) and meat were fried. 22% of the uses referred to mixtures of products; these were mostly pastry (see (53)) or stuffing (see (54)). The fat used for frying was always oil or grease, with the exception of one recipe in which some liquid is also suggested for frying, see (55).

---

66 *Bakemeat* = 'pastry, a pie' (*OED*: s.v. †*bake-meat*, n.).

(53) Take and make a foile of gode past as thynne as paper; kerue it out with a sauces & **fry** it in oile, oþer in grece;

(FC_171)

(54) (...) and do it [pork and hens] in a panne and **frye** it; & make a coffin[67] as to a pye smale & do þerinne,

(FC_193)

(55) & tak myced onyounnes & **frye** hem in <u>oyle dolyf or vynegre or in wyn or in þe same broth</u>,

(UC_9)

In the later recipes *fry* definitely referred to pastry products more often than in the 14th c. (47% of records). The range of individual products which were often fried did not change, and these included: onions (13% of records), meat and fish (18%), fruit (pines, raisins, dates) and nuts (15%); the remaining 7% applied to such products as bread, herbs, oil, peas and yolks. Apart from grease and oil, butter became a frequently used frying fat.

The purpose of frying was, apart from a way of cooking, to colour food, see for instance (56). Sometimes frying was preceded or followed by other cooking procedures such as parboiling, boiling, seething, roasting, baking, etc., e.g., (57)–(58).

In the 15th c. material, the compound *frying pan* appears 17 times (RNF: 2 / 10,000 words). Despite its name, next to frying, it could also have been used for boiling (see (59)–(60)) or baking (see (61)).

(56) þen take alknete & **fry** it esely <u>for brynnyng of þe colour</u>;

(GR_eMus_44)

(57) Have yolkes of eyron **sodyn** hard & **fryed** a lytyll;

(OP_37)

(58) Put theryn clere oylle – lete them be **fryed** therin **byfore the boylyng** (...)

(OP_1)

(59) þan tak water & **well** [= 'cook/boil'] it **in a frying panne**;

(Ht_Hrl_64)

(60) Cut venson or moton smale lytell thynne leshys & put them in a **fryyng panne** with ale by wese & **boyle** them welle tylle they be ny tendour.

(GR_Rwl_281)

(61) þan cast þam in to a **frying pann** with batur & ole & **bake** team & serof.

(Ht_Hrl_37)

---

67 *coffin* = 'pastry shell'.

4.3.1.4 *roast*

Roast derives from the Anglo-Norman *roster, roister, roistir* and AN, OF, MF *rostir* – denoting 'to roast, to cook on an open fire, to warm oneself' (*OED*: s.v. *roast*, v.) and 'to heat; to roast; to bake, to cook' (*AND*: s.v. *rostir*). It was recorded in English from the end of the 13th c. with the sense 'to cook (food, esp. meat) by prolonged exposure to heat at or before a fire or similar source of radiant heat'. Following the *OED*, it was first used with reference to the method of cooking meat over an open fire, usually on a spit, but its later uses indicate the sense similar to that of *bake*, i.e., 'to cook in an enclosed oven, usually with the use of fat' (*OED*: s.v. *roast*, v.; cf. *OED*: *bake*, v. 1a).

In the 14th c. 102 occurrences [RNF: 35.1] of the verb were found. The majority of records were in the form of a passive participial adjective (68%). 27.5% of forms were transitive. The 15th c. corpus revealed 328 records [RNF: 33] of the verb. The ratio of particular forms has changed, comparing to the earlier material, i.e., the majority of uses were transitive (50%) and participial (44%), see Fig. 13. This can be accounted for by the fact that the later a recipe, the more descriptive it became. Thus, in the 14th c. instead of instructing the cook what to do step by step, the recipes were rather lists of ingredients which should be added in a particular order, and very often the ingredients were first processed in various ways, hence, the cook was instructed 'to take roasted meat' with no details of how to roast it, or he was instructed what to do next when 'the meat is roasted to a particular degree', see for instance (62).

(62) Take capouns half yrosted and smyte hem on pecys, and do þerto pynes and hony clarified; salt it and colour it with safroun,

(FC_64)

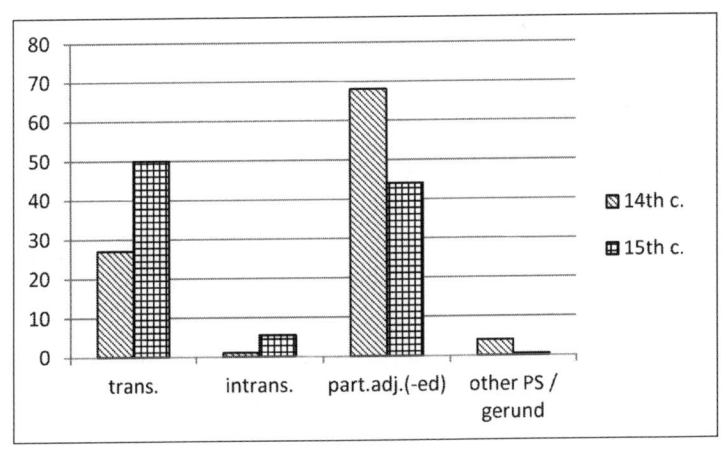

Fig. 13: The percentage of particular forms of *roast*

Semantically, both in the 14th and 15th c. almost all the occurrences of *roast* referred to various meats and fish (96% in both periods); the variety of meats which could have been roasted can be seen in some of the menus enumerating the dishes, e.g., (63). The remaining 4% of occurrences referred to milk, cake (sweet / non-meat), figs, raisins, dates and almonds, see (64), and in the 15th c. also to eggs and some fruit, e.g., (65).

(63) (...) pyggys **rostyd**, crunes **rostyd**, fesaintis **rostyd**, herones **rostyd**, pekokys **rostyd**, breme, sartes, broken brawn, conyng **rostyd**, & i soteltee. Potage callyd bruet of almayne, new lombard, venesoun **rostyd**, egret **rostyd**, pekokys **rostyd**, perteryches **rostyd**, pegones **rostyd**, rabetes **rostyd**, qualys **rostyd**, larkes **rostyd**, (...)

(Cos_2)

(64) Take fyges iquarterid, raysouns hool, dates and almaundes hole, and ryne hem on a spyt and **roost** hem;

(FC_195)

(65) þen take **rostede egges** & take þe 3olkes schrede small as þe comen use,

(GR_eMus_78)

In the analyzed recipes roasting was conducted over an open fire, on a spit or a griddle. Additionally, a few recipes suggest a skewer, an oven or a pan, see (66). The 15th c. meats were also frequently roasted on a 'roastiron', which is 'an iron grid, sometimes also fitted with hooks or spikes, for roasting meat, fish, etc., on' (*OED*: s.v. *roastiron*, n.). However, despite its name, the tool was also used for other procedures, such as toasting or broiling, e.g., (67).

Only sporadically was the use of fat indicated, e.g., (68)–(69); however, taking into consideration the fact that the majority of records of *roast* were applied to meat or fish, fat must have obviously been present.

Meat was usually prepared for roasting by parboiling or larding (70), which prevented it from drying out. However, single occurrences (15th c.) suggest that roasting might have been also conducted in order to dry food, see (71). Moreover, similarly to frying, roasting was applied to meat in order to colour it.

(66) he [lobster] schal be **rostyd** in his scalys in a ouyn oþer by þe feer vnder a panne,

(DS_75)

(67) take & tost hit a lytyll on a **rost yron** that hit be somdell broun. Dip hit a lytyll in the wyn & ley hit a lytyll ayen on the **rost yron** & tost hit.

(OP_187)

(68) capones **rostyd** of hy grece

(Cos_2)

(69) Put the laumprey on a spyt; **roost** hym & kepe wel the grece.

(FC_130)

(70) HARYS in CIUEE schul be perboyled & lardyd & **rostid**;

(DS_8)

(71) Lay þam [venison] a3eyne on þe roste yren; late **rost** tyl hit be drye.

(GR_Rwl_82)

4.3.2 Discussion

Three of the verbs, i.e., *bake, fry* and *roast* seem to have been common in the analyzed period. However, the number of occurrences of the verbs seems to depend on the foodstuffs particular actions were applied to, i.e., baking was applied mostly to bread and pastry (Wilson 1991), which was such a basic activity that there was no need to describe it in the recipes, hence the smallest number of records. The basic character of this activity can be also seen in the fact that the verb was mostly used in the headings rather than within the body of the recipes. Frying and roasting referred to more sophisticated procedures, thus a higher number of their occurrences. All of the three verbs seem to have been pretty stable in terms of their frequencies (see Table 4b and Fig. 14 below). Only in the case of *fry* can we observe a significant decrease in the number of records. This drop could be accounted for by the fact that the verb *fry* changed its reference – earlier it referred to meat and fish (which were the most frequent element of dishes in the analyzed recipes) much more frequently than in the later period. Instead it was used mostly with reference to flour dishes. The fourth verb, i.e., *broil*, entered English only in the 2nd half of the 14th c., which explains its rare occurrence in the corpus.

In the recipes, the cook was often given the choice between baking, frying and roasting, see for instance (72)–(73), which would suggest that the difference between the three processes was not very significant. Sometimes the choice was between the verbs of 'cooking with fat' and those of 'cooking in liquid', as in (74). But on the other hand, the 14th c. menus show that a specific verb might have been used with specific foodstuffs when particular dishes were enumerated, e.g., (75).

Table 4: *The number of occurrences of the 'verbs of cooking with fat' found in the analyzed material*

4a. Absolute frequencies:

	bake	broil	fry	roast
14th c.	37	2	93	102
15th c.	147	15	212	328
Total:	184	17	304	429

4b. Normalized frequencies (to 10,000 words):

	bake	broil	fry	roast
14th c.	12.7	0.7	32	35.1
15th c.	14.8	1.5	21.4	33

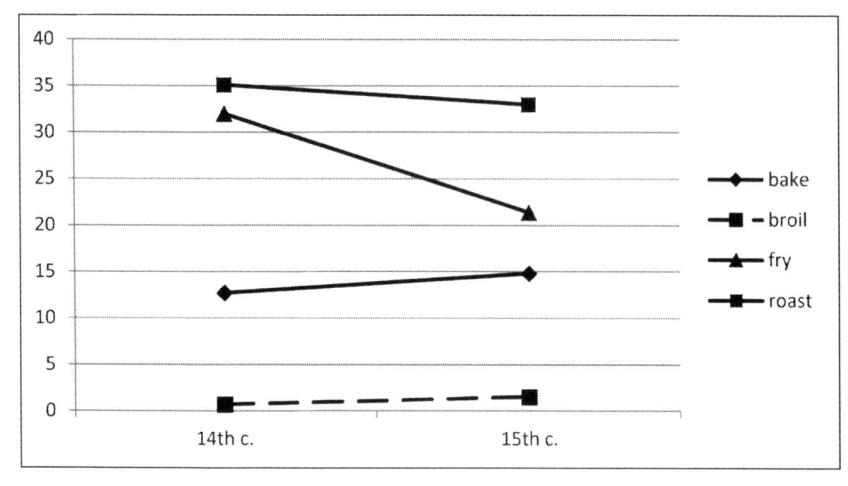

Fig. 14: *Distribution of the verbs at particular periods (normalized to 10,000 words)*

(72) Take Conyng, Hen, or Mallard, and **roste** him al-moste ynowe; or elles choppe hem, and **fry** hem in fressh grece;

(BK_63)

(73) (…) & so he is kut & close with-al, & **bake** or **frye** it, & þanne serue it forth.

(BM_10)

(74) Sole **boyled**, **roste**, or **fryed**.

(GR_Pen_129)

(75) Perchys in graue & gele, þerwith cheuettes of frut, hake ifarsed, rosyn **rosthenes**, eles **ibake**, lampreys **irosted**, grete luces **isoden**.

(Cosin_8)

Already in the earlier studies the similarities between the verbs were noticed (Lehrer 1969, Leaf 1971, Sihler 1973, see also section 2.2.2). However, in these studies, it was *fry* and *bake* which were compared. Taylor (2005: Online) compares the medieval *roast* and *bake*, claiming that *roast* "was originally semantically the same as *bake*, but they diverged with the prestigious French word applied generally to meat, while *bake* is now more often used for non-meat items, such as breads, cakes, or maybe potatoes". The present study shows that all the three verbs (*bake, fry* and *roast*) show some degree of overlapping, especially in terms of the use of fat, the foodstuffs affected and the type of fire to which the food was exposed. *Broil* was very close to *roast*. The two were identical in all categories, except for the grammatical forms in which they were used, i.e., *broil* was not used as a participial adjective, which can be accounted for by the fact that it was still rather infrequent. The most frequently occurring features of each of the four 'verbs of cooking with fat' have been presented in Table 5.

To conclude, *fry* and *bake* resemble each other only in terms of the foodstuffs affected, and only to a certain degree, since the latter process was applied to a wider range of products, and flour dishes gained popularity in terms of frying only in the 15th c. Earlier it was rather the individual products which were fried. As far as the use of fat is concerned, *bake* resembles *roast* rather than *fry*. The type of fat was hardly ever specified, although it must have been used in order not to burn the dish.

Table 5: *The most frequently occurring features of the 'verbs of cooking with fat'. In brackets ( ) the less frequent elements have been enumerated*

	bake	broil	fry	roast
etymology	Com.Germ.	Fr	Fr	Fr
use of fat[68]	[− fat]	[− fat]	[+ fat] oil / grease / butter	[− fat]

---

68 Under the 'use of fat' we mean the indication of the use of grease in the recipes. Thus [+ fat] means that the cook is instructed to use a specific type of grease, whilst [− fat], in turn, means that it has not been mentioned in most of the recipes. All of the procedures required some extra fat to be added during the process of cooking in order not to burn the dish.

		bake	broil	fry	roast
foodstuff		flour dishes (filling, closed)	meat / fish	14th c. meat/fish, fruit, nuts, onion (flour dishes: battered, closed)	15th c. flour dishes (filling, closed); meat/ fish, fruit, nuts, onion	meat /fish
type of tool		[± open] trap, pan, oven	[+ open] griddle, roastiron	[+ open] frying- / pan	[+ open] griddle, roastiron, spit, skewer
type of verb[69]		14th c. [+ T]	15th c. [± T]	[+ T]	[+ T] –	14th c. 15th c. [+ ed] – [+ T]
derived nouns		bakemeat	–	fries, fritour, frying pan	roastiron, rost (n)

4.4 Verbs of cooking with any or no medium

This group comprises five verbs (*burn*, *flamb*, *heat*, *scorch* and *toast*) which referred to actions connected with heating, but the medium in which these were conducted was not important. They were rather infrequent in the analyzed material (see Table 6).

Table 6: The number of occurrences of the 'verbs of cooking in fat' in the analyzed material. [RNFs / 10.000 words]

verb:	14th c.	15th c.
burn	10 [3.4]	4 [0.4]
flamb	2 [0.7]	1 [0.1]
heat	3 [1]	17 [2]
scorch	3 [1]	0 [0]
toast	8 [3]	32 [3]

---

69 [T] = transitive.

The most prominent of the verbs was *toast*. It was derived from French *toster* 'to roast or grill' (from Lat. *tostāre*). It entered English in the 14th c. with the sense 'to burn as the sun does, to parch, to heat thoroughly' (*OED*: s.v. *toast*, v.[1] 1a). Following the dictionary, the first reference of *toast* to cooking comes from the middle of the 15th c., when it was recorded with the sense 'to brown (bread, cheese, etc.) by exposure to the heat of a fire, etc.' (ibid.: 2a). The present material shows that the verb was used earlier; we have identified eight records [RNF: 3] of *toast* in the 14th c. (e.g., (76)) and 32 [RNF: 3] a century later. All of them referred to bread.

Heat is a Common Germanic verb denoting 'to make hot; to raise the temperature'. It was found in the corpus 3 [RNF: 1] and 17 times [RNF: 2] in the respective centuries. Not only food might have been heated but also vessels. Any medium for heating food in might have been used, i.e., either some liquid or grease. Sometimes the temperature was indicated, e.g., (77)–(78). *Heat* was also used in phrases, such as 'give it a heat' or 'take a heat', e.g., (79).

(76) **Toste** wyte bred & do yt in dischis,

(DS_65)

(77) Take a schouyl of yron, & **hete** it brennyng hote;

(BM_28)

(78) **hete** milke scalding hoote

(Aus_Douce_12)

(79) (...) & sette it on þe fyre, an **3if it an hete**;

(PD_87)

All the other verbs categorized in this group were extremely rare (the relative normalized frequencies being equal to or lower than 1). *Flamb* was derived from French *flamber* 'to singe', and originally was a variant of *flammer* 'to flame'. According to the *OED*, its first record comes from 1440. It is still used in Scottish English with the senses 'to baste roasted meat' and 'to besmear oneself with the food which one is eating' (*EDD*: s.v. *flamb*, v.). In the analyzed recipes it was found twice in the 14th and once in the 15th c. All of these records referred to clarified honey.

The last two verbs belonging to this group are *burn* and *scorch*. The former "represents two OE verbs: (i) an intr. str. vb. *birnan, beornan*; (ii) a trans. wk. vb. *bærnan*" (Hoad: s.v. *burn*[2]). *Burn* was found 10 times in the 14th c. and 4 times in the 15th c. However, it functioned either as a gerund or participial adjective, e.g., (80)–(81).

The latter is of obscure etymology. According to the *OED*, it appears in the 15th c. with the sense 'to heat to such a degree as to shrivel, parch, or dry up, or to char

153

or discolour the surface; to burn superficially' (s.v. *scorch*, v.[1]), whilst the analyzed corpus contains it only in the 14th c. material. All of its records refer to 'lamprey'.

(80) Take hony and sugur cipre and clarifie it togydre, and boile it with esy fyre, and kepe it wel fro **brennyng**.

(FC_68)

(81) Take a shouell of yren, and hete him **brennyng** hote in þe fire; (...) and sette þe pan and þe salt ouer the fire ayen, til þe salt be **brennyng** hote;

(BK_118)

4.5 Conclusions

The verbs of cooking can be divided into three groups depending on the medium in which the action of the cooking takes place: (i) verbs of cooking in liquid, (ii) verbs of cooking with fat, and (iii) verbs of cooking in any / no medium. They were not very numerous in terms of their types (with only 7 verbs of cooking in liquid, 4 verbs of cooking with fat and 5 in any / no medium). However, most of the verbs were very frequent in terms of tokens, both in the 14th and 15th c. Taking into account that the cooking procedures seem to have been so common that very often the activities are not described in the recipes, but only their result is mentioned, we may expect that if the recipes were more detailed (especially in the earlier period), the verbs of cooking would have been much more numerous.

Some of the verbs were still infrequent due to the fact that they had entered English shortly before the time the recipes were written down, e.g., *stew* or *broil*. In the case of other verbs we can observe some rivalry leading to semantic changes, e.g., *seethe* and *boil*. The former decreased in frequency and narrowed its meaning as a result of the growing popularity of its synonym of French origin, which takes over the dominance within the semantic field. Such a phenomenon leads to a more drastic result of the French influence, i.e., the obsolescence of some of the verbs, e.g., *well* or *ouerstep*, which being used with the same meaning as *seethe* and *boil*, became redundant in the language.

Additionally, the analyzed material revealed some form of a hierarchy of the verbs of cooking in liquid, i.e., some of the activities were more basic than others. For instance, parboiling seems to have been the preliminary action to seething and boiling, whilst seething was preliminary to boiling, and boiling was the most advanced of the cooking procedures.

Due to the French influence on the semantic field of the verbs of cooking, more specific meanings of verbs have been introduced – see for instance verbs such as *stew*, *parboil* or *scald*. The native vocabulary items were used with a more general sense than the words of French origin, e.g., *seethe*, or were used with reference to more basic (less sophisticated) preparations and less expensive dishes, e.g., *bake* (which was used with reference to pastry) vs. *roast* (used for meats).

In the later period, we may also observe the fixing of collocations to a certain extent, that is, a particular verb is used with a particular foodstuff, e.g., *bake* usually refers to flour products, *broil* or *roast* to meat and fish, and *seethe* became specific for cooking eggs, which were never boiled, etc.

Chapter Five: Verbs of Preparing

5.1 Introduction

The present chapter gathers a wide range of verbs which refer to any activities conducted in the process of food preparation other than cooking or cutting. They have been divided into 7 groups, i.e.,

(i) Verbs of cleaning
(ii) Verbs of adding and combining
(iii) Verbs of straining
(iv) Verbs of seasoning
(v) Verbs of decoration
(vi) Verbs of taking
(vii) Verbs of serving

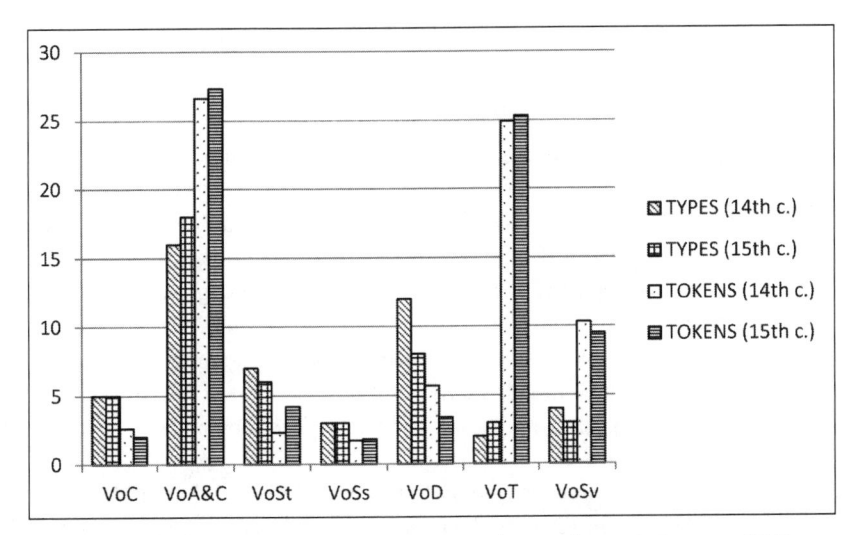

Fig. 1: *Types and tokens (RNFs / 1,000 words) of particular verbal groups (VoC = verbs of cleaning; VoA&C = verbs of adding and combining; VoSt = straining; VoSS = seasoning; VoD = decoration; VoT = taking; VoSv = serving)*

157

5.2 Verbs of cleaning

This group contains verbs which refer to the process of removing unwanted elements from foodstuff without the use of a knife (unlike the removing verbs, see section 3.4). Verbs of cleaning may refer either to the removal of the integral parts of the foodstuff (such as hulls) or the external substances (such as dirt). Levin (1993: 122–128) categorized such verbs as a subgroup of 'verbs of removing'; however, in order to avoid confusion with the verbs discussed under 3.4, which involved the use of a sharp instrument such as a knife, a different label has been adopted.

This group contains only 5 verbs: *draw₃, fan (out), make clean, wash* and *winnow out*. Table 1 shows their number of occurrence in the 14th and 15th centuries.

Table 1: The number of occurrences of the 'cleaning verbs' in the analyzed material. Relative normalized frequencies have been given in brackets [RNFs / 10.000 words]

verb:	14th c.	15th c.
draw₃	0	47 [4.7]
fan (out)	1 [0.3]	4 [0.4]
make clean	4 [1.4]	23 [2.3]
wash	65 [22.4]	89 [9]
winnow (out)	1 [0.3]	0

Wash, which referred to cleaning foodstuffs by removing the dirt from their surface, is the most frequent of all the 'cleaning verbs' found in the analyzed material, with 65 records [RNF: 22.4] in the 14th c. and 89 [RNF: 9] in the 15th c. It was the only verb which referred to the removal of dirt. The drop in its frequency in the 15th century may be accounted for by the fact that, even though the later recipes were more precise and longer than the 14th c. ones, washing was such a basic procedure that it might have been omitted from the instructions. What is more, the social awareness concerning hygiene was growing (see for instance Smith, V. 2007) and thus it is suggested that the cook did not have to be reminded of the need to wash meat or vegetables.

The phrase *make clean* occurred only four times [RNF: 1.4] in the 14th c. material and 23 [RNF: 2.3] in the 15th c., and was always used with reference to the entrails of fish or parts of animals such as ears, feet, tongue, bowels, etc. (see for instance (1)–(2)).

(1) Take the guttes of samoun and **make hem clene**;

(FC_114)

(2) Take the bowels of veel: **make ham clene**. Seth them in fresshe brothe; (...)

(OP_42)

The removal of the unwanted parts of food was also expressed with such verbs as *draw₃, fan (out)* and *winnow out*. *Draw₃* referred to the process of cleaning meat and fish of the unwanted hair, feathers and scales. The other two verbs referred to the removal of hulls and were used from the Old English period. The former was derived from the Old English noun *fann* (borrowed from Latin *vannus*). However, it is believed that its Middle English use was enhanced by the French *van*. The latter stems from OE *windwian* 'to expose to the wind or to a current of air so that the lighter particles are separated or blown away' (*OED*). Both *fan (out)* and *winnow out* were peripheral (with single occurrences in the analyzed material), *draw₃* was found only in the 15th c.

5.3 Verbs of adding and combining

Due to the fact that sometimes it is impossible to distinguish between the specific meanings, this group comprises verbs denoting mixing, adding, but also putting one ingredient into the others (this includes stuffing). For the ambiguity of meanings see (3). Altogether 18 verbs will be discussed in the present section: *ally/ lye, beat₂, cast, couch, do (thereto/therein), draw₁, farce, fill, meddle, mell, ming, plant, pour, stir, stop, stuff, swing* and *temper*. Table 2 shows the number of their occurrence in the analyzed material. For the sake of clarity, they have been subdivided into three subsections: 'verbs of combining', 'verbs of adding', and 'verbs of stuffing'.

(3) mynce oynouns and seeþ hem in grece and gode broth; **do þerto** [= add]. Drawe a lyre of brede, blode, vyneger, and broth; **do þerto** with powdour fort [= mix, put together].

(FC_27)

Verbs which referred to the process of mixing ingredients usually carried some additional information, such as the way of mixing, the tool used for the mixing, the purpose of mixing, etc.

Table 2: The number of occurrences of the 'combining verbs' in the analyzed material. Relative normalized frequencies have been given in brackets [RNFs / 10.000 words]

verb:	14th c.	15th c.
ally/lye[70]	60 [20.7]	115 [11.6]
beat$_2$	4 [1.4]	21 [2.1]
cast	180 [62]	1058 [106.6]
couch	5 [1.7]	76 [7.7]
do$_2$	273 [94]	582 [58.6]
draw$_1$	48 [16.5]	179 [18]
farce	4 [1.4]	11 [1.1]
fill	8 [2.8]	42 [4.2]
meddle	34 [11.7]	52 [5.2]
mell	0	43 [4.3]
ming	9 [3.1]	19 [1.9]
plant	6 [2]	31 [3.1]
pour	7 [2.4]	96 [9.7]
stir	28 [9.6]	130 [13]
stop	8 [2.8]	28 [2.8]
stuff	0	6 [0.6]
swing	11 [3.8]	20 [2]
temper	86 [29.6]	205 [20.7]

5.3.1 Verbs of combining

The present subsection presents those verbs whose major reference was mixing rather than adding ingredients, even though some of them might have referred to the latter as well (the two senses often merged).

Ally, from AN and OF *alier*, was used from the 14th c. with the sense 'to combine, mix (ingredients)'. This sense became obsolete in the 15th c. (*OED*: s.v. *ally*, v. 2). In the analyzed material, the verb was used with the meaning 'to mix', but

---

70 It is suggested that *ally* and *lye* might have been perceived as two forms of the same verb. They were definitely used with the same meaning, and the spelling variants found in the analyzed editions often do not allow us to state which of the two is being represented.

more often it occurred with a more specific sense 'to mix in order to thicken', usually by mixing with flour of rice, starch, the yolks of eggs, bread, etc. Similarly, *lye* (from Fr. *lier* 'to thicken') was used with the same sense. Following the *OED*, it was used only in the 14th and 15th c. (s.v. *lye*, v.[1]). Due to the similarity of forms and meanings, it is suggested that the two verbs might have been used interchangeably, as two forms of the same verb. In the 14th c. they were found 60 times [RNF: 20.7], a century later 115 times [RNF: 11.6]. For examples of the two senses of the verbs see (4)–(7). The drop in frequency of occurrence in the 15th c. material shows that this sense of the verb was becoming obsolete. Following the *OED* (s.v. *ally*, v. 2), the culinary reference of *ally* disappeared from the written language in the 15th c.

(a) 'to mix':

(4) (…) and take þe first mylke & **alye** it **vp** wiþ a penne [= a feather].

(FC_119)

(5) take almaundes blaunched, grynde hem & **alay** hem **vp** with the same broth.

(FC_38)

(b) 'to mix + to thicken':

(6) þan sette it from þe fyre, & **a-lye** it **vp** with raw 3olkes of eyroun,

(PD_36)

(7) & if it be no3t þikke ynow, **lye** it with floure of rys or with amodyne (…)

(UC_16)

Meddle and *ming* were used with the sense 'to mix, blend (together)'. The former is of Anglo-Norman origin (from *meddler* 'mix, mingle'). The latter is a Germanic verb (OE *mæncgan*). Although synonymous, the borrowed verb was much more frequent in the 14th c. material, with 34 records [RNF: 11.7] (*ming* occurred only 9 times [RNF: 3.1]). A century later, *meddle* was found 52 times [RNF: 5.2] and *ming* 19 times [RNF: 1.9]. Both decreased in number in the 15th c. Both actions referred to mixing or blending with the use of one's hands (as the 'instrument'), which in a way specified the meaning of the verbs, see for instance (8). Moreover, a number of examples suggest that *minging* might have been used not only to mix ingredients but also to thicken the dish, as one of the ingredients was often flour or the yolks of eggs.

(8) Take rawe creme & yolkes of egges all rawe with oute any whyete & **menge** togedure with þy handes,

(GR_eMus_66)

Temper (from OE *temprian* < from Latin *temperāre* 'to divide or proportion duly, to mingle in due proportion, to combine properly') was found 86 times [RNF:

29.6] in the 14th c. and 205 [RNF: 20.7] in the 15th c. Following the *OED*, the verb denotes 'to bring to a proper condition, state or quality, by mingling with something else' (s.v. *temper*, v. I.1). In the 14th c. *temper* referred to mixing ingredients, of which at least one was liquid (broth, wine, ale, etc.) or liquid-like (the yolks of eggs), so that the mixture took the form of a paste, e.g., (9)–(12).

(9) Make a past **tempred** wiþ ayren,

(DC_45)

(10) & **tempre** floure of rys with almound melk & boyle it til it be chargeaunt,

(UC_22)

(11) Take rawgh almondes & grynd hem small, & **temper** hem with wyne and water.

(GR_Raw_5)

(12) Make a mylke of almonds yblaunchyd, & **temper up** the fisch therwith;

(OP_80)

Another popular 'verb of combining' was *stir* (OE *styrian*). It was found 28 times [RNF: 9.6] in the 14th c. and 130 [RNF: 13] a century later. In the recipes, the verb was often accompanied by a specifying phrase referring to the 'degree of mixing', e.g., (13)–(14). Stirring with one's hands was also possible (15).

(13) After, take gode mylke of almaundes & put þe brawn þerin, & **stere** it wel togyder

(FC_201)

(14) þan sett it fro þe fyre & **stere** it a lyttyll wyth þi spatyll

(GK_11)

(15) sette it fro þe fourneys and euermore **stere** with 3oure hand

(GK_11)

Similarly, *swing* (from OE *swingan*), which following the *OED*, denoted 'to beat up, whip', was used with reference to mixing ingredients, one of which was always an egg (or a part of it). Only in one 14th-c. recipe does swinging not involve an egg. It instructs to 'swing mallard over the fire' (see (16)). The verb was found 11 times [RNF: 3.8] in the 14th c. and 20 times [RNF: 2] in the 15th c.

(16) tak a mallard & pul hym drye, & **swyng** ouer þe fyre.

(DS_52)

Additionally, in the 15th c. the verb *mell* appeared 43 times [RNF: 4.3]. Even though such a sense has not been found in the *OED*, in the analyzed corpus the verb referred to mixing ingredients together, e.g., (17). The dictionary recognizes the sense of *mell*, but only with reference to people, and no culinary context has been presented (s.v. *mell*, v. 2).

(17) sethe it [beef or veal] tyl it be y-now; þan hew cold oþer hote, & **melle** togederys þe eggys, þe Bef, or vele, & caste þerto Safroun, & Salt, & pouder of Pepir, & **melle** it togederys;

(LV_57)

And finally, one of the senses of *beat* referred to mixing. It was found only four times [RNF: 1.4] in the 14th c. and 21 times [RNF: 2.1] in the 15th c. All of its records referred to the mixing of ingredients in order to form some kind of pastry, thus, eggs and flour were always involved.

5.3.2 Verbs of adding

The most frequent verb referring to 'adding/putting in' was *cast*, with 180 records [RNF: 62] in the 14th c. and 1058 [RNF: 106.6] in the 15th c. The verb was borrowed from Old Norse *kasta* 'to throw' and surfaced in written English in the 13th c. In the analyzed texts it is usually accompanied by a particle suggesting the direction of throwing, e.g., *thereto, thereon, therein, into*, etc. Figures 2 and 3 show the ratio of occurrence of the particular particles in the 14th and 15th centuries, respectively. Its popularity can be accounted for by the fact that in the analyzed period it was well established in the language, and being general in meaning it could have been used with a wide variety of more specific senses (with the use of particles following the verb).

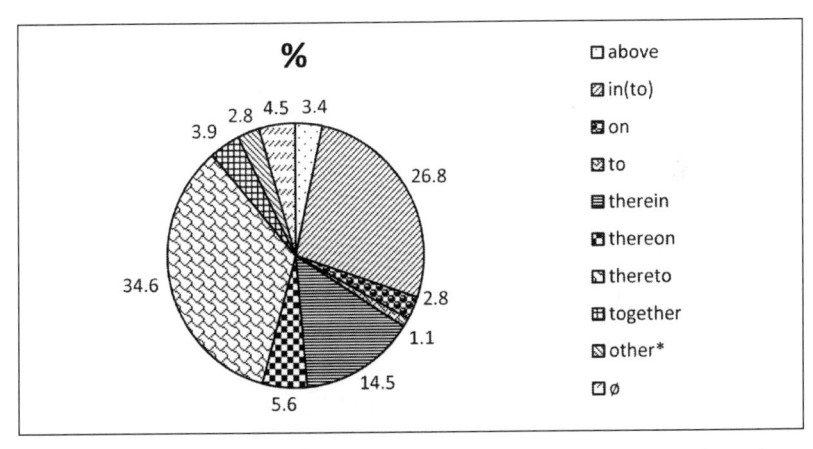

Fig. 2: *The ratio of occurrence of the particular particles accompanying the verb* cast *in the 14th c. (*'other' refers to all those particles whose RNF was equal to or below 1)*

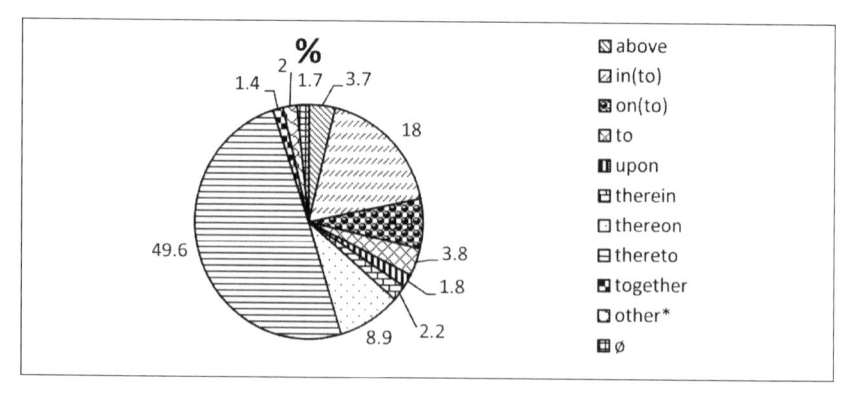

Fig. 3: *The ratio of occurrence of the particular particles accompanying the verb* cast *in the 15th c. (*'other' refers to all those particles whose RNF was equal to or below 1)*

A similar verb to *cast*, i.e., do_2, which was also used with the sense 'to add, to put in(to)', was found 273 times [RNF: 94] in the 14th c. and 582 [RNF: 58.6] in the 15th c. Apart from a few occurrences (2.6% in the 14th c. and 1.5% in the 15th c.), it was always followed by a particle specifying its meaning, such as *thereto, therein, thereupon, in, to*, etc. Figures 4 and 5 show the ratio of occurrence of the particular particles following *do* in the 14th and 15th c., respectively.

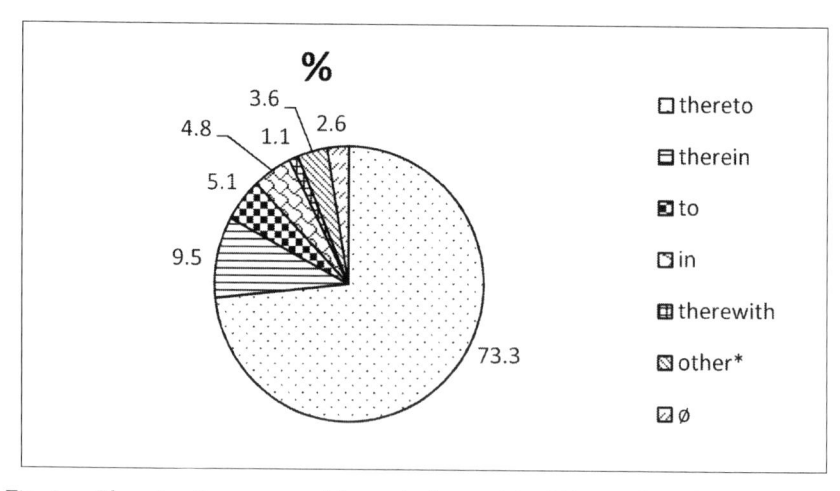

Fig. 4: *The ratio of occurrence of the particular particles following the verb* do_2 *in the 14th c. (*'other' refers to all those particles which had 1% or less of occurrences)*

164

%

2.9 4 1.6
6.7
39.9
32
7.9 5

□ thereto
▤ therein
▨ to
▨ in(to)
▦ together
▨ on
▨ other*
▨ ∅

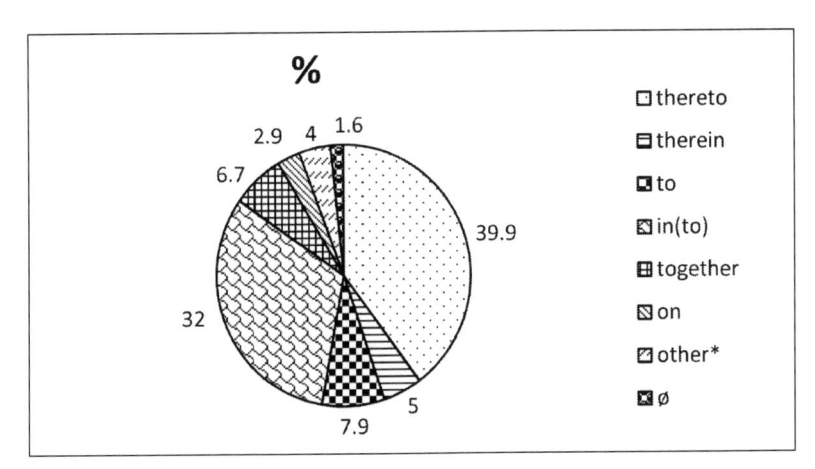

Fig. 5: The ratio of occurrence of the particular particles following the verb do$_2$ in the 15th c. (*'other' refers to all those particles which had 1% or less of occurrences)

The next verb which belongs to the present group is *draw*, with 77 records [RNF: 26.6] in the 14th c. and 606 [RNF: 61] in the 15th c. However, its records show that it should be categorized into several groups of verbs: (i) 'adding and combining' (= *draw$_1$*), (ii) 'straining' (= *draw$_2$*), (iii) 'cleaning' (= *draw$_3$*), and (iv) 'cutting' (= *draw$_4$*). In the present section only *draw$_1$* will be discussed. According to the *OED*, the verb was used with reference to cookery with the sense 'to bring to the proper consistency' (s.v. *draw*, v. 4). Following the dictionary, the meaning was present only in the 15th c. We have found the verb with a culinary reference already in the 14th c. It occurred with a variety of senses:

(i) 'to add, mix (also in order to thicken)';
(ii) 'to strain' – with 24 records [RNF: 8.3] in the 14th c. and 262 [RNF: 26.4] in the 15th c. – see section 5.4;
(iii) 'to clean' – found only 47 times [4.7] in the 15th c. material – see section 5.2;
(iv) 'to cut' – with two records [RNF: 1.7] in the 14th c. and 96 [RNF: 9.7] in the 15th c. – see section 3.5.1.3;
(v) 'to take out (of a vessel)' – with three records [RNF: 1] in the 14th c. and 6 [RNF: 0.6] in the 15th c.[71]

---

71 This sense was so rare in the analyzed corpus that we have decided not to discuss it in detail.

The majority of its 14th -century occurrences referred to adding/mixing, i.e., 48 [16.5] in the 14th c. A century later this sense was represented 179 times [RNF: 18], which makes it one of the two most frequent senses of *draw* (see Fig. 6).

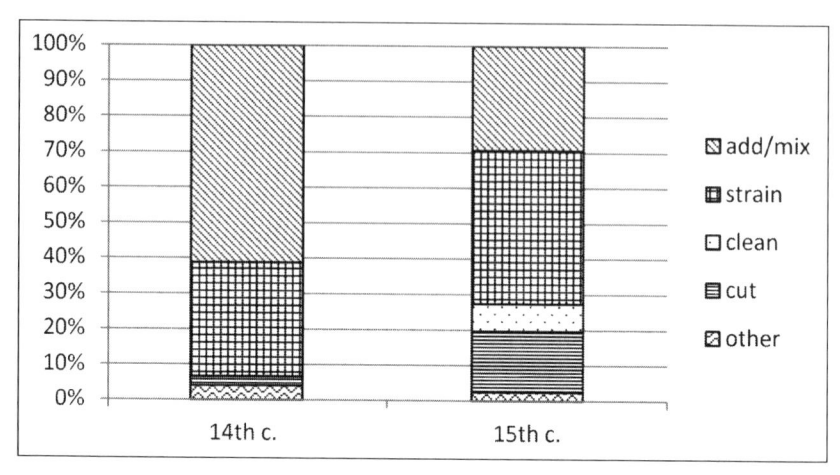

Fig. 6: The percentage of the occurrence of the particular senses of draw *in the 14th and 15th centuries*

Additionally, we should mention the verb *pour*. Its origin is uncertain, but it might be related to Middle (Norman) French *purer* 'to decant, pour out (a liquid)' (*OED*: s.v. *pour*, v.). It belongs to the group of 'verbs of adding', but it is specific in terms of the nature of the ingredient which was added, i.e., it was always liquid. According to the *OED*, *pour* was used in English from the 14th c. We have found only 7 records [RNF: 2.4] in the 14th c. and 96 [RNF: 9.7] in the 15th c.

Two of the verbs categorized into this group, apart from 'to put (usually into a vessel)', denoted 'to fill (e.g., with stuffing)'. These are *couch* and *plant*. The former, from Fr. *coucher*, which according to the *OED* (s.v. *couch*, v.[1]) entered English in the 14th c. with the sense 'to lay down flat', was found only 5 times [RNF: 1.7] in the early material. In the 15th c. the verb was much more frequent, with 76 occurrences [RNF: 7.7], which proves its good adaptation into English. The records suggest that it was used with the senses (i) 'to put, lay flat' (in a dish), e.g., (18), (ii) 'to cover, sprinkle' (with powder), e.g., (19)–(20), and in the 15th c. (iii) 'to fill with stuffing/filling', e.g., (21).

Similarly, *plant*, borrowed into Old English from Latin *plantāre* and later reinforced by AN *planter, plaunter*, was rare in the 14th c. with only 6 occurrences [RNF: 2]. A century later it was slightly more frequent, with 31 records [RNF:

3.1]. Apart from its regular meaning, i.e., (i) 'to set or place', see for instance (22), it seems to have denoted (ii) 'to flourish', e.g., (23), and (iii) 'to fill (with stuffing, etc.)', e.g., (24). The few occurrences of the verb suggest that the Old English form must have disappeared from the language earlier and in the analyzed period it was re-introduced due to the French influence.

(18) Take obleys oþer wafrouns in defaute of loseyns, and **cowche** in dysshes.
(FC_26)

(19) & tak bothe [eels, pines] togedere & **couche** hem in blaunche poudere, & in ceucre, & **couche** aboue poudere of gyngere as þe quantite of þy seruise nedeth.
(UC_1)

(20) Take lamprounys & skald hem with [blank in MS] & make fayre paste, & **couche** ij or iij lamprounys with pouder of Gyngere, Salt, Pepir, & lat hem bake;
(BM_22)

(21) þan take fyne past of flowre an water, Sugre, Safroun, & Salt, & make fayre cakys þerof; þan rolle þin stuf in þin hond, & **couche** it in þe cakys & kyt it,
(LV_58)

(22) Pare peris & quarter them; **plante** tham in dyschis & poure the syrip abowne.
(GR_Sl7_10)

(23) (...) & dresse v or vj lechys in a dysch & **plante** it with florys of vyolet & serve it forth.
(GR_Sl7_3)

(24) (...) **Plante** hem full of almoundes iblaunchede, & mynce hem smale & c.
(GR_eMus_33)

5.3.3 Verbs of stuffing

Apart from the two verbs mentioned in the previous section (*couch* and *plant*), which apart from their major sense referred to stuffing, the corpus contains four lexemes which denoted 'to fill with stuffing/filling', i.e., *farce, fill, stop* and *stuff*. All of them are more specific in meaning than *couch* and *plant*. Two of the verbs, *stop* and *fill*, are of Germanic origin. *Farce* and *stuff* were borrowed from French. The former derives from OF *farsir* (from L. *farcīre* 'to stuff'), while the latter comes from OF *estoffer* 'to furnish, equip, garrison'. In the case of *stuff*, the analyzed material agrees with the dictionary. Following the *OED* (s.v. *stuff*, v.[1] 6), its culinary reference, i.e., 'to fill (the inside of a bird or animal, a piece of meat, etc.)

167

with forcemeat, herbs, etc. as a stuffing', was first recorded in 1430. This agrees with the analyzed material, in which *stuff* was found only 6 times [RNF: 0.6] in the 15th c. All the occurrences referred to meat and fish. The earlier material did not contain the verb. *Farce* was used in English slightly earlier than the previous verb. We have found 4 records [RNF: 1.4] in the 14th c. material and 11 [RNF: 1.1] in the 15th c. Similarly to *stuff*, all the records of *farce* refer to meat and fish. *Farce* was slightly more frequent than *stuff*; however, the dominance among the verbs referring to stuffing belonged to the Germanic verbs: *fill* and *stop*. The former was found 8 times [RNF: 2.8] and 42 times [RNF: 4.2] in the respective centuries, the latter 8 times [RNF: 2.8] and 28 times [RNF: 2.8] in the respective centuries. The higher frequency of usage of the native verbs might be accounted for by the fact that the borrowings were relatively new and thus they were only just making their way into English. However, a closer look at the usage of the four verbs shows that the Germanic lexemes had a broader usage. They were used not only with reference to meat and fish, but also to pastry, vegetables, fruits, etc., see for instance (25)–(26). The native verbs were often followed by the particle 'full'.

(25) þan take <u>datis</u>, & wasshe hem clene, & pyke owt þe Stonys, & **fylle** hem fulle of blaunche poudere

(PD_104)

(26) Recipe [= take] fayre <u>quynces</u> & payr þam clene, & cut þeam oute þe kyrnyls; þan tak sugur enogh & a lityll powdyre of gynger **Stop** þe hole full;

(Ht_Hrl_83)

The 'verbs of adding and combining' represent a wide range of meanings. The particular senses of these verbs often overlap, and some of the verbs cannot be clearly categorized into one of the subgroups. Moreover, the medieval recipes seldom give a satisfactory explanation when it comes to the instructions. That is why we have decided to create such a numerous and general verbal category. The attempt to subdivide the verbs into smaller groups lacks precision, but it has been undertaken in order to make the presentation of the data clearer and better systemized.

This group has definitely been dominated by verbs of Germanic origin, which contributes to the suggestion that the non-sophisticated activities were expressed with native vocabulary. It is also worth noting that the most general (Germanic) verbs were often accompanied by a particle specifying their meaning. The two most frequent verbs in the 14th c., i.e., do_2 and *cast* seem to have changed places in the 15th c. The former decreased, while the latter rose in number. This can be accounted for by the fact that, being synonymous, the simpler term was preferred by speakers. *Do* had to be followed by a particle specifying its meaning, which was not the case with *cast*. Moreover, the latter was not as broad as the former; *do*, incorporated into phrases, could have referred to almost any culinary activity, e.g., *do clean* (= 'wash'), *do therein* (= 'put in/add'), *do through* (= 'strain'), *do with saffron* (= 'colour'), *do to leaches* (= 'cut'), etc.

5.4 Verbs of straining

This group comprises verbs which refer to the action of filtering food, i.e., putting it through a strainer or a cloth in order to separate certain parts of it, remove unwanted lumps, or to obtain the proper consistency of food, etc. However, very often the verbs could be categorized both as cleaning (straining was to remove the unwanted parts) and adding (straining was to combine ingredients together). The verbs belonging to this group are: *clarify, draw₂, make, run, *searce, skim, strain* and *wring*. Table 3 shows the number of occurrences of the particular verbs.

Table 3: The number of occurrences of the 'straining verbs' in the analyzed material. The relative normalized frequencies have been given in brackets [RNFs / 10,000 words]

verb:	14th c.	15th c.
clarify	21 [7.2]	59 [5.9]
draw₂	24 [8.3]	262 [26.4]
make	2 [0.7]	0
run	2 [0.7]	1 [0.1]
skim	4 [1.4]	42 [4.2]
strain	8 [2.8]	65 [6.5]
**searce*	1 [0.3]	2 [0.2]
wring	9 [3.1]	20 [2]

The verb *clarify*, of French origin, denoted 'to make clear and pure (a liquid or liquefied substance); to render pellucid; to free from all impurities or extraneous matters held in suspension' (*OED*: s.v. *clarify*, v. 3b). It was found 21 times [RNF: 7.2] in the 14th c. and 59 [RNF: 5.9] in the 15th c. It mostly referred to honey. However, other foodstuffs might have been clarified as well, e.g., butter, sugar, wine. Usually, the process was applied to some mixtures, such as sugar, spices or honey mixed with wine, broth or the white of eggs, see examples (27)–(28).

(27) **Clarifie** hony with wyne & vyneger

(FC_150)

(28) Take and **claryfye** the sugur with a quantite of wyne

(FC_22)

Draw₂, already mentioned in the previous section, referred to straining 24 times in the 14th c. [RNF: 8.3] and 263 [RNF: 26.5] a century later. The tool used for filtering food was usually specified. Thus, 75% of the 14th c. occurrences of *draw₂* referred to putting food through a strainer (e.g., (29)), and 25% to filtering food through a cloth (e.g., (30)). In the 15th c. a strainer was used in 94% of cases, whilst 5.7% occurrences of *draw₂* referred to cloth, and 0.3% to straining through a colander, see example (31). The instrument did not depend on the ingredients to be strained. Sometimes the same mixture was drawn through different utensils (see (32)–(33)).

(29) (...) & tak bred, & stepe in þe same broth, & **drawe** it þorw a streynour.

(UC_2)

(30) Tak vp þe pykys & elys & hold hem hote, & **draw** þe broþ þorwe a cloþe.

(DS_92)

(31) nym crostes of whyt bred, resons, & canele, bray hit, tempre it vp with good wyn, **drawe** it thorw a colonur / let hit be al ycoloured with canele,

(Aus_Laud_11)

(32) Take crustes of brede and grynde hem smale (...); temper it vp with vyneger, and **drawe it vp þurgh a straynour**,

(FC_142)

(33) Take brede and blode iboiled, and grynde it and **drawe it thurgh a cloth** with vyneger;

(FC_145)

The verbs *searce* and *strain*, both of French origin, usually referred to putting food through a sieve and a strainer, respectively. The former occurred only once [RNF: 0.3] in the 14th c. and 3 times [RNF: 0.3] in the 15th c. The latter was found 8 times [RNF: 2.8] in the 14th and 66 [RNF: 6.6] in the 15th c. Filtering food through a cloth was usually referred to with more general verbs, usually of Germanic origin, such as *run*. Additionally, the verb *wring* could have been used with both a strainer and a cloth. Although the reference of all these verbs is quite narrow, the first two (*searce* and *strain*) are much more specific in meaning. They both bear formal resemblance to nouns denoting the instrument that is used for the activity. *Searce* has been formed by the process of conversion from the noun *searce*. *Strain*, on the other hand, gave rise to the noun *strainer* (later also †*strain* n.). However, it seems that in the later material *strain* might have referred to filtering food through a cloth, with 9.2% of all its 15th c. occurrences, e.g., (34). The other records were either not specified at all (i.e., 67.7%) or referred simply to a strainer (23.1% of occurrences), e.g., (35).

The verbs which referred exclusively to filtering food through a cloth, were *make* and *run*. However, they were very rare, with only single occurrences. Due to the fact that they were general in meaning, they were always specified in the recipes, e.g., (36)–(37).

Additionally, *wring*, of Germanic origin, was used for both activities, i.e., straining through a strainer or filtering through a cloth. It was found only 9 times [RNF: 3.1] in the 14th c. and 20 times [RNF: 2] in the 15th c. Its 14th-century usage seems to have been narrowed in terms of reference, i.e., it was used for filtering eggs only, e.g., (38)–(39). In the following century the reference is broader (eggs, whey, etc.).

(34) Take Strawberys, & waysshe hem in tyme of ȝere in gode red wyne; þan **strayne** þorwe a cloþe,

(PD_123)

(35) theym take and **streyne** theym thorough a streyner

(GR_SA_5)

(36) Nym þe grete bonys & grynd hem al to dust, & kest hem al in þe broth & **mak it þorw a cloþe**,

(DS_11)

(37) Take ... ounces kanel & galinga, greyns de paris, and a lytel peper, & make poudur, & temper hit wyt god wyte wyne & þe þrid perte hony & **ryne hit þorow a cloþ**.

(FC_205)

(38) (...) **wryng** ayren thurgh a straynour

(FC_93)

(39) Breke ayren and **wryng** hem thurgh a cloth

(FC_161)

The last verb belonging to this category, i.e., *skim*, was introduced into English in the 14th c. from French. According to the *OED* (s.v. *skim*, v.), it was borrowed from French with the sense 'to clear (a liquid or a liquid mass) from matter floating upon the surface, usually by means of a special utensil; to deprive (milk) of cream by this method'. It gained in frequency in the 15th c. material. We have found 4 occurrences [RNF: 1.4] in the early material and 42 [RNF: 4.2] in the 15th c. corpus. Both in the 14th and 15th centuries *skim* referred to broth, honey, and honey with wine (sometimes spices were added).

5.5 Verbs of seasoning

Verbs belonging to this group referred to the addition of herbs and spices to the prepared dishes. They were either general (i.e., could refer to any herbs or spices, e.g., *season, enforce*) or specific (i.e., could refer to a specific spice, e.g., *salt, saffron*). Table 4 shows the number of occurrences of the most prominent verbs.

Table 4: *The number of occurrences of the 'seasoning verbs' in the 14th and 15th c. Relative normalized frequencies have been given in brackets [RNFs / 10,000 words]*

verb:	14th c.	15th c.
(en)force	7 [2.4]	6 [0.6]
salt	36 [12.4]	48 [4.8]
season	7 [2.4]	127 [12.8]

The major verb which referred to the addition of spices was *season*. It originates from Old French *saisonner*, Modern French *assaisonner*. According to the *OED*, the verb was used with the sense 'to render (a dish) more palatable by the addition of some savoury ingredient' and dates from the early 14th c. In the 14th c. material *season* occurred only 7 times [RNF: 2.4], and all of the records were found in the collection *Utilis coquinario* (UC) dated to the end of the century. In the 15th c. the verb was more frequent, with 127 occurrences [RNF: 12.8]. *Season* was general in meaning, i.e., it could be applied to any spices. In both periods the exact spices to be used were enumerated in each case, e.g., (40)–(41). There are also examples in which the reader is advised to 'season the dish up', without any specific list of spices to be added, in which case it is the cook who is to decide at his own discretion what and how much to add. The increase in the number of occurrences of the verb suggests that it entered English in the 14th c. and became well established in the following century.

Additionally, two other, more specific, verbs were used with reference to the action of adding particular spices to a dish, i.e., *saffron* and *salt*. *Salt* was the more popular of the two. It was partly derived from the Germanic *sealtan* and partly was a new formation on the noun *salt* (*OED*: s.v. *salt*, v.[1]). In the culinary sense it denoted 'to season with salt'. In the 14th c. *salt* was found 36 times [RNF: 12.4] and 48 [RNF: 4.8] in the 15th c. The decrease in number may be accounted for by the growing popularity of the general verb *season*. Additionally, in the 15th c. corpus one occurrence of the verb *saffron* was found, see (42). Although, the *OED* (s.v. *saffron*, v.) dates the introduction of the verb to the end of the 14th c., the material shows it was not well established in English.

Salt and *saffron* were the only specific verbs formed on the basis of the conversion of the noun denoting the particular spice. The addition of other spices was expressed with the use of a number of general verbs such as *cast* + *'spice'*, *put/do thereto* + *'spice'*, *take* + *'spice'*, etc. This can be accounted for by the fact that salt and saffron were the most frequently used spices both in the 14th and 15th centuries. What is surprising is that no verb was formed with reference to adding sugar or ginger, which were also very popular, the former in both the analyzed centuries, the latter in the 15th c. (On the analysis of terms for herbs and spices see Bator 2013b). Additionally, 3 records of the phrase *lie with spices* were found in the 14th c. (exclusively in the DC collection), see (43).

Finally, the verb *enforce* (also in the form *force*) was used with the sense 'to season up'. According to the *OED*, it was a peripheral meaning of the verb *farce* (from OF *farsir*) 'to stuff, to fill full of something', used from the 15th until the 18th c. We have come across only a few occurrences of this sense (7 [RNF: 2.4] and 6 [RNF: 0.6] in the respective centuries), see (44)–(45).

(40) (…) charge it with rosted braun, & **sesen** it with sugre & salt,

(UC_21)

(41) then **seson** hit with powder of peper, ginger, and salt;

(BK_16)

(42) take & caste Sugre y-now þerto, & Vynegre a quantyte, & pouder Gyngere, & **Safroun** it wel, & Salt;

(PD_141)

(43) & soþþen do a lute bred of wastel, & **lye wel wiþ speces** & ayren

(DC_37)

(44) And do þerto safroun & salt, and **force** it with powdour douce.

(FC_6)

(45) **A-force** it with stronge pouder of Canelle & of Galyngale,

(PD_124)

5.6 Verbs of decoration

The group of 'verbs of decoration' is one of the most numerous subgroups of the preparing verbs. This proves that the way a dish looked – its appearance – was extremely important in the Middle Ages. Food could have been decorated for instance by the introduction of various colours into the dish or by flourishing the dish or the plate with flowers and spices. Table 5 shows the number of occurrences of the 'verbs of decoration' in the particular centuries.

Table 5: The number of occurrences of the 'verbs of decoration' in the 14*th* and 15*th* c. The relative normalized frequencies have been given in brackets [RNFs / 10,000 words]

verb:	14*th* c.	15*th* c.
anoint	6 [2]	0
colour	91 [31.4]	174 [17.4]
endore	4 [1.4]	41 [4.1]
flourish	11 [3.8]	23 [2.3]
flour	6 [2]	2 [0.2]
gild	3 [1]	5 [0.5]
paint	1 [0.3]	2 [0.2]
powder$_2$	1 [0.3]	12 [1.2]
silver	2 [0.7]	0
spring	2 [0.7]	0
stray (about)	12 [4.1]	0
straw	25 [8.6]	81 [8.2]

Often the same dish, in order to be more attractive, contained various colours, or the cook was given the choice as to which colour to use within the same recipe, e.g., (46). Various colours were obtained with the use of herbs and spices, such as alkanet (= red), saffron (= yellow), sanders (= red), parsley (= green), etc. Additionally, the colour gold was obtained with the use of foil, black with blood, and other colours might have been acquired by the use of various flowers. The most frequent verb which referred to the process of colouring food was *colour*, with 91 records [RNF: 31.4] in the 14*th* c. and 174 [RNF: 17.4] in the 15*th* c. It was derived from Anglo-Norman and Middle French *colorer, coulourer, coulorer* 'to be coloured'. It was the most general verb denoting colouring and could have been used with various colourants. Table 6 shows the number of occurrences of particular colourants used with the verb *colour*.

(46) Yf thu wilt, thu may draw some therof with the same broth & with a perty of wyne without mylke, coloured as bryght as lambur with saffron. (…) Or thu may turne hit anothir colour: yf thu wilt have a grene colour, draw hit with mylke of almondes & grynde indebaudeas into a morter, & safron therwith; or els put safron when hit ys growndyn, muche of lytyll, after thu wylt make thi colour, & colour hit therwith when thu takyst hit from the fyre, (…), or thu

may put theryn a grete quantyte of canell & of gynger & of sawndres to make hit brown, (...) Or, yf thu wilt, thu may take turnsole & wesch hit & wryng hit well in wyn that thu sesonyste hit up with; and when hit ys boylyd, coloure hit up with blou or sangueyn, whether thu wilt (...)

(OP_89)

Table 6: The number of occurrences of the particular colourants following the verb colour. Relative normalized frequencies have been given in brackets [RNFs / 10,000 words]

colourant:	14th c.	15th c.
alkanet	6 [2]	11 [1.1]
blood	6 [2]	3 [0.3]
cannel	2 [0.7]	2 [0.2]
parsley	0	2 [0.2]
saffron	52 [17.9]	115 [11.6]
sanders	11 [3.8]	30 [3]
turnsole	0	4 [0.4]
other	11 [3.8]	12 [1.2]
ø	8 [2.8]	9 [0.9]

Another verb which referred to colouring a dish was the verb *paint*. This verb, of Latin origin, but derived from Anglo-Norman *peindre, paindre, peinter* and Old French *peindre* 'to decorate with coloured motifs; to represent with lines and colour; to depict in words', can be found in English from the 13th c. However, the verb was extremely rare in the analyzed corpus, with single occurrences in both centuries. In the 14th c. it referred to colouring a dish so that it is of two colours, whilst in the 15th c. it was synonymous with the verb *silver*.

Sporadically, a number of more specific verbs referred to colouring a dish with a particular colour, e.g., *gild* (with a golden colour), *silver, endore* or *anoint*. The first represents Old English *gyldan* and denotes 'to cover entirely or partially with a thin layer of gold, either laid on in the form of gold-leaf or applied by other processes' (*OED*: s.v. *gild*, v.[1]). It was found only 3 times [RNF: 1] in the 14th c. and 5 [RNF: 0.5] in the 15th c. *Silver*, also of Germanic origin[72], was found only twice in the 14th c. [RNF: 0.7], with *the* sense 'to cover or plate with silver; to coat with silver-leaf' (*OED*: s.v. *silver*, v.). A similar effect to gilding could have been

---

72 For a discussion on the etymology of *silver* see Boutkan and Kossmann (2001).

achieved by 'endoring' food; however, it could have also referred to the application of a different colour than gold (see Hieatt and Butler 1985: 185). The verb *endore*, from Old French *endorer* 'to gild', was used from the end of the 14th c. until the late 17th c. with the sense 'to cover with a yellow glaze of yolk of egg, saffron, etc.' (*OED*: s.v. *endore*, v.). Due to its late appearance in English, only 4 records [RNF: 1.4] were found in the 14th c. Two of them referred to endoring with the yolk of eggs, while the other two recipes do not specify the ingredient used for colouring. In the 15th c. *endore* was slightly more frequent with 41 records in the analyzed material [RNF: 4.1]. Additionally, in the later period 3 occurrences of the nominal form 'endoring' was found, which supports the statement that the term became better adapted into English. Finally, one more verb might have been used with reference to the change of colour of food, i.e., *anoint*. It was derived from the adjective *anoint*, which in turn stems from OF *enoint* (Lat. *inunctum*), used from the 14th c. It referred to the action of moistening or rubbing a surface with oil or grease, but the 14th c. recipes reveal also another sense of *anoint*, i.e., 'to moisten a surface with a substance'. Apart from oil (almond oil or sweetmeat oil), e.g., (47), food could have been anointed with the glaze of an egg, or with various mixtures with the addition of the glaze of eggs, e.g., (48). We have found the verb only in the 14th c. material, with only 6 records [RNF: 2]. However, taking into account that it had only just entered English, the small number of occurrences should not be surprising.

(47) **Anoynte** it wyth swetemete oyle as thyne as it may be anointed and (...)
(GK_14)

(48) (...) **noynte** þem wyth gleyre of egge and gilde þem or siluer þem, (...), take ynde wawdeas ii penywey3te, ii penyweyte of saffron, þe water of þe gleyr of ii egges, and stampe all wele togeder and **anoynte** it wyth all.
(GK_15)

Apart from colouring, decoration of food was also possible by flourishing the dish or the plate with various motifs, flowers, powders, etc. scattered on the surface of the dish or over the plate as a whole. For these actions such verbs were used as *flourish, flour, powder, spring, stray,* and *straw*. For the number of records of the particular verbs see Table 5 above.

Flourish, particularly with reference to cookery, meant 'to ornament or garnish (a dish)' and was used from the late 14th c. until the 16th c. (*OED*: s.v. *flourish*, v. II.5.b). The verb was derived from OF *florir* (Latin *flōrēre*). It was infrequent in the analyzed material, with 11 records [RNF: 3.8] in the 14th c. and only 23 [RNF: 2.3] in the 15th c.

Flour, with the culinary reference denoted 'to sprinkle with flour; to powder', and according to the *OED* (s.v. *flour*, v.), was used in English from the 2nd half of the 17th c. However, the verb occurs in the analyzed corpus already in the 14th c., with 6 records [RNF: 2] found in the database, e.g., (49). In the 15th c. material only two occurrences of *flour* as a verb were found.

(49) lay the sewe onoward, **flour** it with powdour douce, and serue it forth.
(FC_42)

Sporadically, the Germanic verb *spring* was used with the sense 'to sprinkle'. It was found only twice in the 14th c.

The verb *powder*, which has been already discussed in section 3.3.1.8 with reference to (i) 'the reduction to powder' (= *powder₁*), might have been also used with the senses (ii) 'to sprinkle or treat with powder, or something in the state of powder' and (iii) 'to sprinkle (food) with a powdery condiment; to season, spice' (= *powder₂*). The latter sense (iii) became obsolete in the middle of the 15th c. (*OED*: s.v. *powder* v.¹ I.2.a). *Powder₂* was found only once [RNF: 0.3] in the 14th c. and 12 times [RNF: 1.2] in the 15th c.

The most frequent verb, which referred to the action of sprinkling powders or scattering flowers or leaves, was *straw*. Following the *OED*, the verb represents a dialectal form of OE *streowian* (PDE *strew*). It was found 25 times [RNF: 8.6] in the 14th c. and 81 [RNF: 8.2] in the 15th c. According to the *EDD*, *straw*, denoting 'to strew, spread' has been used in the dialects of Scotland, Northumberland, Durham and Yorkshire (s.v. *straw*, v.²). Another synonymous verb was found in the 14th c. material, i.e., *stray*, from OE *strégan*. It was found 12 times [RNF: 4.1] in the 14th c. The verb has been restricted to dialectal use. The *EDD* finds it in the dialect of Cheshire (s.v. *stray* v.).

Summing up, on the one hand, the action of colouring food was expressed with the most general verb, i.e., *colour*. The general verb might have been preferred over the specific ones in order not to impose any particular colour upon the cook, who was usually given the choice concerning the particular colours of the dish. On the other hand, the process of scattering food was usually expressed with the Germanic term *straw*. This could be accounted for by the fact that scattering spices was perceived as a much more basic procedure than colouring the food.

5.7 Verbs of taking

This group of verbs is the most numerous in terms of tokens found in the corpus, but the least numerous in terms of types – only three verbs with the sense 'to take' were found in the analyzed material. There are hardly any recipes which would not contain the verb *take₁* or one of its synonyms, i.e., *nym* or *recipe*. Table 7 shows the number of occurrences of the three verbs in the analyzed corpus.

Table 7:   The number of occurrences of take₁ *and its synonyms in the analyzed material. Normalized relative frequencies have been given in brackets [RNFs / 10,000 words]*

verb:	14th c.	15th c.
nym	112 [38.6]	67 [6.7]
recipe	0	90 [9]
take₁	610 [210]	2356 [237.3]

The high frequency of the *take*-verbs can be accounted for by the nature of the recipe, which is a set of instructions informing the reader what ingredients to incorporate into the dish. The most popular of the verbs, *take*, was borrowed from Old Norse in the late Old English period, initially meaning 'to put the hand on, to touch'. "(…) the sense passed to 'lay hold upon, lay hold of, grip, grasp, seize' (…) By the subordination of the notion of the instruments, and even of the physical action, to that of the result, *take* becomes in its essence 'to transfer to oneself by one's own action or volition'" (*OED*: s.v. *take*, v.). This became its regular sense in English in the 12th c.

Its synonym, *nym* (cognate with Old Frisian *nima, nema*; Old High German *neman*; or early Scandinavian *nam*, Old Icelandic *nema*), corresponded to a variety of senses of *take* (see Rynell 1948: 41–44). The major senses of *nym* were 'to take, pick up; take up, take out; grab, grasp, seize' (*MED*: s.v. *nimen*, v.). The earlier studies of the rivalry between the two verbs (e.g., Wełna 2005, Rynell 1948) show that in the Middle English period the use of *take* and *nym* was geographically dependant, e.g., in the West Midland dialect *take* began to dominate over *nym* in the 2nd half of the 14th c.; *nym* disappeared from the North East Midland dialects already at the beginning of the 13th c. but still prevailed in Norfolk in the middle of the 13th c.

In the culinary material *take₁* definitely prevails, with 610 occurrences [RNF: 210] in the 14th c. and 2356 [RNF: 237.3] in the 15th c. Sometimes the verb is followed by a particle which specifies the direction of the action, e.g., *off/out, down, up*.

Nym was found 112 times [RNF: 38.6] in the 14th c. and 67 times [RNF: 6.7] a century later. We can see a significant drop in the frequency of the verb, which proves its increasing disappearance from the language. What is significant is that only a few recipes contain both verbs (*take₁* and *nym*), e.g., (50)–(52). The examples come respectively from the beginning of the 14th c., the end of the 14th c. and the 15th c. The majority of the 14th c. records of *nym* were found in two of the analyzed collections: *Diuersa cibaria* (DC) and *Diuersa servicia* (DS). Additionally, three records of *nym* were found in the *Forme of Cury* and two in the *Gathering of Medieval English recipes* (both from the end of the 14th c.). The DC originates in Herefordshire, whilst the provenance of the DS has not been established (*LALME, MED*). The former collection can be characterized by the use of *nym* (with the exception of only 2 records of *take$_1$*). The latter contains a mixture of forms, i.e., 92 records of *take$_1$* and 57 of *nym*. It should be noted that out of 92 recipes included in the DS collection, only four contain both verbs. 14 recipes contain neither of the verbs. The rest call either for *nym* or *take$_1$*. This suggests that the DS is a collection of recipes of different provenance / dialects. Fig. 7 illustrates the number of recipes from the 14th c. which contain the particular verbs.

Additionally, the few records of *nym* found in the FC and GR (3 and 2 respectively) also cannot be assigned dialectally to any area. However, the ratio of occurrence of *nym* comparing to *take* in the two collections suggests that these collections were composed in an area where, at the end of the 14th c., *nym* was used sporadically (thus, following Wełna (2005) or Rynell (1948), these could be the West Midland or Northern dialects).

In the 15th c. material, *nym* was found exclusively in the collections edited by Austin, some of which (Aus_Laud) originate in Herefordshire; unfortunately the provenance of most of the recipes could not be established. It seems that only in the Aus_Laud collection did the choice of a particular verb play a role, i.e., the recipes called either for *nym* or *take$_1$* (see Fig. 8). In the other recipes of Austin's collections, the verbs seem to have been used interchangeably and the number of their occurrences proves the dominance of *take$_1$*.

(50) **Nym** plaumen & do out þe stones, & soþþen boill am in watre. Soþþen drauh out of þe crouhhe & wel istured; seoþþen **tak** vers seym, peopur, kanel, (…)

(DC_49)

(51) **Tak** clene whete & braye yt wel in a morter tyl þe holes gon of; seþe it til it breste in water. **Nym** it **vp** & lat it cole. **Tak** good broþ & swete milk of kyn or of almand & tempere it þerwith. **Nym** 3elkys of eyren rawe (…)

(FC_1)

(52) **Take** þe Whyte of the lekys, an seþe hem in a potte, an presse hem vp, & hacke hem smal on a bord. An **nym** gode Almaunde Mylke, (…) þanne **take** powderd Elys,

(PD_45)

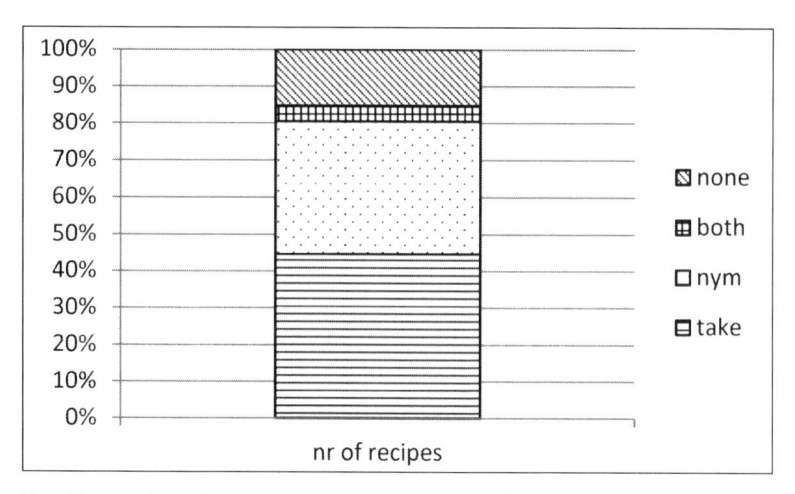

Fig. 7: *The number of recipes in the DS collection (14th c.) containing the particular verbs*

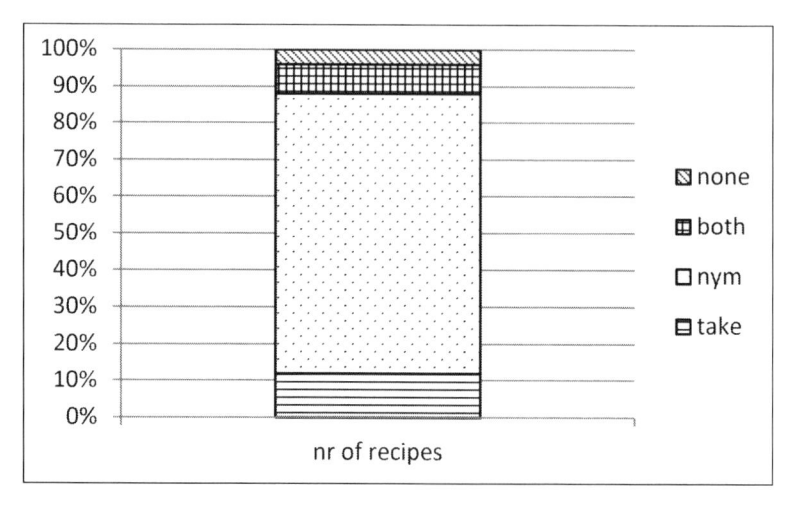

Fig. 8: *The number of recipes in the Aus_Laud collection (15th c.) containing the particular verbs*

In the 15th c. material, the verb *recipe* has also been found. It originates from classical Latin *recipe* 'receive' (*OED*: s.v. *recipe*, v.). The verb was used in the imperative, usually at the beginning of a medical prescription, with the sense 'to take (an ingredient)'. The *OED* records it from 1300 until 1678 (when it became obsolete). The analyzed material has not revealed any occurrences of the verb in the 14th c. It was found 90 times [RNF: 9] in the 15th c. Most of its records were found in one collection, i.e., Ht_Hrl (90% of records). Following *LALME*, the collection comes from Lincolnshire. All of the occurrences of *recipe* were found in recipe-initial position, immediately after the heading. This suggest that *recipe* had a very restricted use, and could have been replaced by any of its synonyms, which had a much broader use. Fig. 9 shows the number of records of *take*-verbs used as imperative in a recipe-initial position.

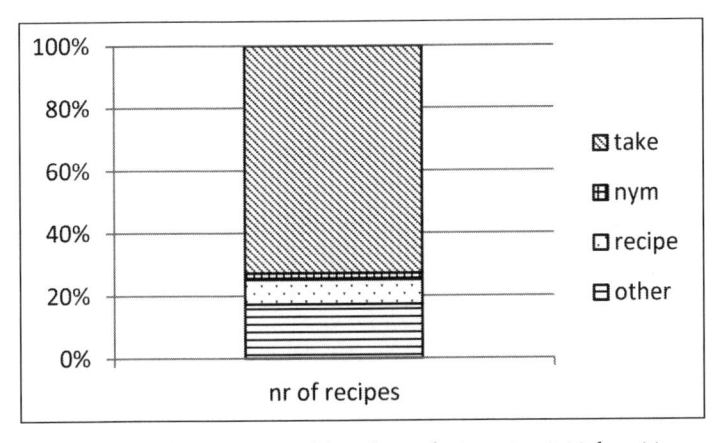

Fig. 9:   *The number of occurrences of the* take-*verbs in recipe-initial position*

Summing up, the use of *nym* and *take$_1$* was definitely geographically determined. The 14th c. distribution of the two verbs in the culinary corpus partly contradicts Wełna's results (2005). According to his analysis, in the West Midland dialect *take* was much more frequent already in the 1st half of the 14th c. (see Wełna 2005: 60–62), whilst the culinary material from Herefordshire, i.e., the DC, (from 1325) shows 96% records of *nym* over *take$_1$*. Unfortunately, this is the only manuscript which can be assigned provenance. The other 14th c. occurrences of *nym* cannot be discussed geographically. However, they all come from the end of the century. In the DS (from 1381) the dominance of *take$_1$* can be observed – *nym* constitutes only 35%. However, due to the fact that the two verbs do not occur in the same recipes (with the exception of 4 recipes), we may assume that the collection contains recipes from at least two different dialectal areas. What is interesting, is the comparison of the use of *take$_1$* and *nym* in the recipes from Herefordshire from the two analyzed centuries (see Fig. 7 and 8 above). Even though it is *take$_1$* that should have become more frequent with time, the two collections show an opposite trend, which suggests that the dominance of *take₁* was much later in this area than expected (cf. for instance Wełna 2005).

Finally, the verb *recipe*, which appeared in the 15th c. material, was restricted both geographically (90% of its occurrences were found in the collection from Lincolnshire) and contextually (it was found only as the imperative at the beginning of recipes, immediately after the heading), which was typical of the medieval medical recipes. This suggests that the author of the collection perceived the culinary recipe as being the same as the medical recipe (= prescription).

5.8 Verbs of serving

Four verbs referred to the action of serving food: *(a)dress, dish, mess* and *serve*. *Serve* stems from Old French *servir* (from Latin *servīre* 'to be a servant or slave, to serve'). It was present in English from the 13th c. However, according to the *OED*, the sense 'to set (meat or drink) on the table or before a person; to bring in or dish up (a meal)' was first recorded in 1400 (s.v. *serve*, v¹ IV.42.a). *Mess* was derived from the Anglo-Norman noun *mes* meaning 'portion of (cooked) food, dish, course' (*AND*: s.v. *mes²*). The verb, with the sense 'to serve up (food); to divide or measure out (ingredients or portions)', was used from the end of the 14th c. (*OED*: s.v. *mess*, v.). *Dress* is a borrowing of Old French *dresser* 'to arrange'. Its culinary reference 'to prepare for use as food, by making ready to cook, or by cooking; to season (esp. salad)' is found from the early 14th c. And finally, *dish* is a formation based on the Germanic noun *dish*. Following the *OED* (s.v. *dish*, v.¹), it denotes 'to put (food) into a dish, and set it ready for a meal'. In the analyzed corpus it seems to be extremely incidental, with only two records in the 14th c.

The verb *serve* was definitely the dominant verb in the database. It was found 176 times [RNF: 60.6] in the 14th c. and 835 [RNF: 84] in the 15th c. *(A)dress* was recorded 52 times [RNF: 17.9] in the 14th and 84 times [RNF: 8.5] in the 15th century, whilst *mess* occurred 69 times [RNF: 23.8] in the 14th c. and 24 [RNF: 2.4] in the later century (see Table 8). Neither of the verbs is typical of any of the analyzed collections, though they appeared in a wide range of recipes. Even though the three verbs seem to have been synonymous, certain differences in their use could be noticed. The majority of the records of *serve* and *mess* were followed by the particle *forth*, which was not the case with *(a)dress*, see Fig. 10. A closer look at the recipes shows that *(a)dress* was more often used with reference to the manner of serving food, for instance 'in dishes', 'in the manner of the partridge', etc., see (53) and not to the readiness of a dish to be served, as in (54). Sometimes different verbs were used in the same recipe, which proves there must have been some difference in their reference, e.g., (54).

Table 8: The number of occurrences of the 'serving verbs' in the analyzed material. Relative normalized frequencies have been given in brackets [RNFs / 10,000 words]

verb:	14th c.	15th c.
(a)dress	52 [17.9]	84 [8.5]
mess	69 [23.8]	24 [2.4]
serve	176 [60.6]	835 [4]

(53) (…) and **dresse** þe gees <u>in disshes</u> & lay þe sewe onoward.

(FC_32)

(54) & seþ reysouns in wyn & do þerto & after **dresse yt forth**.

(DS_81)

(55) (…) & wan it is sodyn **dresse** it <u>into dischis</u> & strew þeron powder & **serue it forth**.

(DS_76)

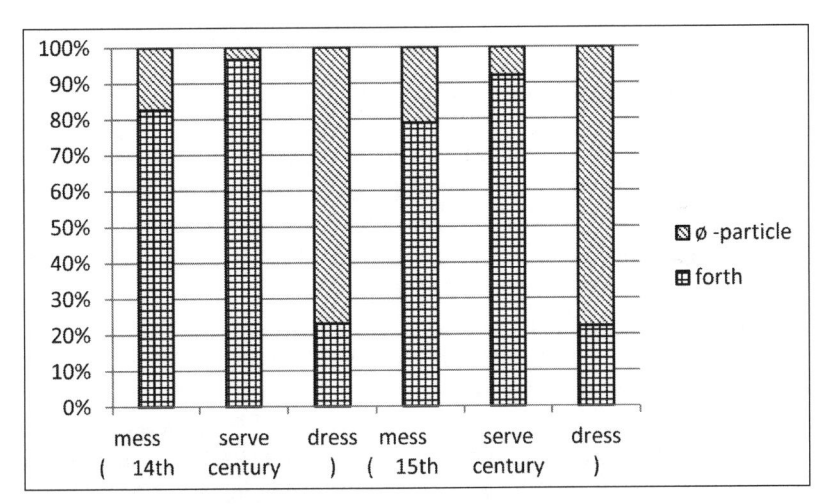

Fig. 10: The ratio of occurrence of the verbs followed or not by forth.

When it comes to the verbs *serve* and *mess*, in the majority of the recipes they must have been synonymous since they seem to have been used interchangeably, i.e.,

183

they occur in very similar recipes in exactly the same contexts. However, sporadically, the same recipe contains both *mess* and *serve*, e.g., (56)–(57). These records indicate a slight difference in the sense of the two verbs. Thus, *mess* referred to the way of serving a particular dish, e.g., with sauce/herbs/etc., whilst *serve* meant that a dish was ready to be taken to the table.

>(56) Cast þerto safroun, sugur, & salt, & **messe** it **forth** with colyaundre in confyt rede, & **serue** it **forth**.
>
>(FC_132)
>
>(57) (...) & tak hem vp & **messe** hem wyþ þe frutours & **serve** forþe.
>
>(DS_26)

The drop in the number of records of *mess* shows that it was becoming archaic. However, the verb has still been used dialectally. According to the *EDD* (s.v. *mess*, v.[1] 7), *mess* 'to serve up a dish; to divide food amongst a number of people' has been retained in the dialects of Lancashire and Cheshire.

The analyzed material shows that, even though the three verbs were synonymous, there were different shades of meaning: *(a)dress* referred to the way of serving (in particular dishes, etc.), whilst *mess* referred to the way of serving (with a particular dressing, sauce, etc.), and *serve* referred to the readiness of a dish to be taken to the table.

5.9 Miscellaneous verbs

This group comprises those verbs which refer to culinary procedures and which do not fit in with any of the groups discussed above. They should not be omitted from the study, thus they will be briefly presented in the present section.

A verb which, following the *OED*, could be categorized in a few of the sections included in the present chapter is *dight*. Following the dictionary (s.v. *dight*, v. 14b), *dight* in its culinary sense denoted 'to prepare, make ready (food, meal); to cook; to prepare or mix (a portion or medicine)'. This sense is stated to have been used from the beginning of the 14th c. until the 18th c. Thus, it could be as well categorized as a 'verb of cooking' or 'combining'. However, the records of the verb found in the analyzed corpus (it occurred 15 times [RNF: 1.5] in the 15th c.), suggest that it was used with the senses 'to serve' or 'to prepare'. The former was more sporadic than the latter (i.e., 4 records vs. 11).

A group of verbs which did not fit into any other included in the present chapter, are verbs which refer either to temperature (but do not qualify as 'verbs of cooking') or to the consistency of food. These are: *cool, dry, melt,* and *wet*. Table 9 shows their number of occurrences in the respective centuries. All of them are of Germanic origin, and all of them dropped in frequency in the 15th c., which could be explained by the fact that they referred to some of the most basic culinary procedures.

Table 9: The number of occurrences of the verbs in the analyzed material. Relative normalized frequencies have been given in brackets [RNFs / 10,000 words]

verb	14th c.	15th c.
cool	36 [12.4]	59 [5.9]
dry	16 [5.5]	31 [3.1]
melt	2 [0.7]	4 [0.4]
wet	12 [4.1]	32 [3.2]

Two synonyms referred to the insertion of bacon or other fat to a the dish before cooking it. These were: *enarm* and *lard*. Both were borrowed from French. However, *enarm* was found only in the 14th c. (6 records [RNF: 2]), and *lard* occurred 6 times [RNF: 2] in the 14th c. and 23 [RNF: 2.3] in the 15th c. It is believed that the former disappeared from the 15th c. corpus due to the fact that its culinary reference was peripheral, and since a synonym was at hand there was no need to adapt/restore the verb *enarm*.

Finally, the verb *baste* should be mentioned. Its origin is unknown. It was found in the 15th c. material, even though the *OED* states that the verb surfaced only in the 16th c. It referred to the action of moistening food "by the application of melted fat, gravy or other liquid, so as to keep it from burning" (*OED*: s.v. *baste*, v^2). The verb occurred 20 times [RNF: 2] in the 15th c. No synonyms of *baste* were found in either of the centuries.

5.10 Conclusions

The verbs of preparing constitute the most varied group of verbs. They can be further subdivided into more specific groups, i.e., verbs of cleaning, adding and combining, straining, seasoning, decoration, taking, and serving. The particular groups varied in terms of their representation, i.e., the number of types categorized to each of the groups. The most numerous were the verbs of adding and combining. This can be accounted for by the broad reference of the category, as opposed to, for instance, 'verbs of taking' or 'serving'.

The presented material has shown that the most basic instructions, such as adding ingredients, or washing them, were expressed by the native vocabulary. The borrowings of French origin were usually used with a more specific meaning, and mostly referred to the more sophisticated activities. In a number of cases, the general verbs were specified by the use of particles, or specifying phrases, which narrowed their meaning, e.g., *make through a cloth* vs. *strain*. This may seem odd if we think of the fact that the early recipes were very imprecise and lacked detailed information which may be crucial to the preparation of the dish, such as measures. Why then was the cook told which utensil to use for filtering food if at the same time he was not told how much of particular ingredients to add for certain dishes or at which temperature to cook them?

Conclusion

The present work aimed at the presentation of verbs found in the available culinary collections from the 14th and 15th centuries. Altogether, 431 and 1157 recipes from the respective centuries were analyzed. The verbs were divided into three major categories: the verbs of cutting, of cooking, and of preparing. Each of the three categories was further subdivided on the basis of some characteristics of the particular verbal group. Thus, the verbs of cutting were divided due to the outcome of the cutting procedure into dividing, reducing, removing, and penetrating verbs. The verbs of cooking were subdivided due to the medium in which the action took place into verbs of cooking in liquid, with fat and in no/any medium. And finally, the verbs of preparing were subdivided on the basis of the meaning of the verbs into: verbs of cleaning, adding and combining, straining, seasoning, decoration, taking and serving. Additionally, in the group of the 'verbs of preparing' we have included those verbs which refer to some culinary procedures but which do not fit in any of the above mentioned subgroups, which have been tagged as 'miscellaneous'.

The analysis covered 122 verbal types. Some of the verbs, due to their polysemous character, had to be categorized into more than one group. The greatest variety of verbs was found among the verbs of cutting, with 59 types. The most frequently used verbs (with the highest number of tokens) were verbs of taking (*take, nym*), verbs of cooking in liquid (*boil, seethe*), as well as verbs of adding and combining (*cast, temper*). Thus, these are verbs which referred to the most basic culinary instructions.

Two fundamental conclusions can be drawn from this work and applied generally to the culinary verbs in Middle English. First of all, despite the general belief that the French influence on the semantic field of food and cooking was enormous (see for instance, Baugh and Cable 2006, Bator 2011, or Miller 2012), in the culinary recipes of the 14th and 15th c. the Germanic verbs tend to be more frequent than those of French origin, see Fig. 1. This seems to be justified by the fact that the former were usually general and more basic in terms of their meaning, and thus could have been applied in a wider range of contexts. This leads to the second conclusion, i.e., that the verbs of French origin were usually very specific and referred to a very narrow context, which influenced their frequency in the analyzed recipes. The borrowings usually filled in lexical gaps, which earlier were occupied by phrases (i.e., general verbs, often polysemous, which were accompanied by specifying phrases). This can very well be seen in the group of the cutting verbs. The introduction of such verbs as *dice, slice, leach, quarter*, etc. replaced the phrases such as *cut in four, hew in slices*, etc. However, not all the verbs follow the division French = specific, Germanic = general. There are also cases, in which two verbs of different origins were synonymous and started to compete against each other. The most prominent example would be *seethe* and *boil*. As a result of this rivalry, the former became limited in denotation, which led to the creation of a certain hierarchy of the 'verbs of cooking in liquid'. Further research into the relation between *seethe* and *boil* would show that in the later period the former was restricted to a figurative meaning.

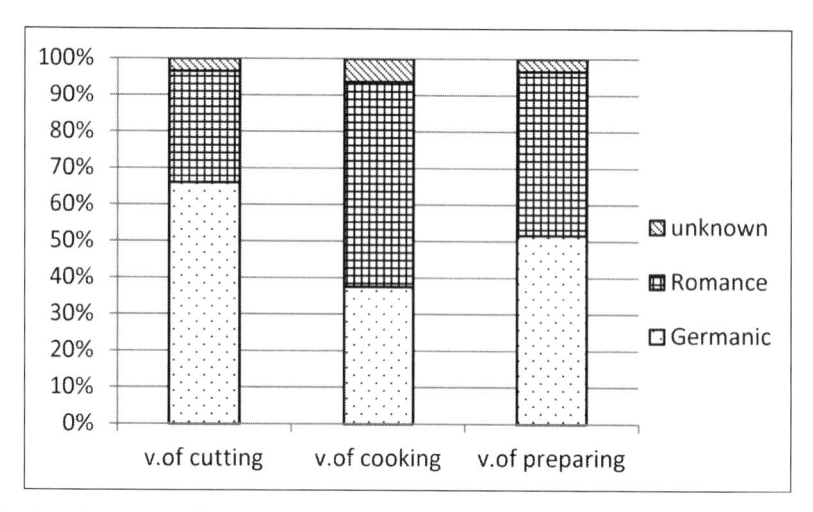

Fig. 1: *The ratio of the culinary verbs (types) of particular origin, as found in the analyzed material*

In the analytical process in this work some other minor conclusions have been reached. First, a number of verbs turn out to have been used earlier than stated in the available dictionaries, especially the *OED*, e.g., *toast, gobbon, skin*, etc. Second, a significant number of the analyzed verbs were formed from the related nouns on the basis of conversion, e.g., *hull, shell, leach*, etc.

Additionally, a number of conclusions can be drawn specifically with relation to the particular groups of culinary verbs. And thus, the cutting verbs, which were especially numerous in terms of the types, comprise a number of rather infrequent verbs (in terms of the tokens). The infrequent ones are mostly items of specific meaning and of French etymology. The French items had been recently introduced and filled in the lexical gaps, earlier expressed with the use of phrases (i.e., a general verb + a specifying phrase), e.g., *carve in half, hew in leaches*, etc. The limited frequency of the specific verbs can also be justified by the fact that some of these verbs referred to a particular foodstuff, hence their use depended on the popularity of the particular foods, e.g., *grate* referred to reducing bread to crumbs. Moreover, a certain rivalry took place between the general verbs of cutting. The dividing verbs *carve, hew* and *hack*, which were the regular general terms for cutting in the Old English and early Middle English periods, lost frequency in favour of *cut* and *chop*, both of which surfaced in the early Middle English period and both being of dubious etymology[73]. This shows that the French origin of the verbs was not the necessary factor for the popularity of particular verbs. Additionally, certain semantic areas seem to have been extremely reluctant to accept verbs of French origin. For instance, the group of the removing verbs consists of 21 types, only three of which were borrowed from French. This suggests that certain activities were more appropriate to be referred to with borrowed vocabulary than others. It should be noted that the three verbs of French etymology, belonging to this group, are extremely specific in meaning, e.g., *blanch* refers exclusively to almonds, *scale* to fish, etc. Similarly, the penetrating verbs were all of Germanic origin.

Unlike the verbs of cutting, the verbs of cooking were limited in terms of types but most of them had a high number of tokens found in the analyzed material. Moreover, the French element was definitely dominant and outnumbered the verbs of Germanic origin, e.g., within the group of verbs of cooking in liquid there are 4 borrowings and 3 native items (the latter being extremely rare), the group of verbs of cooking with fat contains only one verb of Germanic origin (i.e., *bake*). A certain rivalry can be observed within both these groups of verbs. In the former, the verbs *boil* and *seethe*, which used to be synonyms, seem to have competed, and as a result, *seethe* was pushed to narrow its meaning and become closer to *parboil* than *boil*. In the latter group, the verbs *fry*, *bake* and *roast* seem to have competed to a certain extent; however, in this case their distribution depended on the product (e.g., *roast* was applied to meat and fish, *bake* to pastry and *fry* was used with both), and on the way of exposure to heat (e.g., roasting took place on a roast-iron or griddle, frying in a pan, and baking in the oven).

The present author hopes that the void in scholarship concerning the linguistic analysis of the early culinary material has, at least partially, been reduced.

---

73   *Cut* has been suggested to be of Scandinavian origin (e.g., *ODEE*).

Nevertheless, much more work needs to be conducted on the culinary language of the period. Not only when it comes to the analysis of the language of the available recipes but also in terms of editing. As Hieatt noted (2008), there is still a lot of culinary evidence to be explored, she mentions about 2000 recipes which have not even been edited, and there are still more being found in various manuscripts. Moreover, a comparative study of the culinary and the medical recipes also awaits a thorough investigation.

References

Primary Sources

1970   *A collection of ordinances and regulations for the government of the Royal household, made in divers reigns. From King Edward III. to King William and Queen Mary. Also receipts in ancient cookery.* London: the Society of Antiquaries by John Nichols. ECCO Print Editions.

Anderson, J.L.
1962   *A fifteenth century cookry boke.* New York: Scribner.

Austin, T. (ed.)
2000   *Two 15th-c. cookery books.* Oxford: Oxford University Press.

Furnivall, Frederick James (ed.)
1931   *Early English meals and manners: John Russels 'Boke of Nurture',*
[1868]   *Wynkyn de Worde's Boke of keruynge, The boke of curtasye, R. Weste's Booke of demeanor, Seager's Schoole of vertue, The babees book, Aristotle's A B C, Urbanitatis, Stans puer ad mensam, The lytille childrenes lytil boke, for to serve a lord, Old Symon, The birched schoolboy, &c. &c.: with some forewords on education in early England.* London: Oxford University Press. (Early English Text Society).

Hieatt, Constance B.
1996   "The Middle English culinary recipes in MS Harley 5401. An edition and commentary", *Medium Aevum* 65.1: 54–71.
2004   "The third 15th-century cookery book: A newly identified group within a family", *Medium Aevum* 73.1: 27–42.

Hieatt, Constance B. (ed.)
1988a   *Ordinance of pottage: An edition of the 15th c. culinary recipes in Yale University's MS Beinecke 163.* London: Prospect Books.
2008   *A gathering of Medieval English recipes.* (Textes Vernaculaires du Moyen Age 5). Turnhout: Brepols.

Hieatt, Constance B. – Sharon Butler (eds.)
1985   *Curye on Inglysch: English culinary manuscripts of the 14th c.* (Early English Text Society, SS 8). London: Oxford University Press.

Hieatt, Constance B. – Robin F. Jones
   1986   "Two Anglo-Norman culinary collections edited from British Library manuscripts Additional 32085 and Royal 12.C.xii", *Speculum* 61: 859–882.
Meyer, Paul
   1893   "Notice sur le MS. Old Roy. 12.C.XII du Musée britannique", *Bulletin de la Société des anciens texts français* 19: 38–56.
Morris, Richard
   1862   *Liber cure cocorum*. Berlin: A. Asher & Co. Available at: http://www.pbm.com/~lindahl/lcc/parallel.html. (date of access: November 2010).
Napier, Alexander (ed.)
   1882   *A noble boke off cookry*. London: Elliot Stock.
Pegge, Samuel (ed.)
   1780   *The forme of cury. A roll of Ancient English cookery*. London: J. Nichols.
Pynson, Richard
   1500   *A noble boke of festes ryalle and cokery*. London: No indication of the publisher.
Warner, Richard
   1791   *Antiquitates culinariae or curious tracts relating to the culinary affairs of the Old English*. London: R. Blamire Stranc.
Worde de, Wynken
   1508   *The boke of keruynge*. [Reproduction of the original in the Cambridge University Library]. (Early Social Customs). Anon.

Secondary Sources

Abram, Annie
   1913   *English life and manners in the later Middle Ages*. London: George Routledge & Sons.
Adamson, Melitta Weiss
   2004   *Food in Medieval times*. London: Greenwood Press.
Adamson, Melitta Weiss (ed.)
   2002   *Regional cuisines of Medieval Europe. A book of essays*. New York; London: Routledge.

Albarella, Umberto
2006 "Pig husbandry and pork consumption in Medieval England", in: Woolgar, C.M. et al. (eds.), 72–87.

Ammon, Ulrich – Harald Haarmann (eds.)
2008 *Wieser Enzyklopädie. Sprachen des europäischen Westens.* Vol. 1. Klagenfurt: Wieser Verlag.

Anglo-Norman dictionary (AND)
Online Available at: www.anglo-norman.net (date of access: June 2012–February 2014).

Banham, Debby – Laura Mason
2002 "Confectionary recipes from a fifteenth-century manuscript", *Petits Propos Culinarires* 69: 45–69.

Bator, Magdalena
2011 "French culinary vocabulary in the 14th c. English", in: Fisiak, J. – M. Bator (eds.), 287–301.
2013a "Verbs of cooking in Middle English: *Fry, roast* and *bake*", in: Fisiak, Jacek – Magdalena Bator (eds.), 125–138.
2013b "Sugar and spice and all things nice – an analysis of the culinary vocabulary in Middle English", *Kwartalnik Neofilologiczny* LX, 4/2013: 425–438.
2013c "*Boil* vs. *seethe* in Middle English", *Medieval English Mirror* 9: 27–40.

Bauer, Renate – Ulrike Krischke (eds.)
2011 *More than words: English lexicography and lexicology past and present. Essays presented to Hans Sauer on the occasion of his 65th birthday.* 2 Parts. (Münchener Universitätsschriften 36). Frankfurt a/M.: Peter Lang Verlag.

Baugh, Albert C. – Thomas Cable
2006 *A history of the English language.* (5th edition). London: Routledge.
[1951]

Beck, Simone – Louisette Bertholle – Julia Child
1961 *Mastering the art of French cooking.* Oxford: Penguin Books.

Biber, Douglas – Ulla Connor – Thomas A. Upton
2007 *Discourse on the move. Using corpus analysis to describe discourse structure.* (Studies in Corpus Linguistics 28). Amsterdam: John Benjamins Publishing Company.

Biber, Douglas – Edward Finegan (eds.)
1994   *Sociolinguistic perspectives on register.* Oxford: Oxford University Press.

Bickerdyke, John
1889   *The curiosities of ale and beer: An entertaining history.* London: Swan Sonnenschein & Co.

Black, Maggie
1981   "Health food heritage", *History Today* 31.7: 54–55 (July 1981).

Bosworth, Joseph – T. Northcote Toller (eds.)
Online   *An Anglo-Saxon dictionary.* (*ASD*). Available at: http://bosworth.ff.cuni.cz/ (date of access: June 2012 – February 2014).

Boutkan, Dirk – Maarten Kossmann
2001   "On the etymology of *silver*", *NOWELE* 38: 3–15.

Brears, Peter
2008   *Cooking and dining in Medieval England.* Wiltshire: Prospect Books.

Brown, Duncan
2002   *Pottery in Medieval Southampton c.1066–1510.* (Research Report 133). York: CBA.

Brown, Gillian – George Yule
1983   *Discourse analysis.* Cambridge: Cambridge University Press.

Campbell, Bruce M.S.
2000   *English seigniorial agriculture, 1250–1450.* (Cambridge Studies in Historical Geography). Cambridge: Cambridge University Press.

Carlin, Martha
2008   "*What say you to a piece of beef and mustard?*: The evolution of public dining in Medieval and Tudor London", *Huntington Library Quarterly* 71.1: 199–217.

Carlin, Martha – Joel T. Rosenthal (eds.)
1998   *Food and eating in Medieval Europe.* London: Hambledon Press.

Carroll, Ruth
1997   *Verbs of cooking in fourteenth-century English. A semantic class and its syntactic behaviour.* [Ph.D. dissertation]. Oxford: University of Oxford.
1999   "The Middle English recipe as a text-type", *Neuphilologische Mitteilungen* 100: 27–42.

2004 "Middle English recipes: Vernacularisation of a text-type", in: Taavitsainen, I. – P. Pähta (eds.), 174–196.

Clark, Priscilla P.
1975 "Thoughts for food, I: French cuisine and French culture", *The French Review* 49.1: 32–41.

Cortonesi, Alfio
1999 "Self-sufficiency and the market. Rural and urban diet in the Middle Ages", in: Flandrin, Jean-Louis – M. Montanari (eds.), 268–274.

Culy, Christopher
1996 "Null objects in English recipes", *Language Variation and Change* 8.1: 91–124.

Darby, Henry Clifford
1936 *An historical geography of England before A.D. 1800.* Cambridge: Cambridge University Press.

Davidson, Alan
2006 *The Oxford companion to food.* Oxford: Oxford University Press.
[1999]

Dendle, Peter – Alain Touwaide (eds.)
2008 *Health and healing from the medieval garden.* Woodbridge: The Boydell Press.

Durkin, Philip
2012 "Etymological research on English words as a source of information about Anglo-French", in: Trotter, David (ed.), 101–107.

Dyer, Christorpher C.
1988 "Changes in diet in the Late Middle Ages: The case of harvest workers", *The Agricultural Historical Review* 36: 21–37.
1998 *Standards of living in the Later Middle Ages: Social change in England c. 1200–1520.* (2nd ed.). Cambridge: Cambridge University Press.
2006 "Gardens and garden produce in the Later Middle Ages", in: Woolgar, C.M. et al. (eds.), 27–40.

Ferguson, Charles A.
1994 "Dialect, register, and genre: Working assumptions about conventionalization", in: Biber, D. – E. Finegan (eds.), 15–29.

Fisiak, Jacek – Magdalena Bator (eds.)
2011 *Foreign influences on Medieval English.* (Studies in English Language and Literature 28). Frankfurt a/M., New York: Peter Lang Verlag.

2013 *Historical English Word-Formation and semantics.* (Warsaw Studies in English Language and Literature 15). Frankfurt a/M., New York: Peter Lang Verlag.

Flandrin, Jean-Louis
1999 "Seasoning, cooking, and dietetics in the Late Middle Ages", in: Flandrin, Jean-Louis – M. Montanari (eds.), 311–327.

Flandrin, Jean-Louis – Massimo Montanari (eds.)
1999 *A culinary history: Food.* New York: Columbia University Press.
[1996] [translated by Albert Sonnenfeld].

Fox, H.S.A.
1991 "Farming practice and techniques: Devon and Cornwall", in: Miller, E. (ed.), 303–323.

Frantzen, Allen J.
2011 "Food words in the Anglo-Saxon penitentials", in: Bauer, Renate – Ulrike Krischke (eds.), 83–99.

Freedman, Paul
2007 "Some basic aspects of Medieval cuisine", *Annales Universitatis Apulensis, Series Historica* 11.1: 44–60.

Görlach, Manfred
1992 "Text-types and language history: The cookery recipe", in: Rissanen, M. – O. Ihalainen – T. Nevalainen – I. Taavitsainen (eds.), 736–761.
2004 *Text types and the history of English.* Berlin, New York: Mouton de Gruyter.

Grig, Gwynhwyvaer
Online "Common herbs in Roman cooking according to Apicius", available at: www.housedragonor.org/A&S/herbs-gwen.html (date of access: May 2013).

Haan de, Ferdinand
2010 "Building a semantic map: Top-down versus bottom-up approaches", *Linguistic Discovery* 8.1: 102–117.

Hagen, Ann
1994 *A handbook of Anglo-Saxon food and drink: Processing and*
[1992] *consumption.* Pinner, Middlesex: Anglo-Saxon Books.
1995 *A second handbook of Anglo-Saxon food and drink: Production and distribution.* Hockwold-cum-Wilton, Norfolk: Anglo-Saxon Books.
2010 *Anglo-Saxon food and drink. Production, processing, distribution*

[2006]   *and consumption.* Hockwold-cum-Wilton, Norfolk: Anglo-Saxon Books.

Hammond, Peter
2005 *Food and feast in Medieval England.* Thrupp: Sutton Publishing.
[1993]

Harvey, Barbara F.
1993 *Living and dying in England, 1100–1540.* Oxford: Clarendon Press.

Henisch, Bridget Ann
2009 *The Medieval cook.* Woodbridge: The Boydell Press.

Hieatt, Constance B.
1988b "Further notes on the *Forme of Cury* et al.: Additions and corrections", *Bulletin of the John Rylands University Library of Manchester* 70: 45–52.
1998 "Making sense of Medieval culinary records: Much done, but much more to do", in: Carlin, Martha – Joel T. Rosenthal (eds.), 101–116.
2002 "Medieval Britain", in: Adamson, Melitta Weiss (ed.), 19–45.
2006 *Concordance of English recipes. Thirteenth to fifteenth centuries.* Tempe, Arizona: MRTS.

Hoad, T.F.
1993 *The concise Oxford dictionary of English etymology.* (*ODEE*). Oxford: Oxford University Press.

Horsey, Richard
1998 *Null arguments in English registers. A minimalist account.* Bundoora, Victoria, Australia: La Trobe University. Available at: http://cogprints.org/1538/3/thesis_master_%28with_trees%29.pdf (date of access: January 2013).

Jespersen, Otto
1912 *Growth and development of the English language.* Oxford: Basil Blackwell.

Johansen, T.K.
2007 *Aristotle on the sense-organs.* Cambridge: Cambridge University
[1997] Press.

Knowles, Gerry
1997 *A cultural history of the English language.* London: Arnold.

Kornexl, Lucia – Ursula Lenker
2011 "Culinary and other pairs: Lexical borrowing and conceptual differentiation in Early English food terminology", in: Bauer, Renate – Ulrike Krischke (eds.), 179–206.

Laurioux, Bruno
1985 "Spices in the medieval diet: A new approach", *Food and Foodways* 1: 43–76.
1999 "Medieval cooking", in: Flandrin, Jean-Louis – Massimo Montanari (et al.) (eds.), 295–301.

Leach, Edmund
1972 "Claude Levi-Strauss. Oysters, smoked salmon, and stilton cheese", available at: http://www.colorado.edu/envd/courses/envd4114-001/Fall07/ENVD%204310/Levi-Strauss.pdf (date of access: December 2011).

Leaf, Murray
1971 "Baking and roasting: A compact demonstration of a cultural code", *American Anthropologist* 73.1: 267–268.

Lee, Christina
2007 *Feasting the dead. Food and drink in Anglo-Saxon burial rituals.* Woodbridge: The Boydell Press.

Lehrer, Adrienne
1969 "Semantic cuisine", *Journal of Linguistics* 5: 39–55.
2007 "Can wines be brawny? Reflections on wine vocabulary", in: Smith, Barry C., 127–139.

Levin, Beth
1993 *English verb classes and alternations: A preliminary investigation.* Chicago: University of Chicago Press.

Lloyd, T.H.
1977 *The English wool trade in the Middle Ages.* Cambridge: Cambridge University Press.

Lutz, Angelika
2013 "Language contact and prestige", *Anglia* 131.4: 562–590.

Mäkinen, Martti
2004 "Herbal recipes and recipes in herbals – intertextuality in early English medical writing", in: Taavitsainen, I. – P. Pahta (eds.), 144–173.

Martilla, Ville
2009 "Mincing words: A diachronic view on English cutting verbs", in: McConchie, R.W. – A. Honkapohja – Jukka Tyrkkö (ed.), 104–122. Also available at: http://www.lingref.com/cpp/hel-lex/2008/paper21 71.pdf (date of access: 10.12.2010).

Massam, Diane
1992 "Null objects and non-thematic subjects", *Journal of linguistics* 28.1: 115–137.

Massam, Diane – Yves Roberge
1989 "Recipe context null objects in English", *Linguistic Inquiry* 20.1: 134–139.

McConchie, R.W. – Alpo Honkapohja – Jukka Tyrkkö (eds.)
2009 *Selected proceedings of the 2008 Symposium on New Approaches in English Historical Lexis (HEL-LEX 2)*. Somerville, MA: Cascadilla Proceedings Project.

McIntosh, Angus – M. L. Samuels – M. Benskin (eds.)
1989 *A linguistic atlas of Late Medieval English. (LALME)*. Aberdeen: Aberdeen University Press.

Mennel, Stephen
1996 *All manners of food: Eating and taste in England and France from*
[1985] *the Middle Ages to the present.* (2nd edition). Urbana; Chicago: University of Illinois Press.

Mettig, Robert
1910 *Die französischen Elemente im Alt- und Mittelenglischen.* Marburg: Lahn.

Middle English dictionary (MED)
Online Available at: http://quod.lib.umich.edu/m/med/ (date of access: June 2012 – February 2014).

Miller, Edward (ed.)
1991 *The agrarian history of England and Wales.* (Vol. 3: 1348–1500). Cambridge: Cambridge University Press.

Miller, Gary D.
2012 *External influences on English: From its beginnings to the Renaissance.* Oxford: Oxford University Press.

Moffett, Lisa
2006 "The archaeology of Medieval plant foods", in: Woolgar, C.M. et al. (eds.), 41–55.

Montanari, Massimo
1996 "Towards a new dietary balance", in: Flandrin, Jean-Louis – M. Montanari (eds.), 247–250.
2012 *Let the meatballs rest and other stories about food and culture*. New York: Columbia University Press.

Myers, Daniel
Online "Making sense of strawberries. An analysis of six related recipes", available at: medievalcookery.com (date of access: February 2011).

Myers, Alec Reginald (ed.)
1959 *The household of Edward IV: The Black Book and the ordinance of 1478*. Manchester: Manchester University Press.

Murphy, Margaret
1998 "Feeding Medieval cities: Some historical approaches", in: Carlin, M. – J.T. Rosenthal (eds.), 117–131.

Oxford English dictionary (OED)
Online Available at: www.oed.com (date of access: June 2012 – February 2014).

Radford, Andrew
2005 *Transformational grammar*. Cambridge: Cambridge University
[1988] Press.

Redgrove, Herbert Stanley
1933 *Spices and condiments*. London: Isaac Pitman.

Riera-Melis, Antoni
1999 "Society, food, and feudalism", in: Flandrin, Jean-Louis – M. Montanari (eds.), 251–267.

Rissanen, Matti – Ossi Ihalainen – Terttu Nevalainen – Irma Taavitsainen (eds.)
1992 *History of Englishes: New methods and interpretations in historical linguistics*. Berlin; New York: Mouton de Gruyter.

Rothwell, William
1998 "Anglo-Norman at the (green)grocer's", *French Studies* 52: 1–16.
1999 "Sugar and spice and all things nice: From Oriental bazar to English cloister in Anglo-French", *Modern Language Review* 94: 647–659.
2001 "English and French in England after 1362", *English Studies* 2001/6: 539–559.

Römer, Ute – Stefanie Wulff
2010 "Applying corpus methods to written academic texts: Exploration of MICUSP", *Journal of Writing Research* 2(2): 99–127.

Russell, John
    The Boke of Nurture, in: Furnivall, Frederick J. (ed.) 1931 [1868], 1–123.

Rynell, Alarik
1948   *The rivalry of Scandinavian and native synonyms in Middle English especially* taken *and* nimen. Lund: Gleerup.

Savelli, Mary
2011   *Tastes of Anglo-Saxon England.* Oakville: David Brown Book Co.
[2002]

Scheler, Manfred
1977   *Der englische Wortschatz.* Berlin: Erich Schmidt Verlag.

Schmidt, Kari Anne Rand
1994   "*The index of Middle English prose* and late Medieval English recipes", *English Studies* 5: 423–429.

Scully, Terence
1995   *The art of cookery in the Middle Ages.* Woodbridge, U.K.: Boydell Press.
1997   *The Vivendier: A fifteenth century French cookery manuscript. A critical edition with English translation.* Totnes: Prosper Books.
2008   "A cook's therapeutic use of garden herbs", in: Dendle, P. – A. Touwaide (eds.), 60–71.

Serjeantson, Dale
2006   "Birds: Food and a mark of status", in: Woolgar, C.M. et al. (eds.), 130–147.

Serjeantson, Dale – Chris M. Woolgar
2006   "Fish consumption in Medieval England", in: Woolgar, C.M. et al. (eds.), 102–130.

Serjeantson, Mary S.
1962   *A history of foreign words in English.* London: Routledge & Kegan
[1935]   Paul Ltd.

Shaw, Patricia
1991   "'Of fish and flesh and tender breede of win both white and reede': Eating and drinking in Middle English narrative texts", *SELIM Journal of the Spanish Society for Medieval English Language and Literature* 1: 2–28.

Sherman, Paul W. – Geoffrey A. Hash
2001   "Why vegetable recipes are not very spicy", *Evolution and Human Behavior* 22: 147–163.

Sihler, Andrew L.
1973   "Baking and roasting", *American Anthropologist* 75.5: 1721–1725.

Smith, Barry C. (ed.)
2007   *Questions of taste: The philosophy of wine*. Oxford: Signal Books.

Smith, Virginia
2007   *Clean – a history of personal hygiene and purity*. Oxford: Oxford University Press.

Soyer, Alexis
2004   *Food, cookery and dining in Ancient times. Alexis Soyer's Pantropheon*. Mineola, New York: Dover Publications Inc.

Spencer, Judith
1984   *The four seasons of the house of Cerruti*. New York: Facts On File Inc.

Stone, David J.
2006a   "The consumption of field crops in Late Medieval England", in: Woolgar, C.M. et al. (eds.), 11–26.
2006b   "The consumption and supply of birds in Late Medieval England", in: Woolgar, C.M. et al. (eds.), 148–161.

Super, John C.
2002   "Food and history", *Journal of Social History* 36.1: 165–178.

Sykes, Naomi Jane
2006a   "From *cu* and *sceap* to *beffe* and *motton*", in: Woolgar, C.M. et al. (eds.), 56–71.
2006b   "The impact of the Normans on hunting practices in England", in: Woolgar, C.M. et al. (eds.), 162–175.

Taavitsainen, Irma
2001a   "Middle English recipes: Genre characteristics, text type features and underlying traditions of writing", *Journal of Historical Pragmatics* 2.1: 85–113.
2001b   "Changing conventions of writing: The dynamics of genres, text types, and text traditions", *European Journal of English Studies* 5.2: 139–150.

Taavitsainen, Irma – Päivi Pahta (eds.)
2004   *Medical and scientific writing in Late Medieval English*. Cambridge: Cambridge University Press.

Taavitsainen, Irma – Päivi Pahta — Marti Mäkinen (eds.)
2005 *Middle English Medical Texts (MEMT)*. CD-ROM with MEMT Presenter software by Raymond Hickey. Amsterdam/Philadelphia: John Benjamins.

Tannahill, Reay
1988 *Food in history*. New York: Three Rivers Press.
[1973]

Taylor, Rosalie
2005 "More garbage, anyone? Eating and cooking meat in medieval England", available at: http://homes.chass.utoronto.ca/~cpercy/courses/6361taylor.htm (date of access: September 2013).

Thomas, Valerie
2011 "Do modern-day medical herbalists have anything to learn from Anglo-Saxon medical writings?, *Journal of Herbal Medicine* I (2011): 42–52.

Trotter, David
2008 "Anglo-Norman (Anglonormannisch)", in: Ammon, Ulrich – Harald Haarmann (eds.), 13–18.

Trotter, David (ed.)
2012 *Present and future research in Anglo-Norman: Aberystwyth Colloquium, July 2011*. Aberystwyth: The Anglo-Norman Online Hub.

Weiss, Corinna
2009 "*Ox, beef* and company: Story-telling in historical linguistics", Unpublished manuscript.

Wełna, Jerzy
2005 "*Nim* or *take*? A competition between two high frequency verbs in Middle English", *SAP* 41: 53–69.

Wilson, C. Anne
1991 *Food and drink in Britain: From the Stone Age to the 19th c.*
[1973] Chicago: Academy Chicago Publishers.

Woolgar, Chris M.
1999 *The great household in Late Medieval England*. New Haven: Yale University Press.
2006 "Meat and dairy products in Late Medieval England", in: Woolgar, C.M. et al. (eds.), 88–101.
2009 "Food and the middle ages", *Journal of Medieval History* 36: 1–19.

Woolgar, Chris M. – Dale Serjeantson – Tony Waldron (eds.)
2009 *Food in Medieval England: Diet and nutrition.* (Medieval History
[2006] and Archeology). Oxford: Oxford University Press.

Wright, Joseph (ed.)
1898–1905 *The English dialect dictionary.* Oxford: Oxford University Press.

Appendix: List of collections and editions used for the research

collection	abbreviation	date	nr of recipes	length (nr of words)[74]
Austin	Aus_Ashm	1410	19	992
Austin	Aus_Laud	1430	25	1,286
Austin	Aus_Douce	1450	12	1,096
Bake metis	BM	1435	41	4,462
Boke of kokery	BK	1450	182	18,464
Diversa cibaria	DC	1325	63	3,608
Diversa servisa	DS	1381	92	5,894
Forme of Cury	FC	1390	205	12,610
Gathering of ME recipes	GR_AshmB	1390	5	202
Gathering of ME recipes	GR_Har	1395	2	150
Gathering of ME recipes	GR_Ashm	1410	35	1,522
Gathering of ME recipes	GR_Sl	1420	11	734
Gathering of ME recipes	GR_Whit	1425	6	282
Gathering of ME recipes	GR_Raw	1435	1	145
Gathering of ME recipes	GR_ASC GR_Roy	1445	2	40 70
Gathering of ME recipes	GR_Rwl GR_Har	1450	85	6,968 46
Gathering of ME recipes	GR_TC	1465	7	388
Gathering of ME recipes	GR_WW	1470	19	1,165
Gathering of ME recipes	GR_Sl GR_SA	1480	31	1,601 1,130
Gathering of ME recipes	GR_CUL GR_Pen	1485	111	4,913 3,507
Gathering of ME recipes	GR_TCC GR_Hunt	1490	6	129 302

---

74 Based on the automatic count in .docx files.

collection	abbreviation	date	nr of recipes	length (nr of words)
Gathering of ME recipes	GR_eMus GR_Hus	1495	36	2,734 29
Goud kokery	GK	1340	2	133
Goud kokery	GK	1380	7	801
Goud kokery	GK	1395	9	1,857
Goud kokery	GK	1410	1	82
Goud kokery	GK	1420	1	81
Goud kokery	GK	1425	1	62
Goud kokery	GK	1450	3	213
Goud kokery	GK	1480	1	90
Hieatt_Harley	Ht_Hrl	1490	96	5,976
Hieatt_Medium Aevum	MAe	1450	8	678
Historical menus	Cosin	1397	9	661
Leche viaundez	LV	1435	64	6,063
Liber cure cocorum	LCC	1460	127	
Ordinance of pottage	OP	1460	197	19,912
Ordinance of pottage	OP	1475	3	241
Potage diverse	PD	1435	153	13,861
Utilis coquinario	UC	1395	37	3,107

Index of verbs

(a)dress	5.8	*cut$_2$*	3.4.1.3
ally/lye	5.3.1	*cut$_3$*	3.5.1.2
anoint	5.6	*depart*	3.2.1.5
bake	4.3.1.1	*dice*	3.2.1.6
bard	3.2.1.15	*dight*	5.9
baste	5.9	*dish*	5.8
beat$_1$	3.3.1.1	*dismember*	3.2.1.15
beat$_2$	5.3.1	*do$_1$*	3.4.1.9
blanche	3.4.1.1	*do$_2$*	5.3.2
boil	4.2.1.1	*draw$_1$*	5.3.2
bone	3.4.1.10	*draw$_2$*	5.4
bray	3.3.1.2	*draw$_3$*	5.2
break$_1$	3.2.1.1	*draw$_4$*	3.5.1.3
break$_2$	3.3.1.3	*dry*	5.9
break$_3$	3.4.1.2	*enarm*	5.9
break$_4$	3.5.1.1	*endore*	5.6
broil	4.3.1.2	*enforce*	5.5
bruise	3.3.1.4	*fan (out)*	5.2
burn	4.4	*farce*	5.3.3
carve	3.2.1.2	*fill*	5.3.3
cast	5.3.2	*flamb*	4.4
chine	3.2.1.15	*flay*	3.4.1.4
chop1	3.2.1.3	*flour*	5.6
chop off	3.4.1.10	*flourish*	5.6
clarify	5.4	*fry*	4.3.1.3
cleave	3.2.1.15	*gild*	5.6
colour	5.6	*gobbon*	3.2.1.15
cool	5.9	*grate*	3.3.1.6
couch	5.3.2	*grind*	3.3.1.7
crumb	3.3.1.5	*hack*	3.2.1.7
culpon	3.2.1.15	*heat*	4.4
cut$_1$	3.2.1.4	*hew*	3.2.1.8

hild	3.4.1.4	*season*	5.5
hull	3.4.1.10	*seethe*	4.2.1.4
lard	5.9	*serve*	5.8
leach	3.2.1.9	*share*	3.2.1.15
make	5.4	*shave*	3.4.1.8
make clean	5.2	*shell*	3.4.1.10
meddle	5.3.1	*shred*	3.2.1.11
mell	5.3.1	*silver*	5.6
melt	5.9	*skim*	5.4
mess	5.8	*skin*	3.4.1.4
mince	3.3.1.8	*slit$_1$*	3.2.1.12
ming	5.3.1	*slit$_2$*	3.5.1.5
nym	5.7	*smite*	3.2.1.13
open	3.5.1.4	*smite off*	3.4.1.10
ouerstep	4.2.1.5	*spring*	5.6
paint	5.6	*stamp*	3.3.1.12
parboil	4.2.1.2	*stew*	4.2.1.6
pare	3.4.1.5	*stir*	5.3.1
peel	3.4.1.6	*stop*	5.3.3
pick	3.4.1.7	*strain*	5.4
plant	5.3.2	*straw*	5.6
pluck	3.2.1.15	*stray*	5.6
pour	5.3.2	*strip*	3.4.1.10
powder$_1$	3.3.1.9	*stuff*	5.3.3
powder$_2$	5.6	*swing*	5.3.1
press	3.3.1.10	*take$_1$*	5.7
quarter	3.2.1.10	*take$_2$*	3.4.1.9
quest	3.3.1.11	*tear*	3.2.1.15
recipe	5.7	*tease*	3.2.1.14
roast	4.3.1.4	*temper*	5.3.1
run	5.4	*toast*	4.4
salt	5.5	*wash*	5.2
scald	4.2.1.3	*well*	4.2.1.7
scale	3.4.1.10	*wet*	5.9
scorch	4.4	*whiten*	3.4.1.1
scrape	3.4.1.8	*winnow*	5.2
searce	5.4	*wring*	5.4

Studies in English Medieval Language and Literature

Edited by Jacek Fisiak

Vol. 1 Dieter Kastovsky / Arthur Mettinger (eds.): Language Contact in the History of English. 2nd, revised edition. 2003.

Vol. 2 Studies in English Historical Linguistics and Philology. A Festschrift for Akio Oizumi. Edited by Jacek Fisiak. 2002.

Vol. 3 Liliana Sikorska: In a Manner of Morall Playe: Social Ideologies in English Moralities and Interludes (1350-1517). 2002.

Vol. 4 Peter J. Lucas / Angela M. Lucas (eds.): Middle English from Tongue to Text. Selected Papers from the Third International Conference on Middle English: Language and Text, held at Dublin, Ireland, 1-4 July 1999. 2002.

Vol. 5 Chaucer and the Challenges of Medievalism. Studies in Honor of H. A. Kelly. Edited by Donka Minkova and Theresa Tinkle. 2003.

Vol. 6 Hanna Rutkowska: Graphemics and Morphosyntax in the Cely Letters (1472-88). 2003.

Vol. 7 The Ancrene Wisse. A Four-Manuscript Parallel Text. Preface and Parts 1-4. Edited by Tadao Kubouchi and Keiko Ikegami with John Scahill, Shoko Ono, Harumi Tanabe, Yoshiko Ota, Ayako Kobayashi and Koichi Nakamura. 2003.

Vol. 8 Joanna Bugaj: Middle Scots Inflectional System in the South-west of Scotland. 2004.

Vol. 9 Rafal Boryslawski: The Old English Riddles and the Riddlic Elements of Old English Poetry. 2004.

Vol. 10 Nikolaus Ritt / Herbert Schendl (eds.): Rethinking Middle English. Linguistic and Literary Approaches. 2005.

Vol. 11 The Ancrene Wisse. A Four-Manuscript Parallel Text. Parts 5–8 with Wordlists. Edited by Tadao Kubouchi and Keiko Ikegami with John Scahill, Shoko Ono, Harumi Tanabe, Yoshiko Ota, Ayako Kobayashi, Koichi Nakamura. 2005.

Vol. 12 Text and Language in Medieval English Prose. A Festschrift for Tadao Kubouchi. Edited by Akio Oizumi, Jacek Fisiak and John Scahill. 2005.

Vol. 13 Michiko Ogura (ed.): Textual and Contextual Studies in Medieval English. Towards the Reunion of Linguistics and Philology. 2006.

Vol. 14 Keiko Hamaguchi: Non-European Women in Chaucer. A Postcolonial Study. 2006.

Vol. 15 Ursula Schaefer (ed.): The Beginnings of Standardization. Language and Culture in Fourteenth-Century England. 2006.

Vol. 16 Nikolaus Ritt / Herbert Schendl / Christiane Dalton-Puffer / Dieter Kastovsky (eds): Medieval English and its Heritage. Structure, Meaning and Mechanisms of Change. 2006.

Vol. 17 Matylda Włodarczyk: Pragmatic Aspects of Reported Speech. The Case of Early Modern English Courtroom Discourse. 2007.

Vol. 18 Hans Sauer / Renate Bauer (eds.): Beowulf and Beyond. 2007.

Vol. 19 Gabriella Mazzon (ed.): Studies in Middle English Forms and Meanings. 2007.

Vol. 20 Alexander Bergs / Janne Skaffari (eds.): The Language of the Peterborough Chronicle. 2007.

Vol. 21 Liliana Sikorska (ed.). With the assistance of Joanna Maciulewicz: Medievalisms. The Poetics of Literary Re-Reading. 2008.

Vol. 22 Masachiyo Amano / Michiko Ogura / Masayuki Ohkado (eds.): Historical Englishes in Varieties of Texts and Contexts. The Global COE Program, International Conference 2007. 2008.

Vol. 23 Ewa Ciszek: Word Derivation in Early Middle English. 2008.

Vol. 24 Andrzej M. Łęcki: Grammaticalisation Paths of *Have* in English. 2010.

Vol. 25 Osamu Imahayashi / Yoshiyuki Nakao / Michiko Ogura (eds.): Aspects of the History of English Language and Literature. Selected Papers Read at SHELL 2009, Hiroshima. 2010.

Vol. 26 Magdalena Bator: Obsolete Scandinavian Loanwords in English. 2010.

Vol. 27 Anna Cichosz: The Influence of Text Type on Word Order of Old Germanic Languages. A Corpus-Based Contrastive Study of Old English and Old High German. 2010.

Vol. 28 Jacek Fisiak / Magdalena Bator (eds.): Foreign Influences on Medieval English. 2011.

Vol. 29 Władysław Witalisz: The Trojan Mirror. Middle English Narratives of Troy as Books of Princely Advice. 2011.

Vol. 30 Luis Iglesias-Rábade: Semantic Erosion of Middle English Prepositions. 2011.

Vol. 31 Barbara Kowalik: Betwixt *engelaunde* and *englene londe*. Dialogic Poetics in Early English Religious Lyric. 2010.

Vol. 32 The Katherine Group. A Three-Manuscript Parallel Text. Seinte Katerine, Seinte Marherete, Seinte Iuliene, and Hali Meiðhad, with Wordlists. Edited by Shoko Ono and John Scahill with Keiko Ikegami, Tadao Kubouchi, Harumi Tanabe, Koichi Nakamura, Satoko Shimazaki and Koichi Kano. 2011.

Vol. 33 Jacob Thaisen / Hanna Rutkowska (eds.): Scribes, Printers, and the Accidentals of their Texts. 2011.

Vol. 34 Isabel Moskowich: Language Contact and Vocabulary Enrichment. Scandinavian Elements in Middle English. 2012.

Vol. 35 Joanna Esquibel / Anna Wojtyś (eds.): Explorations in the English Language: Middle Ages and Beyond. Festschrift for Professor Jerzy Wełna on the Occasion of his 70th Birthday. 2012.

Vol. 36 Yoshiyuki Nakao: The Structure of Chaucer´s Ambiguity. 2013.

Vol. 37 Begoña Crespo: Change in Life, Change in Language. A Semantic Approach to the History of English. 2013.

Vol. 38 Richard Dance / Laura Wright (eds.): The Use and Development of Middle English. Proceedings of the Sixth International Conference on Middle English, Cambridge 2008. 2012.

Vol. 39 Michiko Ogura: Words and Expressions of Emotion in Medieval English. 2013.

Vol. 40 Anna Czarnowus: Fantasies of the Other´s Body in Middle English Oriental Romance. 2013.

Vol. 41 Hans Sauer / Gaby Waxenberger (eds.): Recording English, Researching English, Transforming English. With the Assistance of Veronika Traidl. 2013.

Vol. 42 Michio Hosaka / Michiko Ogura / Hironori Suzuki / Akinobu Tani (eds.): Phases of the History of English. Selection of Papers Read at SHELL 2012. 2013.

Vol. 43 Vlatko Broz: Aspectual Prefixes in Early English. 2014.

Vol. 44 Michael Bilynsky (ed.): Studies in Middle English. Words, Forms, Senses and Texts. 2014.

Vol. 45 Bożena Duda: The Synonyms of *Fallen Woman* in the History of the English Language. 2014.

Vol. 46 Magdalena Bator: Culinary verbs in Middle English. 2014.

www.peterlang.com